THUNDEROUS SILENCE

THUNDEROUS SILENCE
A FORMULA FOR ENDING SUFFERING

A Practical Guide to the Heart Sutra

DOSUNG YOO

Wisdom Publications • Boston

199 Elm Street
Somerville, MA 02144 USA
www.wisdompubs.org

Library of Congress Cataloging-in-Publication Data
Yoo, Dosung.
 Thunderous silence : a formula for ending suffering : a practical guide to the Heart sutra / Dosung Yoo.
   pages cm
 Includes bibliographical references and index.
 ISBN 1-61429-053-9 (pbk. : alk. paper)
 1. Tripitaka. Sutrapitaka. Prajñaparamita. Hrdaya—Criticism, interpretation, etc. 2. Religious life—Buddhism. 3. Buddhism—Doctrines. I. Title.
 BQ1967.Y65 2013
 294.3'85—dc23
                              2012022585
 ISBN 9781614290537
 eBook ISBN 9781614290643

17 16 15 14 13
5 4 3 2 1

Interior design by Gopa&Ted2; typset by LC. Set in Diacritical Garamond 12/15.54.
Illustration on page 122 is by Rocky Bracero.

Wisdom Publications' books are printed on acid-free paper and meet the guidelines for permanence and durability of the Production Guidelines for Book Longevity of the Council on Library Resources.

Printed in the United States of America.

This book is dedicated to the teachers who have helped me find and walk on the Dharma path.

CONTENTS

INTRODUCTION

For him to whom emptiness is clear,
Everything becomes clear.
For him to whom emptiness is not clear,
Nothing becomes clear.

—Nagarjuna[1]

HUI KO,[2] a prominent Confucian scholar and practitioner, came to Bodhidharma, the First Patriarch of Zen Buddhism, to become his disciple. Despite all his knowledge, Hui Ko could not attain a peaceful and centered state of mind. When Hui Ko saw Bodhidharma, who was practicing meditation in a cave, he said, "Master! My mind is not at peace. Please put my mind to rest." Bodhidharma replied, "Show me your disturbed mind." Hui Ko paused and searched for his mind. After a while he said, "Master, I have searched for my mind, but I cannot find it." Bodhidharma replied, "Then I have already put your mind to rest."

Bodhidharma did not ask Hui Ko *why* he suffered. He did not ask about Hui Ko's financial problems, nor did he ask about his personal relationships; rather, Bodhidharma asked him *who* or *what* was suffering. What Bodhidharma questioned was the real nature of Hui Ko's mind, his true self.

When a stone hits a dog, the dog chases after the stone. When a stone hits a lion, the lion chases after the person who threw the stone. When we understand the reality of ourselves (the reality of our minds), suffering ceases. That is the core teaching of Buddhadharma. That is the essence of the Heart Sutra.

Several years ago, a Korean journalist conducted a survey to find out what Koreans wanted the most in their lives, and he asked them to express this desire in one word. Most Koreans chose *haeng-bok*, which means "happiness." Whatever our race, ethnicity, or age may be, what we want most in our lives is happiness. That is why we try to have a better job, a better house or car, or more recognition. We constantly try to alter our conditions rather than make the effort to discover our true selves.

Socrates said, "Know thyself." Trying to change our environment to create happiness without knowing the reality of our mind is like building a house on quicksand and expecting to live in it forever. Happiness, suffering, freedom, dissatisfaction, depression, and joy are all words that describe our state of mind. When we clearly see into the reality of our minds, the root of our suffering is severed, and as a result, suffering ends. The happiness or freedom that comes from the realization of our true self is perpetual and indestructible. The happiness that comes from our changing environment, however, is conditional and fragile, and therefore it cannot be everlasting.

This story illustrates this teaching: When a young boy came home from school, he discovered his grandmother diligently looking for something. He asked, "Grandma, what are you looking for?" She replied, "I am looking for a needle." "Where did you lose it?" the boy asked. "I lost it in the living room," she said. The boy asked again, "Then why are you looking for it in the yard?" She replied, "Because it is brighter out here!"

The person who searches for happiness without realizing his or her true self is like that grandmother looking for the needle in the wrong place.

What could be more important and more urgent than realizing our true self when what we want most is not momentary happiness but eternal and unconditional happiness? For what purpose do we live our lives if not for the complete freedom that comes from awakening to the true reality of our mind? For what purpose do we pour our time and energy into our lives? This is what we need to contemplate.

When I was in my teens, whenever I experienced impermanence, I felt as though I were trapped in a very small barrel; it was as though I were imprisoned. The feeling was very strange. Later I came to realize that these experiences were a kind of koan, or spiritual question, arising in my mind. And then I realized that I could escape from all things except from one thing: *my mind*.

When the reality of our mind is revealed, suffering ceases. When emptiness, which is the nature of all things, is clearly understood, the root of suffering is severed. This is the essential teaching of the Heart Sutra. This is the core of Buddhadharma.

Shakyamuni Buddha was born a prince. He lacked nothing and was raised in an environment where he was always satisfied. But when he witnessed old age, illness, and death, the inevitable conditions of human existence, he acutely felt the inherently unsatisfactory aspect of the human condition. His response to this feeling was to leave his palace and search for that which is eternal. Although most people put up with such feelings, the Buddha courageously confronted it face to face. When he attained supreme enlightenment and discovered his true self—when his innate wisdom emerged—he became free from all suffering and was empowered to help all sentient beings.

This book is written to encourage everyone to take the journey that the Buddha took twenty-five hundred years ago. This is the inner journey to discover our authentic self, the journey to our inherent indestructible freedom and to unconditional and everlasting happiness.

It is time to go inside to find the needle instead of searching for it in the yard.

The Heart Sutra

The Bodhisattva of Great Compassion, when deeply practicing prajna paramita, realized that all five aggregates are empty and became free from all suffering and distress.

Here, Shariputra, form does not differ from emptiness, emptiness does not differ from form. Form is emptiness, emptiness is form. The same is true of sensations, perceptions, impulses, consciousness.

Here, Shariputra, all dharmas are empty; they do not appear or disappear, are not tainted or pure, do not increase or decrease.

Therefore in emptiness, no form, no sensations, no perceptions, no impulses, no consciousness. No eyes, no ears, no nose, no tongue, no body, no mind; no form, no sound, no smell, no taste, no touch, no object of mind; no realm of eye, ear, nose, tongue, body, or mind consciousness.

No ignorance, nor extinction of ignorance, no old age and death, nor extinction of them. No suffering, no cause of suffering, no cessation of suffering, no path; no wisdom, no attainment with nothing to attain.

The Bodhisattva relies on prajna paramita, therefore the mind has no hindrance; without any hindrance, no fears exist; free from delusion, one dwells in nirvana. All buddhas of the past, present, and future rely on prajna paramita and attain supreme enlightenment.

Therefore know that prajna paramita is the great mantra, is the great enlightening mantra, is the unsurpassed and unequalled mantra, which is able to eliminate all suffering. This is true, not false.

So proclaim the Prajna Paramita mantra, which says gate gate paragate parasamgate bodhi svaha.[3]

The buddhas have appeared in this world
to liberate all beings
by helping them realize the treasury of Buddha-Wisdom
that they are unaware they possess within themselves.

—The Lotus Sutra

ONE DAY a rabbit happened to discover a precious gem in the forest and brought it to a lion, who was king of the jungle. All the animals gathered together in order to see this gem. They marveled at its beauty and began to fear that the humans might steal it from them.

The lion said, "Why don't we hide it deep in the jungle so that no humans can find it?" The rabbit, who had found the gem, said, "No, that is not a good idea. Humans are so clever that they will eventually find it. We are rapidly losing our forests to them." All of the animals agreed with the rabbit.

The eagle, king of the sky, said, "I can hide that gem so high in the sky that no one will be able to see it." A hawk said, "No, humans are very smart and they have made an iron bird called an airplane. They will eventually find the gem."

The whale, king of the sea, said, "Why don't we hide it deep in the sea where humans cannot go?" All the fish said, "No, humans have a machine called a submarine that can go deep into the ocean. The sea is not a safe place."

The animals became very worried and pondered for a long time where to hide this gem. Finally, they all agreed to hide it "deep, deep, in the human heart, where humans never think to look too deeply."

Studying the Heart Sutra means embarking on the journey to discover this gem, which is hidden very deeply within our hearts. It is the treasure of our authentic self, our buddha nature, our original nature, which has been lost for a long, long time.

The Heart Sutra is the treasure map to locate that gem.

When I first read the Diamond Sutra in my twenties, for some unknown reason my eyes flooded with tears. I felt as though I had found my true home, my source. The Heart Sutra is the picture of our true self, or the ultimate reality. It is the pathless path to reach our true home. It leads us toward the precious treasure called *buddhahood*.

The original title of the Heart Sutra is Maha Prajna Paramita Hridaya Sutra. Let's look in detail at each of the words in that title.

...Maha Prajna...

There are three kinds of knowledge.

The first is borrowed knowledge. It is like the knowledge you attain from reading books or from listening to others speaking. It is not original. Like a plastic flower, it does not have a fragrance.

The second is wisdom. This is the knowledge that you acquire from your own experiences. It is not borrowed: it is yours.

The third is knowledge that comes from another level. It is called *prajna*, innate wisdom, which is inherent within all sentient beings. The Sanskrit word *prajna* has two components: *pra-* means "before" and -jna means "to know."[4] Prajna is neither borrowed nor acquired by experience. It is neither knowledge nor wisdom. It is inherent, innate awareness or consciousness that does not need to be honed or cultivated. It is something that is already there.

One day, Daesan, the Third Head Dharma Master of Won Buddhism, dispatched several Won Buddhist ministers and laypersons to search for a proper site for a retreat center on Jeju Island, Korea. They came back after several months and reported on what they thought was the best site. After listening to their opinions and seeing the pictures of the possible sites, Master Daesan asked them to buy the site that most people thought was the least desirable. The site was located a long distance from the main road, and the path to that site was very muddy. They obeyed him and bought the site, and then built several buildings for the retreat center. A few years later, an expressway was constructed by the local government, and the road from the expressway to the retreat center was paved. The retreat center became such an accessible and convenient place that its value soared, and many more people were able to use it.

Chwasan, the Fourth Head Dharma Master of Won Buddhism, is a celibate monk and does not have the experiences of marriage or raising children. However, he has written a great deal about prenatal education. Although he never studied this subject, the knowledge very naturally arose in his mind due to his advanced practice and meditation. When our practice deepens, prajna, our inner light, begins to be revealed.

Maha in Sanskrit means "great," "big," or "infinite." *Maha Prajna* means "ultimate wisdom" or "supreme enlightenment." It is the wisdom that a buddha, or one who is fully awakened, possesses.

Animals also have wisdom, but it is different from that of humans. The average person's wisdom is different from the Buddha's in its depth and brightness. A burning match has light, but its brightness differs from that of the sun. When the sun rises, the darkness of the whole world is dispelled. The wisdom or power of a completely awakened person is like the bright light of the sun, which shines on the whole world. *Maha Prajna* is the complete or ultimate wisdom. It is supreme enlightenment, the wisdom that a perfectly enlightened person attains.

...Paramita...

Paramita means "crossing over" or "going to the other shore." This represents crossing from this world of suffering to the world of freedom, or nirvana, which is the ultimate goal of practice. This term originates from an ancient Indian tradition when nations were often divided by large rivers like the Ganges. When people felt unhappy or miserable in their country or in their situation—for example, women living in slavery—and they came to the shore of the river, the situation they saw on the other shore appeared far better. This shore is the land of suffering. That shore is the ideal world, nirvana, or the kingdom of God.

...Hridaya Sutra...

"Heart" is the translation of the Sanskrit *hridaya*, which means "center" or "essence." The heart is the most vital of our internal organs. The Sanskrit word *sutra* means "scripture"—mostly referring to the canonical scriptures or the discourses of the Buddha. In ancient India, Hindu and Buddhist scriptures were made by binding leaves together. The word *sutra* is derived from the root verb *siv-*, meaning *to sew* (the English word *suture* has the same root). *Sutra* literally means "a thread that holds things together." So "heart sutra" means the essential scripture, the essential path, or the summary of all dharmas, and "maha prajna paramita hridaya sutra" means the essential path (*hridaya sutra*) to go to the other shore (*paramita*) by means of complete enlightenment (*maha prajna*).

While many Chinese commentators interpret *paramita* to mean "the other shore," another meaning of *paramita* is "perfection." Using this interpretation, the Maha Prajna Paramita Hridaya Sutra means

WHAT IS THE HEART SUTRA? | 11

"the essential path or teaching that perfects innate wisdom," or "the essential Dharma that perfects realization or enlightenment."

When I worked at the Seoul Meditation Center in Korea, I counseled many young men and women. Many single people there said that they would like to meet and marry a good person. In addition, many married people told me that they would have preferred to remain single. It is important to understand that nirvana, or the other shore, is not the place or time when everything goes our way and our situation is perfect. Nirvana is where our minds become empowered and pure, and prajna, our true self, is revealed.

The Greek root of the word *utopia* means "nonexistence" or "the place that does not exist." Materially or technologically, we have already reached an ideal place or state, but people are still unhappy. Nirvana, or utopia, is attained when people regain prajna and attain freedom of mind, regardless of what the circumstances may be. If we restore our true self and have the power and wisdom of our original mind, then our minds will not be disturbed by external causes and we will enjoy our lives, whatever the situation. When we have prajna, we also have the wisdom and power to change our environment and to gain blessings from any situation.

As the original title of the Heart Sutra, Maha Prajna Paramita Hridaya Sutra, implies, we cannot go to the other shore by making a lot of money, meeting an ideal spouse, or having a good job—in other words by changing our external environment. Only when we are awakened to our true self, only when we attain prajna can we go from this shore of suffering to the other shore, nirvana—from a deluded mind to an enlightened mind, from a dreamy state of mind to an awakened state.

In the Gnostic Gospel of Thomas, Jesus said, "If your leaders tell you, 'Look, the kingdom [of God] is in heaven,' then the birds of heaven will precede you. If they say to you, 'It's in the sea,' then the fish will precede you. But the kingdom is inside you and it is outside you. When you know yourselves, then you will be known, and you will understand that you are children of the living father."[5]

Consider the following tale:

> A legend from ancient India tells of a musk deer who, one fresh spring day, detected a mysterious and heavenly fragrance in the air. It hinted of peace, beauty, and love, and like a whisper beckoned him onward. Compelled to find its source, he set out, determined to search the whole world over. He climbed forbidding and icy mountain peaks, padded through steamy jungles, trekked across endless desert sands. Wherever he went, the scent was there, faint yet always detectable. At the end of his life, exhausted from his relentless search, the deer collapsed. As he fell his horn pierced his belly, and suddenly the air was filled with the heavenly scent. As he lay dying, the musk deer realized that the fragrance had all along been emanating from within himself.[6]

People who try to change their environment without first changing their minds are like the person endlessly rowing a boat toward the horizon. In reality, the horizon is already under our boat. When we realize the reality of our selves, and prajna is fully revealed, then we understand that nirvana (the horizon) already exists here and now.[7] As long as all people wish to become happy and free, which can only be possible when we attain prajna, what can be more imperative than awakening to our true selves?

There is a saying in the Zen tradition: "Cultivation of mind for three days will last as a treasure for a thousand years, but material things that were amassed for a hundred years will crumble into dust in one morning." Discovering and restoring prajna is the path to liberation. It is the way to end suffering forever. That is why studying and contemplating prajna paramita literature is so beneficial. The Heart Sutra encompasses the wisdom of all prajna paramita literature.

In the Diamond Sutra, Buddha spoke about these merits:

Subhuti, if there be one who gives away in gifts of alms a mass of the seven treasures equal in extent to as many mighty Mount Sumerus as there would be in three thousand galaxies of worlds, and if there be another who selects even only four lines from this Discourse upon the Perfection of Transcendental Wisdom, receives and retains them, and clearly expounds them to others, the merit of the latter will be so far greater than that of the former that no conceivable comparison can be made between them.[8]

He also said:

Subhuti, if on the one hand a good man or a good woman sacrifices as many lives as the sand-grains of the Ganges, and on the other hand anyone receives and retains even only four lines of this Discourse, and teaches and explains them to others, the merit of the latter will be the greater.[9]

The chances of attaining the buddhas' teachings are as slim as seeing the *udumbara* flower, which is said to bloom only once in three thousand years. According to the Diamond Sutra, the person who has attained the Buddha's teachings and heard about the Heart Sutra or Diamond Sutra is one who has previously planted many meritorious seeds:

Subhuti said to Buddha: World-honored One, will there always be men who will truly believe after coming to hear these teachings [of the Perfection of Transcendental Wisdom]?

Buddha answered: Subhuti, do not utter such words! At the end of the last five-hundred-year period following the passing of the Tathagata,[10] there will be self-controlled men, rooted in merit, coming to hear these teachings, who will be inspired with belief. But you should realize that such men have not strengthened their root of merit under just one Buddha, or two Buddhas, or three, or four, or five Buddhas, but under countless Buddhas; and their merit is of every kind. Such men, coming to hear these teachings, will have an immediate uprising of pure faith, Subhuti; and the Tathagata will recognize them. Yes, He will clearly perceive all these of pure heart, and the magnitude of their moral excellences.[11]

The ancient Korean Zen master Chinul said, "Since you have now arrived at the treasure house, how can you return empty-handed? Once you lose a human body, for ten thousand kalpas it will be difficult to recover. Be careful. Knowing that there is a treasure house, how can a wise person turn back and not look for it—and yet continue to resent bitterly his destitution and poverty? If you want the treasure you must throw away this skin-bag."[12] Since we have already arrived at the treasure house, we should not go back empty-handed.

HISTORICAL BACKGROUND

Shakyamuni Buddha attained the supreme enlightenment under the bodhi tree after six years of ascetic practice. After his enlightenment, Buddha was said to have remained in samadhi for three weeks. His experiences during this period of samadhi are described in the Avatamsaka Sutra, also called the Hua-yen Sutra or Flower Garland Sutra. In this samadhi state, the Buddha delivered a Dharma talk. However, no one could understand his direct explanation of the ultimate reality, so the Buddha taught his Dharma step by step. Buddha taught the Agama, the sacred tradition, for twelve years, emphasizing meritorious actions for practitioners as the foundation of their practice, and explaining the karmic principle of cause and effect. For the next eight years, he taught the Vaipulya Sutra, wherein he explained the dharma of dependent arising. When the Buddha reached his midfifties, he began to teach the Prajna Paramita Sutras, wherein he revealed the ultimate reality. The Buddha taught the Prajna Paramita Sutras for twenty-one years—and Prajna Paramita Sutras were taught for the longest period on Vulture's Peak, a mountain near Rajgir in the present-day state of Bihar.

The Prajna Paramita Sutras contain more than six hundred volumes; the Heart Sutra has about 270 English words. In this way, the Heart Sutra is the summary, or the heart, of all the prajna paramita literature. The Heart Sutra is the innermost essence of the Buddha-dharma. Since the Heart Sutra is both very short and the summation of the Buddha's wisdom, it is the most popular sutra in Mahayana Buddhism and is chanted in many temples during services.

The Prajna Paramita Sutras, which are among the Mahayana scriptures, appeared between 200 B.C.E. and 400 C.E. During the Buddha's time, his teachings were not written down. According to the traditional account, recorded Buddhist sutras date back to the First Council, which was held in Rajgir after Buddha's death in 383 B.C.E.[13] During the great council, five hundred *arhats* (those who had achieved enlightenment) assembled to recall and write down Buddha's teachings. Ananda, the Buddha's attendant, is said to have recalled all of the Buddha's discourses.

But legend has it that originally Ananda was not allowed to join the First Council because he was not yet considered enlightened by Mahakasyapa, the First Patriarch of Buddhism. Additionally Mahakasyapa, to whom the Dharma lineage was transmitted by the Buddha himself, did not allow Ananda to join the council because he thought that Ananda parroted the Buddha's words without understanding their true meaning. Ananda, upset and frustrated that he could not join the council, retreated deep into the forest with profound regret and with a great determination to attain complete enlightenment. He decided not to sleep until he reached the state of great enlightenment. One day he was so exhausted that he lay down. He mistakenly thought there would be a support under his head, which abruptly dropped to the ground. As his head hit the ground, he realized the empty nature of all things. Because of this experience,

Mahakasyapa allowed him to join the council and to recall the Buddha's words.

Most Buddhist sutras begin with "Thus have I heard..." The "I" here refers to Ananda. This type of scripture is exactly what Ananda recalled, or what the Buddha really spoke, rather than Ananda's interpretation of the Buddha's words.

The Tibetan version of the Heart Sutra begins like this:[14]

> Thus did I hear. At one time the Bhagavan [The Blessed One] was abiding at Vulture Peak in Rajagrha with a great assembly of monks and a great assembly of bodhisattvas. At that time the Bhagavan entered into a samadhi on the categories of phenomena called "perception of the profound."[15]

Here "I" does not only mean the bodily form of Ananda, who is said to have had a photographic memory, but rather Ananda's awakened mind and heart, something all human beings inherently possess. In some sense, this beginning seems to reflect Ananda's repentance. He appears to be saying, "In the old days, I heard the Buddha's words with my ears, but now I listen and recall the Buddha's words with my awakened mind and heart." Just as Ananda did, when we chant, read, and study the Heart Sutra, we should also receive the Buddha's words with our awakened mind and heart.

How to Embody the Heart Sutra

The first way to embody the Heart Sutra is through study. By reading and thinking about the meaning of the Heart Sutra, we can begin our journey to restoring prajna. Before Newton's day, many people had seen apples drop to the ground, but it was Newton who discovered the law of gravity because he was thinking and searching for a law that could explain all phenomena in the universe. Pascal, a French philosopher, said, "Man is only a reed, the weakest of nature, but he is a thinking reed." Despite being very weak, humankind has built great civilizations and invented great things, from airplanes and computers to our many social systems. If there were no thinking, a "eureka" moment would never occur in the human mind. From time to time, we should think about the meaning of the Heart Sutra, and its commentary, in order to reveal prajna.

The second way to embody the Heart Sutra, or to reveal prajna, is through contemplation. One Buddhist expression says: "There is a volume of scripture that, although not in written form, continues to illuminate." The Heart Sutra is a picture of our original face, the face that we have before we are conceived. It is a sutra that describes the world before a thought arises. Only when our thinking mind disappears can we see our true face and can prajna, or our innate wisdom, be revealed.

The meaning of the Heart Sutra defies our rational mind. For instance, one Chinese Zen master who read the Heart Sutra when he was a novice monk was surprised to find that the Heart Sutra says, "No eyes, no ears, no nose, no tongue, no body, no mind..." He touched his nose and ears to make sure they were there.

When the curtain of our desires and wandering thoughts is opened widely, we can see the reality of both ourselves and the universe. Studying the Heart Sutra is like entering a furnace: our thoughts and beliefs, and all of our common sense and conventional wisdom, are burned away. For instance, the idea that form is form and nonexistence is nonexistence, which is the starting point of Western logic, is denied in the Heart Sutra, which says: "Form is emptiness, emptiness is form." The passages of the Heart Sutra can be wonderful koans.[16] By pondering these passages, we can center and focus our minds, going very deeply into meditation, and eventually dropping our thinking mind, allowing our true self to manifest.

One day in Korea, on his way to a nearby village, a wandering silk merchant took a nap, leaning against a tree. When he woke up, he discovered that all his rolls of silk were gone. He was so shocked and upset that he immediately rushed to the governor's office and told him what had happened, asking him to apprehend the thief. The governor asked whether there was anyone who had witnessed the silk rolls being stolen. The merchant said that there was no one around him, only a wooden totem pole. The governor earnestly said to him, "In that case, I have to interrogate the totem pole, since it was the only witness." He then asked his men to bring the totem pole to his office immediately and asked his men to announce a court date.

The news of the governor's ridiculous action spread through the village. On the court date, most of the village people gathered in the courtroom, curious about what would happen. The governor sat on his high bench and asked his men, in a stern voice, to bring the totem pole into the courtroom and to bind it with rope. The governor then asked the totem pole in a loud voice whether it saw anyone take the rolls of silk while the merchant was sleeping. Since the totem pole did not answer, the governor became angry and asked the same question again in a louder voice. The totem pole still did not say anything, so the governor grew furious, stood up, and ordered his men to chain the totem pole tightly to a pillar and to beat it with a club until it spoke. With each stroke, the governor shouted to his men, "Hit it harder!" Eventually, the people watching burst out laughing, and the governor made a show of becoming even angrier. So he ordered his men to apprehend all the people who had laughed. Most of the villagers were caught, and they were ordered to pay three rolls of silk within one week.

By the end of that week, most of the villagers who had laughed in the courtroom brought in their rolls of silk. The governor asked the merchant to pick out his silk from among the piles. Then the governor summoned the persons who had brought the silk rolls and asked them from whom they had bought the silk. They all said they bought the silk from the same person, clearly the thief. This is how the governor apprehended the thief.[17]

At first, striking the totem pole with the club seemed to have nothing to do with apprehending the thief, yet eventually this action led to the thief being caught. Likewise, when you first ponder or meditate on a koan or a passage from the Heart Sutra, you may doubt the merits of your actions. But just as striking the totem pole repeatedly led to apprehending the thief, when we ponder and meditate on the Heart Sutra again and again, we can reach the realm where our mind becomes so calm and focused that eventually meaning will be revealed to us.

The third way to embody the Heart Sutra is through practicing meditation. Only when the ripples disappear from the surface of a lake can the moon be reflected accurately on its surface. In order to reveal prajna, stability of mind is essential. At the hydroelectric power plant, if the dam does not hold much water, very little electricity will be generated. Holding a lot of water is of primary importance. Studying or pondering the Heart Sutra is like powering an electric generator, and meditation is like holding a lot of water in the dam.

When we study, contemplate, and ponder the Heart Sutra, we need to simultaneously calm and empower our minds with meditation. Otherwise, our inquiry into the Heart Sutra will not be deep; we cannot become one with the Heart Sutra. Our bodies get stronger the more we use them, but when it comes to our minds, the more our minds are put to rest, the more empowered they become.

Human civilization began to develop dramatically when people moved from a nomadic existence to a more settled, agricultural existence. When our minds settle down, wisdom, compassion, and all manner of merit and potential will be revealed. Just as the dust settles after the rain and we can see the whole world more clearly, when wandering thoughts and desires disappear from our minds, prajna naturally shows itself.

Master Daesan said, "In order to attain great enlightenment, one should always study and ponder koans; this is the key to enlightenment. To get enlightened as soon as possible, one should maintain the one-pointed state of mind."

If thinking about and studying the Heart Sutra is the approach from branches to roots, meditation on the Heart Sutra is the reverse approach, from roots to branches.

The fourth way to embody the Heart Sutra is through chanting the text.

When we recite the Heart Sutra repeatedly, it settles into us on a very deep level. Practicing in this way can lead us to eventually become one with the sutra—and when that happens its meaning will be fully apparent. Reciting the Heart Sutra is such a popular way of offering Buddhist prayer that many Mahayana Buddhists recite or copy the sutra to invoke the power that is inherent within ourselves.

The fifth way to embody the Heart Sutra is through teaching the sutra.

It is said that the best way to learn is to teach. Kyungsan, the current Head Dharma Master of Won Buddhism, studied the Zen text "Secrets on Cultivating the Mind" many times as a student of Won Buddhism. Despite his efforts, many parts of the text refused to become clear. But later when he taught the text as a minister at the Youngsan Zen University, the meaning became crystal clear. I too have taught the Heart Sutra for several semesters, and this was indeed the best way for me to understand its meaning. When one prepares and teaches something to others, one deeply contemplates that subject, and during this process its full meaning becomes clear. Teaching sutras provides a wonderful opportunity to reflect on one's practice and life.

According to the Avalokiteshvara Sutra, the Bodhisattva of Great Compassion said that he would come to the world in a degenerate age in various forms, sometimes as a butcher, sometimes as a bartender, sometimes as a cook, sometimes as a prostitute. The best person to teach Dharma to a butcher is his coworker. The best person to awaken a bartender is his fellow worker. Likewise, the best person to help your loved ones walk on the spiritual path is you, not the Dalai Lama or some prominent Buddhist master. Because we are often available and close to our loved ones, they are able to hear our words better than those of a stranger and they may take our words more seriously. When we consider that the best way to help others is to open their minds and hearts and lead them to spiritual progress, we should become a teacher to them, whether at home or at work. We can become a great bodhisattva by helping them.

The Heart Sutra ends with the chanting phrase "*gate gate paragate parasamgate bodhi svaha*," which means "Gone, gone, gone beyond, gone altogether beyond! Now awakened!"

The Buddha encourages us to go to the other shore of nirvana together with all other sentient beings. The chance to meet the Buddha's teaching is said to be as slim as a blind turtle putting its head through a hole in a piece of wood floating on the ocean, or a mustard seed falling onto the point of a needle. Let us not lose the chance to teach the Dharma to our loved ones and to the people around us.

The sixth way to actualize the Heart Sutra is through altruistic action. The Heart Sutra is about the ultimate reality (or no-self). One of the best ways to conquer ignorance and reveal our true self is through selflessly helping others.

When the ego disappears, the meaning of the Heart Sutra will be revealed. By actively involving ourselves in selfless service to the public, we can let the shadow of our ego disappear so that prajna will be revealed.

A journalist once asked Mother Teresa what motivated her to help the poor and abandoned people with such dedication for such a long period of time. She replied, "Because I know that they are Jesus in disguise." These words are just like the words of Zen masters who have practiced sitting meditation for a long time and have realized the truth. Mother Teresa may not have practiced sitting meditation or worked with koans, but she lived her life in selfless service. Subsequently the light of prajna very naturally shone forth from within her.

When I lived in Korea, the written exam for a driving test was composed of two parts: one set of questions was about the traffic regulations, and the other set was about car mechanics. With only limited experience of opening the hood and looking at the engine, it was hard for me to remember all the functions of the different parts. However, after driving for several years and fixing the car several times, I naturally came to understand how each part of the car works. Likewise, when we live our lives compassionately and without ego, and are always helping others, then the nature of our true self, the emptiness of our reality, is revealed. That is why cultivating *bodhichitta*— the aspiration to attain awakening in order to deliver all beings from suffering—is so important and fundamental for one's awakening. A selfless and compassionate mind is a calm and peaceful mind. A compassionate mind is a wise mind; it is happy and contented, powerful and focused. Wisdom and compassion cannot be separated: they are said to be the two wings of a bird. With these two wings, one can fly to nirvana.

Helping others is also a great way to create blessings, which are important assets for practitioners according to the Buddha's own words. Without many blessings, it is hard for us to find an ideal environment that supports our practice. Without many blessings, we cannot meet a good teacher or a good dharma friend. Letting go of self and helping others is not only a great way to dissolve our sense of self, but it is also a great way to create many blessings. This process is essential if this world is to become a better place.

To completely embody and actualize the Heart Sutra, we need to become one with our true self. We need to be unified with our authentic self in order for prajna to be revealed. To achieve that, we should continuously study, contemplate the sutra, practice meditation, and lead altruistic lives. Then, eventually, the darkness of our ego will disappear, and the light of our innate wisdom will shine. *This is the end of suffering!*

When we finally attain our innate buddha nature, which cannot be tainted or destroyed, we can walk hand in hand with all buddhas.

Go to the Root!
I have no help for those who search for twigs.

—Zen Master Yung Chia

Entering the Path of a Bodhisattva 2

Grass becomes milk when consumed by a cow
But becomes poison when consumed
By a venomous snake.

—Traditional aphorism

THE HEART SUTRA begins with these words: "The Bodhisattva of Great Compassion..." In contrast, most Buddhist scriptures begin with "Thus have I heard," which explains who the speaker is, the time when the sutra was delivered, the place where it was delivered, and to whom the sutra was spoken. The Heart Sutra, however, begins without any introduction because the Heart Sutra is the essence, the condensed form, of all prajna paramita literature.[18]

"The Bodhisattva of Great Compassion" is the English translation of the Sanskrit *Avalokiteshvara Bodhisattva*. The prefix *ava-* means "down," *lokita* means "behold, observe, look," and *ishvara* means "lord, master, ruler." Thus, *Avalokiteshvara* literally means "lord who gazes down at the world," or "master of looking down at the world." The word "world" is absent from the name, but it is implied in the phrase.

Bodhisattva literally means "a being of enlightenment" or "an enlightened existence." *Bodhi* means "awakening" or "enlightenment." *Sattva* means "a being" or "an existence." In Mahayana Buddhism, the bodhisattva is the ideal practitioner who seeks supreme enlightenment not for himself but for the sake of all sentient beings. His goal of practice, his motivation, is to deliver all sentient beings from suffering to complete liberation.

In Mahayana Buddhism there are many bodhisattva figures. For example, Shakyamuni Buddha mentions figures such as Manjushri Bodhisattva, Ksitigarbha Bodhisattva, and Mahasthamaprapta Bodhisattva in various sutras, all of whom are completely enlightened beings. They have already attained supreme enlightenment, yet they remain as bodhisattvas instead of entering final nirvana. This is because at the beginning of their practice, they made a vow not to enter nirvana until all sentient beings are completely liberated. These bodhisattvas continue to help countless beings escape from suffering. In Mahayana Buddhist temples the images of various bodhisattvas are usually shown standing, which symbolizes that they are still diligently working to help sentient beings. In the Heart Sutra, Avalokiteshvara Bodhisattva is the main figure who practices prajna paramita to deliver all beings from suffering.

Chenrezig, the Tibetan name for Avalokiteshvara, means "the one who always looks upon all beings" with the eye of compassion. Here *chen* means "eye," *re* means "continuity," and *zig* means "look."

In the East, as well as in the West, Guan Yin, or Guan Shi Yin, is one of the most common translations of this bodhisattva's name, literally meaning "the one who looks down upon the sounds (cries) of the world." Guan Yin Bodhisattva is the personification of all buddhas' compassion and observes all the suffering of sentient beings in the world. In line with this spirit, Avalokiteshvara Bodhisattva is freely translated as "the Bodhisattva of Great Compassion" and is also called "Bestower of Fearlessness" because he helps to take away the worries and fears of all sentient beings.

In Mahayana Buddhist temples, there are two standing bodhisattva statues inside the Buddha Hall where Shakyamuni Buddha is enshrined, representing the two major bodhisattvas who assist him. One is the Bodhisattva of Great Compassion and the other is Manjushri Bodhisattva ("the Great Wisdom Bodhisattva"). In Pure Land Buddhist traditions, inside the Ultimate Bliss Hall, where Amitabha Buddha is enshrined as the principal Buddha, the Bodhisattva of Great Compassion is one of the two assisting bodhisattvas along with Mahasthamaprapta Bodhisattva, who represents great wisdom and strength.

The images of the Bodhisattva of Great Compassion are diverse. The Bodhisattva sometimes holds a lotus flower, at other times he holds a jar filled with purifying water that quenches the thirst (that is, the desires) of sentient beings, and at still other times he holds a wish-fulfilling gem. In iconographic images, the Bodhisattva sometimes has a thousand eyes and a thousand arms, which symbolize the Bodhisattva's omniscience and omnipotence respectively. The Eleven-Faced Avalokiteshvara image is shown having ten additional faces, which allow him to observe and help all sentient beings in the ten directions. The Horse-Headed Avalokiteshvara, which is a wrathful form, symbolizes the Bodhisattva's manifestation to save ignorant beings in the animal realm. All these images or manifestations represent the many ways Avalokiteshvara has of saving numberless sentient beings, depending on their levels and situations.

In the Lotus Sutra, the Buddha mentions the Bodhisattva of Great Compassion:

> Inexhaustible Intent, this Bodhisattva Perceiver of the World's Sounds has succeeded in acquiring benefits such as these and, taking on a variety of different forms, goes about among the lands saving living beings...
>
> He is endowed with transcendental powers and widely practices the expedient means of wisdom. Throughout the lands in the ten directions there is no region where he does not manifest himself...
>
> You must single-mindedly call on the name of Bodhisattva Perceiver of the World's Sounds. This bodhisattva

can grant fearlessness to living beings. If you call his name, you will be delivered from these evil…[19]

Avalokiteshvara Bodhisattva is a historical figure but also represents the compassionate aspect of our "original mind." As long as we practice with a vow to help others, we are the Bodhisattva of Great Compassion, and we become the leading figure in the Heart Sutra, whether we are a layperson or are ordained, whether celibate or married, living in the monastery or living in secular society.

I once heard a Christian minister telling a story about a ninety-year-old woman. She was very weak, but whenever she found a positive story in a newspaper or a magazine, she would cut it out. When she felt well enough to go outside, she would bring these articles to old folks in the nearby nursing homes. As she visited more and more, bringing her comforting stories and encouraging words, her popularity grew. She had such an influence that many people around her started to do similar things for others in need.

When I worked at the Philadelphia Won Buddhist temple and at the Won Institute of Graduate Studies, I saw many bodhisattvas. Some members came early to prepare refreshments, others volunteered to help arrange various events, and still others helped Korean ministers to improve their English. All of them were fulfilling the mission of Avalokiteshvara Bodhisattva.

The teaching of the Heart Sutra is implied in its title, Maha Prajna Paramita Hridaya Sutra: to transcend suffering through wisdom. Why then is the main figure not Manjushri Bodhisattva (the Bodhisattva of Great Wisdom) but rather is the Bodhisattva of Great Compassion? This choice is related to the idea of *bodhichitta*, or the motivation of our practice, which is significant in Mahayana Buddhism.

This is best explained when we consider the way Hsuan-tsang (602–64 C.E.), one of the greatest Buddhist translators in Chinese history, received the Heart Sutra. Although there were already many translated Buddhist sutras in China during Hsuan-tsang's time, as a young monk he wanted to know the authentic Buddhadharma by means of the original Buddhist sutras written in Pali and Sanskrit. So he embarked on a journey to India at the age of twenty-nine to learn and to bring back the Pali and Sanskrit sutras. This journey was both long and extremely dangerous. He had to cross over the Taklamakan Desert and the Hindu Kush, a western subrange of the Himalayas. Most of his predecessors who embarked on this journey did not come back.

Hsuan-tsang's journey to India was arduous and lasted many years. He had to overcome many perilous situations during his journey. Finally, he reached a small village on the northern side of the Ganges River. He decided that he would stay one night in one of the Buddhist temples before crossing the river the next day. When he searched for a temple, he discovered that the whole village was abandoned. No one was there at all! When he finally located an old Buddhist temple and entered it, he saw an ancient monk who was quite ill and smelled of some skin disease. The old monk almost looked like a leper. When Hsuan-tsang asked what happened to him and where all the villagers had gone, the sick old monk told him that the entire village had been stricken by an epidemic, and all the people had fled to avoid the contagion. He said that because he was so sick and weak, he had decided to remain in the temple.

Hsuan-tsang wondered whether he should remain in that temple to take care of the sick monk or leave the next morning to continue his journey. He decided to stay because he felt that without his help, the sick monk might die. Hsuan-tsang stayed in the temple for the next several weeks and did his best to help the old monk. Because of his sincere and committed care, the monk recovered and thanked him for his help. When Hsuan-tsang left, the old monk gave him a small box, which he said was a temple heirloom. The monk then told Hsuan-tsang that when he encountered any dangerous situation, he could open the box and use the item inside. Hsuan-tsang thanked him for the gift and left the temple.

When he reached the shore of the Ganges River, he searched for a ferry to take him across. There, he encountered several tribesmen who were searching for a human to sacrifice. The tribe regularly sacrificed humans to appease the river god. They tied Hsuan-tsang up and put him in a boat. As he was about to be thrown overboard into the river, he recalled the old monk's words and hurriedly opened the box. Inside he found a short sutra and a note explaining that one could recite this sutra in dangerous situations. It should be recited three times. Hsuan-tsang began to recite the sutra loudly. When he was about to finish the third recitation, a black cloud suddenly began to form in the sky, and it began to rain heavily. Growing frightened, the tribesmen decided that Hsuan-tsang was a man of god and they immediately released him.

During his six-year journey to Nalanda University,[20] where he studied the original Pali and Sanskrit Buddhist sutras for many years, Hsuan-tsang encountered many dangerous situations. With the help of that sutra, he safely overcame every obstacle. When he left Nalanda University to return to China, he looked for the temple where he had met the old monk. He wanted to thank him for the sutra that had helped him overcome so many hardships. He searched the entire countryside but could not find any trace of the village. He asked many people whether they knew of a village that was struck by an epidemic a number of years ago but everyone said they had lived in that area for a long time and had never heard of that village. Hsuan-tsang concluded that the old monk was a manifestation of the Bodhisattva of Great Compassion, who had been testing him.

The sutra which he received from that old monk is known as the Heart Sutra. It has become customary practice to chant the Heart Sutra three times in many Buddhist traditions because of the instruction in the box. In most cases, however, just the last phrase, *gate gate paragate parasamgate bodhi svaha*, is repeated three times.

When Hsuan-tsang came back from India, he was welcomed by the emperor and was entrusted with the grand project of translating the original Buddhist sutras into Chinese. The story of the divine power of the Heart Sutra became well known, and reciting the Heart Sutra grew more popular.

Although there were already many Chinese translations of the Heart Sutra,[21] Hsuan-tsang's 649 C.E. translation became the standard version throughout Asia. Most English translations are based on his Chinese translation.

Whether the story of how Hsuan-tsang received the Heart Sutra is historically true or not, his test before receiving the sutra is significant to Buddhist teachings. Before he received the sutra, he was first tested to see whether he had *bodhichitta* or not, and to see if he was compassionate enough to help others.

Practice is like driving a car. First we must know our destination or goal. And just as important is who is on the journey with us—anyone who has traveled knows how important fellow travelers are. According to the Buddha, the practitioner's final destination is the attainment of buddhahood and liberation from samsara, the cycle of birth and death. However, we are traveling with all sentient beings, and we should attain buddhahood along with them.

Zen Master Seung Sahn, who practiced in the Mahayana tradition, classified meditation into several categories.[22] The first is "outer-path meditation." In Korea, there are many psychics who also meditate and do various forms of spiritual practice. Many of them do ascetic practices in order to make themselves more spiritual. Yet the goal for many of them is to make more money, so we cannot say that they are walking a proper path. Their practice will turn out to be fruitless.

The second is "average people's meditation." Many people meditate or do spiritual practice in order to reduce stress or to attain a peaceful and calm state of mind. Meditation, as well as other forms of spiritual cultivation, works well for these purposes, but this is just the motivation of the average person's meditation or practice.

The third is "Hinayana meditation," where people practice to liberate themselves from the cycle of rebirth, to have complete liberation. Their goal of practice is clear, but as long as they practice solely for the sake of their own salvation, it is still not the highest form of practice.

The last is "Mahayana meditation." This is the practice for the sake of all sentient beings. These meditators practice out of compassion to help free all beings from suffering. *Bodhichitta* is the motivation of their practice.

Yana means "vehicle" or "conveyance." *Maha* means "great" or "big," and *hina* means "small." So Mahayana means "the great vehicle," and Hinayana means "the smaller vehicle." Mahayana and Hinayana do not truly exist as traditions or Buddhist denominations. They only exist in our minds. If we practice with the motivation to help all beings, then we are driving the great vehicle, Mahayana. If we practice for the sake of ourselves, for our own benefit, then we are driving the smaller vehicle, Hinayana.

No bodhisattva attained the great enlightenment without first making a vow. In the case of Avalokiteshvara Bodhisattva, he vowed to attain the great enlightenment and to save all sentient beings from suffering.

In the Diamond Sutra, when Subhuti, one of the Buddha's ten main disciples, asked the Buddha how practitioners could control their wandering minds, the Buddha answered that all practitioners should control and discipline their thoughts by making a great vow to deliver all sentient beings:

> Buddha said: Subhuti, all the bodhisattva heroes should discipline their thoughts as follows: All living creatures of whatever class, born from eggs, from wombs, from moisture, or by transformation whether with form or without form, whether in a state of thinking or exempt from thought necessity, or wholly beyond all thought realms— all these are led by me to attain unbounded liberation nirvana.[23]

When I was in college, I knew a student who was quite sensitive. He was self-conscious and vulnerable to other people's opinions. Whenever he took an exam, he worried that he would not do his best.

In his sophomore year, he became involved in a student movement whose ideology was based upon socialism. He finally felt that he had found his life goal. All of a sudden, he became a focused, tranquil person. He ceased to be nervous or worried about the opinions of others. He did not practice meditation—his tranquillity and calm state of mind came from his clear life goal.

Likewise, in the Diamond Sutra, the Buddha first asks all practitioners to make a vow before practice. This life goal or vow makes the practitioners' minds centered and focused:

> One of the disciples asked, "By what method should I cultivate so that I may eliminate all of the five desires, focus single-mindedly on cultivating the Way, and lead a life of tranquillity and comfort like the Buddha?"
>
> The Founding Master [of Won Buddhism] replied, "Rather than eliminating desires, you should expand them. Once your petty desires are transformed into a great vow, they will naturally subside as you focus single-mindedly on your vow. Then, you will inevitably lead a life of tranquillity and comfort."[24]

Our vow is like a root: it is the foundation of our practice. Like a root, our vow grows and becomes stronger. Just as we plant, water, and nurture a seed, our vow is something that we have to take care of in order for it to grow. That is why in Mahayana temples people chant the Four Great Vows at every service. It is also why they chant the Heart Sutra; they chant the last passage, *gate gate paragate parasamgate bodhi svaha*, three times. With these final words of "gone, gone, gone beyond, gone altogether beyond! Now awakened!" the Buddha asks us to reflect continuously on our vow or where our lives are going.

When the Buddha left his palace, he made two vows: he would attain supreme enlightenment and he would then deliver all sentient beings from suffering. Because of those vows, any time the Buddha sat, he sat with all sentient beings. When he ate, he ate with all sentient beings. Just like the Buddha, if we practice with such a great vow, then when we sit, we sit with all sentient beings; when we eat, it nourishes all sentient beings. Practicing with such a great vow is as powerful as any politician's actions to disarm the military or help the hungry children in Africa. Bodhisattvas are sometimes called *mahasattvas*, or "great beings," not only because their enlightenment is deep, but also because their vow is great and boundless.

It is not only Nelson Mandela or Martin Luther King, Jr., who are bodhisattvas. If we make this great vow, we all become bodhisattvas, mahasattvas. It is not just Gandhi or Mother Teresa who are holy. As long as we have the great vow, we too are holy. A holy person is not merely one who meditates for ten or twelve hours each day. A holy person is not one who practices in the Himalayas. A holy person is one who has made a holy vow and lives according to that vow, practicing to fulfill it. Living a holy life in a secular world is far more difficult and far more holy.

A number of years ago, a bridge collapsed during rush hour because it could not bear the weight of so much traffic. Investigation revealed that it happened because an engineer had miscalculated the weight of the traffic. One person's carelessness led to a great tragedy, and many lives were lost. These days everyone is very closely linked. One person's problem can become a problem for someone else, and one nation's problem can become a world problem. We cannot live or prosper by ourselves. Without others' help, we cannot survive. Whether we like it or not, we are deeply indebted to others, and we have to live and work together.

Let us all plant the seed of *bodhichitta* and make a great vow to help others. Let us nurture that seed until it grows so tall that all sentient beings can rest under its shade.

Life is characterized by suffering and dissatisfaction. As long as we are born and live in this world, we cannot escape from the suffering that is inherent in life, whether it is from old age, sickness, or simply not getting what we want.

Master Seng Tsan[25] had an incurable skin disease similar to leprosy in his youth, which cut him off from other people and eventually drove him to take up the practice of meditation. Like Seng Tsan, many enlightened masters have transformed their adversity into a great vow and passion to practice. All the suffering in their lives was used as fertilizer to help their vow and practice grow and mature.

Consider the story of how the Bodhisattva of Great Compassion first came to make a vow. According to the Jataka Tales, the stories of the previous incarnations of the Buddha, a businessman had two sons. After his wife died, he remarried, but his new wife did not like his two boys. After she gave birth to her own child, her hatred toward the boys deepened, and one day, when her husband was out of town, she decided to get rid of them. She bribed a boatman, who took them to a remote island. While they were absorbed in playing, the boatman left the island, stranding them. When night set in, they grew terrified. They searched for the man and his boat, calling his name all night, but their efforts were futile. As the night deepened, the temperature dropped. Crying, the shivering and hungry boys embraced each other to keep warm. When they were about to die from the cold, they vowed that whenever people called their names, they would rush to them and help them. They would help suffering beings out of their misery. Those were their last thoughts as they died.

When their father came back from his trip to discover that his sons were missing, he abandoned his job and searched for them everywhere. When he finally found their bodies on the remote island, he understood what had happened. He was so disillusioned with the secular world that he left society to become a monk. Many eons later, the father became Amitabha Buddha. The older boy became the Bodhisattva of Great Compassion, and the younger one became Mahasthamaprapta Bodhisattva. Because of this karmic tie, these three enlightened beings are enshrined side by side in the Ultimate Bliss Hall of the Buddhist monasteries and are called "the Three Saints of the Western Pure Land."

Suffering is rich soil where a great vow can sprout. Suffering provides great energy and motivation for many people to begin their practice with sincerity. When everything is going our way, we hardly reflect on our lives. If we live inside of our comfort zone, it is very hard to redirect our lives. Just as a lotus flower grows and blooms in muddy water, our vow and practice grow from adversity and suffering. As long as the seed of our great vow does not wither and die, it will eventually bear the fruit of buddhahood. When we practice with this great vow to help all sentient beings, we are walking hand in hand with all buddhas and bodhisattvas.

EMPTINESS OF SELF

"To this sage who sees what is good
I have come supplicatingly with a question,
'How is anyone to look upon the world so as not to be seen by
the king of death?'"
"Look upon the world as empty, O Mogharagan," said the
Buddha, "being always wakeful; having destroyed the view
of oneself as really existing, one may overcome death;
the king of death will not see the person
who thus regards the world."

—Buddha (Sutta-Nipata)²⁶

The Bodhisattva of Great Compassion, when deeply
practicing prajna paramita, realized that all five aggregates are empty and became free from all suffering and
distress.

IN THIS CHAPTER, we will look closely at some of the terms used
in the excerpt above.

...paramita...

Paramitas are types of training used to perfect or purify ourselves, in order to attain enlightenment. *Paramita* means "perfection," "crossing over," or "going to the other shore." *Prajna paramita*, or the perfection of wisdom, is one of the six paramitas necessary to go to that other shore (nirvana), from the world of suffering to the world of freedom. Besides prajna, the other five paramitas are *dhyana, sila, dana, virya,* and *khanti.* Each paramita reflects and supports all of the others, and all six must be practiced to attain nirvana.

Dhyana is one-pointed concentration or contemplation. It is a state of deep meditative absorption characterized by lucid awareness, which can be achieved by focusing the mind on a single object. Prajna, or innate wisdom, arises when our minds are centered and calm. Just as a pond whose surface is free of ripples can reflect the moon clearly, so one-pointedness of mind is essential to reveal prajna. Prajna and *dhyana* are inseparable. They are two sides of the same coin. The Sanskrit *dhyana* was translated as *seon-na* or *seon* into Chinese. This word was translated again into Korean as *Seon,* and into Japanese as *Zen.*

Sila is virtue, morality, or proper conduct. Ethical conduct, including proper speech and wholesome action, is essential to attaining a calm and centered state of mind. *Sila* and prajna are connected: virtue, or morality, comes from controlling our minds, our speech, and our actions. And yet, without *sila,* our minds cannot be anchored in prajna.

Dana is generosity, or giving of oneself. The root of our desires and our wandering thoughts is our ego. Generosity, especially giving away things that we cherish, is one of the best and most powerful ways to dissolve our sense of self. *Dana* is the manifestation of our true self, or no-self. By practicing *dana* paramita, we can cultivate *bodhichitta,* which allows us to become very compassionate. When our minds become wide open and compassionate, we begin to settle down, and true wisdom begins to arise.

Virya is diligence, energy, vigor, or effort. Without diligence or energy, none of the other paramitas can be perfected. Whether it is meditation, generosity, endurance, or observing the precepts of Buddhism, without vigorous and energetic effort nothing will be realized. Think about it like this: owning a cookbook does not make you a great chef. Just as you actually have to cook the food to make a great meal, for all the paramitas to be realized, you must apply effort and diligence.

Khanti is patience, forbearance, or endurance. Zen Master So San said, "If you have no patience, the limitless compassionate functioning of the six paramitas cannot be attained."[27] To practice all the other paramitas, patience and endurance are essential. How can we expect to harvest a crop immediately after planting the seeds? It takes time for all the paramitas to bear fruit, which requires a great deal of patience. When we walk on the spiritual path, we have to fight with egoistic desires, laziness, greed, and jealousy on a daily basis. When we meditate, we may encounter many obstacles, everything from doubt to boredom to restlessness. Without the paramita of patience, we cannot continue to carry out all the other paramitas successfully.

As you might have noticed, it's difficult to clearly differentiate the six paramitas. Just like the many-faceted jewels of Indra's net,[28] each paramita contains and reflects all the other paramitas. Therefore, in order to practice prajna paramita completely, it is necessary to practice all the paramitas, too. In the sutra Perfection of Wisdom in Eight Thousand Lines, the Buddha tells Ananda, "The paramita of wisdom incorporates the other five paramitas by means of practices that are based on all-embracing knowledge. Thus does the paramita of wisdom include the other five paramitas. The 'paramita of wisdom' is simply a synonym for the fruition of all six paramitas."[29]

Perfecting prajna paramita is the result of practicing all the paramitas completely. The first five paramitas (meditation, morality, generosity, diligence, and patience) correspond to the accumulation of merit (*karma*), whereas the sixth (*prajna*) is focused on the accumulation of wisdom. Prajna paramita both guides the other paramitas and is the culmination of them.

...practicing...

The word "practicing" used in the above passage is the translation of the Sanskrit *caryam caramano*, which literally means "action perform." Thus, prajna paramita is not the object of thinking, discussing, or contemplating, but rather it is something for us to put into action in order to attain enlightenment.

Several years ago, when preparing for a big event at the Won Institute (the graduate school where I was employed), I asked our pre-minister students, who were studying Won Buddhism, to help me by doing some of the work. However, they were very reluctant to help because they said that they had to write term papers. They tried to pass the work of preparing for the event on to other students, which was not very compassionate. And which class required the paper? They told me: "The Theory of Compassion."

Chongsan, the Second Head Dharma Master of Won Buddhism, said, "It is better to contemplate something one time rather than to read about it ten times. Contemplating something one hundred times is not as good as putting it into action one time." Neither compassion nor wisdom is a subject for talking or contemplation. It is, rather, something that must be practiced.

Since the six paramitas are closely related and complementary to one another, without one, the others cannot be complete. Therefore, practicing prajna paramita is practicing meditation, working with koans, studying scriptures, doing altruistic work, and so on, all at the same time.

...deeply...

Whether it is in meditation or enlightenment, the depth of practice is different. Consider sight. You might think "seeing" is the same for everyone, yet some people have 20/20 vision, whereas others have 20/10 vision. "Practicing deeply" means practicing prajna paramita with utmost devotion, with great sincerity, and with great commitment. By doing so, the Bodhisattva of Great Compassion reached the most profound level of enlightenment.

...when...

In this passage, "when" refers to the moment of realization. The truth, to which the Bodhisattva of Great Compassion became enlightened, was the empty nature of himself, which is identical with the nature of ourselves. "Realized" is the translation of the Sanskrit *pashyati vyavalokayati*, which means "to see luminously." Realization or enlightenment is called *kyun-sung* in Chinese, which literally means "seeing the original nature." Hsuan-tsang, whose translation of the Heart Sutra has become the standard version throughout Asia, translated *pashyati vyavalokayati* as *cho-kyon*, which literally means "illuminate and see."

The Heart Sutra says, "In the Buddha's day, a person who saw what others did not see was called a *pashyaka*, or seer. Avalokiteshvara's seeing is 'deep' seeing."[30] Avalokiteshvara's realization was like turning on the light and seeing the truth with his own eyes rather than fumbling and feeling for an object in a dark room. This is the "direct experience" of enlightenment.

During the Buddha's time, there was a blind, brilliant philosopher who denied the existence of light. He said, "If there is such a thing as light, let me smell it or taste it. Put it before me so that I can bump against it or touch it." Many other philosophers tried to disprove his argument, but it was impossible to persuade that blind philosopher. So one day they brought him to the Buddha. The Buddha said to them that he could not persuade the philosopher, but he sent the philosopher to a good physician, who cured the philosopher's blindness. Seeing the light directly with his own eyes, the philosopher no longer doubted or argued about the existence of light.

Intellectual understanding of the truth is like reading a menu in a restaurant. The menu does not make you full. When we actually see into our original mind, our practice and our lives will begin to change. We will become a different person.

When the Bodhisattva of Great Compassion deeply and luminously saw the empty nature of reality, he became free from all suffering and distress.

...five aggregates...

The "five aggregates" mentioned in the passage comes from the Sanskrit *panca skandhas*. *Skandhas* means aggregates, clumps, heaps, piles, or collections. The five aggregates are one of the most significant concepts in Buddhism.

The aggregates are the five elements that comprise a human being. They are the five components of our personality or individuality. According to the Buddha's words, humans are a collection of physical and mental constituents: one material aspect and four nonmaterial aspects of experience.

The Heart Sutra says that when the Bodhisattva of Great Compassion awakened to the empty reality of himself, he became free from all suffering and distress. What people want most is to be free from suffering and to enjoy a happy life. What is the root of our suffering? Where does all this distress come from? It arises from "I." Just as all plants grow from the soil, so too our suffering or happiness arises from our sense of self.

Although we do not know exactly what this "I" or self is, the notion is always following us. Therefore, let us investigate this "I."

Rupa. The first of the aggregates is *rupa*, which in English means "form." This refers to the material aspect of our experience, including the five material sense organs (eye, ear, nose, tongue, and body) and their corresponding sense objects (visible form, sound, smell, taste, and touch). Our bodies and all physical objects are *rupa*.

Next are the nonmaterial aspects.

Vedana. This means "sensations" or "feelings." *Vedana* is derived from the root *vid*, which means "to know," "to experience," or "to feel."

Sensations arise when the eye comes into contact with light or visual form. The same is true when the ear contacts sound, the nose contacts smell, the tongue contacts taste, the body contacts tangible objects, and the mind encounters ideas or thoughts. (In Buddhism, the mind is considered one of the six sense organs, along with the eye, ear, nose, tongue, and body.) Therefore, *vedana* consists of five physical sensations and our emotions.

Samjna. This is "perception." Perception means the apprehension of an object as distinct from other objects. It works to recognize, categorize, conceptualize, and reason. The word *samjna* is composed of the word *sam*, which means "with" or "together," and *jna*, which means "to know" or "to perceive." Perception is recognizing and identifying the object based on the data that comes through our sense organs.

The Chinese translated *samjna* into *sang* (想). The upper part of this character (相) means "mark," "sign," or "appearance," and the lower part (心) means "mind" or "spirit."[31] A perception is a mark or trace that is left in our minds by sensations. On the physical level, it is the discernment of the five objects of our senses as outlined above. On the conceptual level, it is the recognition of identities or names. For instance, when my eyes come in contact with an object that is round, transparent, ten inches high, and bulging in the middle with a spout, I think, "It is a pitcher." This thought is based on my experience or memory that a pitcher looks like this. That is what is meant by perception.

Samskara. *Samskara* means "impulse," "volition," "will," or "mental formations." It is the intention to do something, regarding form, sound, smell, taste, touch, or mental phenomena. For instance, I happened to see a forty-year-old woman who was approximately six feet tall, blonde, and wearing a black leather jacket—much like my ex-wife. When my eyes encountered this woman, visual sensations arose; this is *vedana*, the second aggregate. Based on my memory or knowledge that my ex-wife is forty years old, and six feet tall, blonde, and loved wearing a black leather jacket, the thought can arise, "She is my ex-wife"; this is *samjna* or perception, the third aggregate. These sensations or perceptions can be pleasant, unpleasant, or neutral, depending on how I feel about my ex-wife. From sensations and perceptions, liking and disliking arise. In this moment, the dualistic world is created. Based on liking or disliking, the desire to push or pull arises. This is *samskara*, the stage in which karma is created. The Buddha said, "O bhikkhus, it is volition that I call karma. Having willed, one acts through body, speech, and mind."[32]

Vijnana. This means "consciousness." Consciousness is the basic awareness that makes our experience possible, giving us the ability to maintain, recognize, compare, store, and remember information. Because of consciousness, we can know the other aggregates.

For instance, when the thought arises that the woman I see is my ex-wife, another thought may follow. For example, noticing that she still wears that leather jacket, I may reflect on how she never seemed to grow up and how her immaturity was the root of all our problems. Or I may observe how stylish she looks, and I may want to resume my relationship with her. Seeing her again can strengthen my feelings for her.

Your thoughts become stored in your consciousness just as a seed is sown in the soil. When that seed meets the proper conditions, it sprouts and grows; so too do all the memories stored in your consciousness arise when they meet certain conditions. For instance, when you are lonely, or when you happen to see someone wearing a certain style of leather jacket, the memory of your ex-wife may arise.

In our lives, consciousness plays the most important role. All of our thoughts, actions, and impulses are stored in our consciousness in the form of seeds. This consciousness, storing different karmic seeds, differentiates our self from others and links this life to our next life.

I heard a story from Bhante Rahula, a former American abbot in the Bhavana Society, a Theravadin Buddhist monastery located in West Virginia. One day, while traveling in India as a young man, he went to a Buddhist monastery and attended a service there. Although he was not a Buddhist, nor a spiritual person, when he heard the monk's Dharma talk, all of a sudden, he felt something stir in his mind and heart. Though he didn't understand why, he wanted to stay in that monastery. Later he became a monk.

When I was in high school, I climbed a mountain with my friends. We lost the trail because of a sudden, thick fog, But we happened to find a Buddhist temple, which was tiny and looked abandoned. When I entered the temple, I felt so at home that I thought this was the place where I should live.

One of the Korean Zen masters became a monk when he was in his teens because he said that when he came to the temple with his mother, the sound of the wind blowing inside the temple courtyard aroused in him a strong sense of impermanence.

All these thoughts are seeds that had been planted in previous lives finally sprouting.

These mental aggregates are hard to distinguish from each other because they are closely related and often arise simultaneously. Where does the busy city end and the suburb begin? Where does the cheek end and the chin begin? Yet, these five aggregates share the same nature: they are all dependently arising. This means that whatever the aggregate, it arises depending on causes and conditions. The five aggregates cannot exist in and of themselves.

Let us now examine the five aggregates from the perspective of dependent arising:

Form. Our body comes into being relying upon what we eat, drink, and breathe. Without our parents and our grandparents, we could not exist. This body exists temporarily as the combination of elements comprising it is dispersed over time.

Sensations. Sensations are all conditional, meaning that when a sensory organ meets a sense object (such as a sound or smell), the corresponding sensation arises. For instance, sorrow arises when my ear hears the news that my mother has passed away. Resentment or anger arises when a certain unpleasant memory pops up. Whatever the sensation is, it arises dependently.

Perceptions. Just like form and sensations, perceptions dependently arise and have conditional existence. In the earlier example, the thought that the woman I saw was my ex-wife arose based on my visual sensation (I saw a forty-year-old woman who was blonde, six feet tall, and wearing a leather jacket) and my memory (I recall that my ex-wife is blonde, tall, and used to wear a leather jacket). Without sensations, perceptions cannot arise.

Impulses or Volition. Without sensations or perceptions arising, impulses or volition cannot arise. Without seeing the tall, blonde woman wearing a leather jacket, and without my memory, the impulse to approach her or to avoid her cannot arise.

Consciousness. Whether the consciousness is visual, auditory, olfactory, gustatory, tactile, or mental, it is conditional. No consciousness can arise in and of itself. Each arises when our sense organs come into contact with sense objects.

...all five aggregates are empty...

The Buddha says, "With the arising of contact there is the arising of feeling... With the arising of contact there is the arising of perception... With the arising of contact there is the arising of volitional formations [impulses]."[33]

Whether it is physical, mental, or emotional, all of the five aggregates dependently arise and have conditional nature. They are all devoid of any inherent existence or intrinsic nature. This is the meaning of "all five aggregates are empty."

In Sanskrit this passage says, *"panca skandhas tams ca sva bhava sunyam,"* which means, "five aggregates are empty of self-existence."

Although most of the Chinese or English translations of the Heart Sutra use the expression "five aggregates are empty," the real meaning is best expressed in the Sanskrit, "five aggregates are devoid of self," and "they are empty of inherent existence or self-abiding nature."

Just as the concept of "fullness" always means "full of something"—for instance, a hall may be full of people—emptiness here means the absence of any substance in the aggregates.

Whether it is physical, mental, or emotional, everything is dependently arising. Since all things are empty of inherent or true existence, in the absolute sense, they do not exist.[34] Aggregates have no inherently defining characteristics or self-abiding nature. They arise under certain conditions and are continually disappearing without cessation. They are constantly changing into another form. For instance, our bodies are always changing: our hair and nails are continually growing, and between 2 and 2.5 million red blood cells are born and die every second. Even when we are angry or full of resentment for an entire day, the quality and intensity of the anger or resentment changes moment to moment.

The five aggregates exist just like a river. They never stop flowing. The water is there, but it is different at each moment. Impermanence is the nature of the five aggregates as well as of all things. The Buddha said, "When the Aggregates arise, decay and die, O bhikkhu, every moment you are born, decay and die."[35]

Everything exists as a flux. Impermanence is the nature of all things. All existence is conditional and momentary. Things arise from nothingness and return to nothingness.

Just as a scientist investigates and analyzes water as the chemical components that make up H_2O, the Bodhisattva of Great Compassion investigated "I" or self and found that the ground where all our suffering arises does not actually exist. It is truly empty. That means that the idea of an ego entity is just a mental construct or illusion. Self only exists as a name or an idea; in the absolute sense, it does not exist at all.

...free from all suffering...

Just as a weed cannot grow when there is no ground, the realization of the empty nature of ourselves eliminates the foothold where our suffering arises (see the next chapter for more detail). This realization is the way to end suffering permanently. Enlightenment is the way to sever the root of suffering.

Master Hui-ching says, "Once someone understands that the *skandhas* are empty, what does suffering have to rest on?... But when bubbles disperse and become water, they aren't bubbles. Bubbles represent beings and water represents our buddha nature."[36]

Master Chen-k'o says, "by viewing the mind as the four *skandhas*, they also can't find anyone who suffers."[37]

When Avalokiteshvara Bodhisattva investigated "who" suffers, rather than "why" one suffers, he saw the empty nature of the self. He realized that the root of suffering does not exist, and he became free from *all* suffering and distress (for further explanation see the next chapter).

Many times we blame a certain situation or some environment (e.g., our boss, our work, our financial situation, etc.) for our suffering. The Bodhisattva of Great Compassion turned the light inward to illuminate the true source of suffering, which is "I," or the "self."

In Buddhism, there are three common traits that all phenomena share. They are called the "three characteristics" or "three marks" of existence:

    1. Everything is impermanent.
    2. Everything is without self.
    3. Everything is suffering or dissatisfaction.

No-self (emptiness) and impermanence describe the conditional and momentary existence of all things. Because everything is impermanent, everything is suffering; however pleasant something is, it will eventually pass away. The Buddha said, "Whatever is impermanent is dukkha."[38]

No-self, impermanence, and suffering are the three characteristics of all things, and are the three aspects of the one ultimate reality. This is the Buddhist trinity.

The *Samyukta Agama* says:

> Thus have I heard: Once, when the Buddha was dwelling near Shravasti at Anathapindada Garden in Jeta Forest, the Bhagavan [Buddha] told the monks, "Whatever is form is impermanent. And whatever is impermanent is suffering. And whatever is suffering is devoid of a self. One who views things like this sees things as they really are. So, too, are sensation, perception, memory, and consciousness impermanent. And being impermanent, they are suffering. And being suffering, they are devoid of a self and anything that might belong to a self. One who views things like this sees them as they really are. Those noble disciples who view things like this are repulsed by sensation, perception, memory, and consciousness. And because they are repulsed by them, they do not delight in them. And because they do not delight in them, they are free of them. And those who are free give rise to the knowledge of how things really are and can claim: 'My life is finally over, I have set forth on the path of purity, I have done what had to be done, and now I know I will experience no future existence.'" Hearing these words of the Buddha, the monks were pleased and put them into practice.[39]

A college friend in Korea told me about one of his female classmates, who dated a very handsome and intelligent young man for several years. She enjoyed his intelligence and spirituality. Right after she graduated from college, her family moved to the United States, so she and her boyfriend were separated. While she was working on her

Ph.D. at an American university, she heard that the boyfriend got a job at a securities firm and was married. She still, however, loved him and thought about him from time to time. Immediately after finishing her Ph.D., she visited Korea and called him. They met in a café located on the second floor overlooking a beautiful outdoor courtyard. When she saw him entering the café, she was shocked to discover the change in his appearance and personality. He had become bald and gained a lot of weight, and he constantly talked about the stock market and how to make money. She remembered that he had been a romantic and idealistic man who loved to discuss philosophy. But listening to him now, she realized that the image of him that she had kept for such a long time was no longer accurate. Looking at a display of fine china in the courtyard below, she felt as though her image of him was like a piece of fine china that had been shattered.

An image may remain constant, yet everything changes without exception. This is true whether in regard to a person or a thing. However beautiful a flower is, it will eventually wither.

We should embrace every changing aspect in our lives.

Just as we cannot capture a sound, a light, or a fragrance, we cannot deny the reality of impermanence. If we do, we are like a child who cries over a melting snowman, unable to understand why the snowman can't last.

As practitioners, we should learn to enjoy every aspect of our lives just as we enjoy each movement of a symphony or every stage of a flower's growth, from bud to fully blossomed. When we understand and embrace the truth of impermanence, the amount of freedom that we have in our everyday life will become greater and greater.

The Buddha said, "Of all footprints, the elephant's are outstanding; just so, of all subjects of meditation for a follower of the Buddhas, the idea of impermanence is unsurpassed."[40]

Instead of saying, "Today is the first day of the rest of my life," a practitioner might better say, "Today may be the last day of my life."

A number of years ago in Korea, there was a literary contest for middle school students under the auspices of *Hanwoolan* newspaper.

The subject of the composition was "What would you do if you had only three days left to live?" The best composition was published in the newspaper.

One student wrote that if he had only three days left to live, he would visit all the people whom he had known to say thank you on the first day. He wanted to express his heartfelt appreciation for their just being. On the second day, he would visit several nursing homes and orphanages to comfort and assist the inhabitants. On the last day, he wrote that he would retreat to a nearby mountain and spend the night looking at the sky filled with countless stars, and contemplate the mystery of the universe and the human condition.

Is this not what all buddhas ask us to do in our daily lives? What would you do if you had only three days left to live?

Tao Hsin (580–651 C.E.) met Seng Tsan, the Third Patriarch of Zen Buddhism, when he was only fourteen years old. Tao Hsin said, "I ask for the Master's compassion; please instruct me on how to achieve liberation."

Seng Tsan replied, "Is there someone who binds you?"

Tao Hsin paused and pondered for a moment and said, "There is no such person."

Seng Tsan said, "Why then seek liberation when you are bound by no one?"

Upon hearing these words, Tao Hsin was enlightened.

He attended to Seng Tsan for the next nine years.

Tao Hsin became the Fourth Patriarch of Zen Buddhism.

The Bodhisattva of Great Compassion, when deeply practicing prajna paramita, realized that all five aggregates are empty and became free from all suffering and distress.

ALL PEOPLE dream of attaining happiness. No matter where they're from or where they live, their life goal is the same: happiness. The reasons why we suffer are diverse.

Sometimes we suffer because of financial issues or a bad relationship. Other times, we suffer because of a broken dream or simple anger or depression. Whatever the reason, the source of our suffering is always "I," or the self. Just as a tree has many branches but one trunk, we may have many sufferings, but the ultimate cause is "I," or our sense of self.

The above passage from the Heart Sutra says that when the Bodhisattva of Great Compassion was enlightened to his real nature, he became permanently liberated from all suffering and distress.

Let us investigate this "I" more deeply so that we can fundamentally remove the source of our suffering.

What is "I"? Surely "I" is related to our body and mind. When you cut your finger, you say, "I cut myself." In that case, "I" or "myself" means your body. When pointing to a childhood picture, you say, "That is me." "Me" here indicates your body. When we say, "I am tall," "I am fat," "I am beautiful," or "I am ugly," the "I" means our body.

When you say, "I am happy," "I am upset," or "I feel wonderful," the "I" indicates your mind.

Yet our sense of self goes beyond our body and mind. After you have cosmetic surgery, you may still think that you are basically the same person, even though some part of your body has changed.

Though our personalities, moods, habits, and mental faculties constantly change, we still perceive ourselves as the same person. In other words, we just think "my body" or "my mind" has changed.

The expressions "my body" and "my mind" imply that there is some invisible entity or substance that exists permanently beyond our body and mind. Just as fruits belong to a tree, or a pet belongs to its owner, most people believe that our experiences belong to some unchanging entity. Many people identify themselves with this invisible entity, calling it their "true" or "authentic" self.

Yet when the Heart Sutra says "the five aggregates are empty," this means that our belief in this permanent substance is just an illusion. We are just simply the collection of the five components, or *skandhas*, discussed in chapter 3: physical form, sensations, perceptions, impulses, and consciousness. The above passage means that the sense of self that exists beyond our body and mind is just an idea, or mental construct, not reality.

CONCEPT VERSUS REALITY

To better understand this, a clear distinction between concept and reality will be of great help.

When I was very little, whenever I cried, my mother used to say, "Gom-ji is going to catch you if you do not stop crying!" I did not know then what Gom-ji was. From the tone of my mother's voice, I could tell that Gom-ji was a very fierce and strong animal that especially hated crying children (*gom* means "bear" and *ji* means "rat" in Korean). When I grew up, I realized that there was no such thing as Gom-ji: it was just an idea or name that would make children stop crying. As a child, I thought that when people named something, there must be a correspondingly real object. Yet this is not always the case.

In ancient China, an arms dealer sold weapons in the marketplace. He pointed to a spear and said that it was so sharp and strong that it could penetrate any shield. Pointing to the shield next to the spear, he said that this shield was so strong that it could protect against any spear. Upon hearing this, a boy asked the man, "If you strike that shield with that spear, what would happen? Would the shield protect against the spear, or would the spear penetrate the shield?" From this story came the word *mo-soon*, which means "contradiction." *Mo* means "spear" and *soon* means "shield."

The *sharpest* spear, the *strongest* shield, the *biggest* or the *smallest*, the *greatest* or the *least*, these words are purely ideas without any reference based in reality. They exist in our minds only as ideas, not as reality. The belief that every word conveys reality is simply false.

This being said, let us think about whether a fruit is reality or just a concept: does the fruit *really* exist or is it just a name?

You can show me an apple, a pear, or an orange and say that "fruit" is a real thing that actually exists. However, what really exists is a specific type of fruit, the apple, pear, or orange you are holding. "Fruit" is just a concept or name for a category. "Fruit" is an idea rather than reality.[41]

How about color? Is color a reality or just a concept? You can show black, red, or yellow and say that color is a reality. Yet what really exists is a black color, a red color, or a yellow color. In other words, a specific color is what *really* exists. "Color" is just a name for a category of various colors. "Color" is a pure concept rather than reality.

What then is *mind*? Is it a reality or just a concept?

When my teacher was young, she asked a Zen master, "What is the mind?" The master replied, "What you are asking is the mind." My teacher said, "Is not my speaking coming from my mind?" The master just smiled. Later she realized how ignorant she was. Like many people, she believed that there was some invisible entity called "mind," from which our mental faculties originate. Just as fruit and color are pure concepts, "mind" is just a name for various mental faculties. What *really* exist are sensations, perceptions, impulses, and consciousness. They are the reality.[42]

It is not true that from the core called "mind" all kinds of mental or emotional faculties arise. All these mental and emotional faculties dependently arise under certain causes and conditions (see the previous chapter for details). They do not have any inherent substance. Hence the master's reply, "What you are asking is the mind," is truthful.

The following is a well-known analogy regarding our true self, which is no-self.

> Just as the word "chariot" is but a mode of expression for axle, wheels, chariot-body, pole, and other constituent members, placed in a certain relation to each other, but when we come to examine the members one by one, we discover that in the absolute sense there is no chariot. And just as the word "house" is a mode of expression for

wood and other constituents of a house, surrounding space in a certain relation, but in the absolute sense there is no house... "tree" for trunk, branches, foliage, etc., in a certain relation, but when we come to examine the parts one by one, we discover that in the absolute sense there is no tree; in exactly the same way the words "living entity" and "Ego" are but a mode of expression for the presence of the five attachment groups [*skandhas*], but when we come to examine the elements of being one by one, we discover that in the absolute sense there is no living entity there to form a basis for such figments as "I am," or "I"; in other words, that in the absolute sense there is only name and form. The insight of him who perceives this is called knowledge of the truth.[43]

In the *Samyutta Nikaya*, the Buddha says that "just as the word 'chariot' exists on the basis of the aggregation of parts, even so the concept of 'being' exists when the five aggregates are available."

We humans are made up of five elements, which are constantly changing. Our sense of a self that transcends our body and mind is a complete illusion and pure ignorance. There is no permanent, unchanging entity behind our body and mind, where our experiences belong. The Buddha described this reality as "actions without an actor, doings without a doer."

As Buddhaghosa says, "Mere suffering exists, but no sufferer is found..."[44] He further says in the *Visuddhimagga*, "There is a path to walk on, there is walking being done, but there is no traveler. There are deeds being done, but there is no doer."[45]

When you peel off the layers of an onion, what is ultimately left is nothing. Onion-ness exists in all the aggregates or layers of the onion. Similarly, we are just the five aggregates. Our experience does not refer back to any entity. There is no self behind the changing events to whom they are all happening.

The *Samyutta Nikaya* says:

> Lord, why is the world called empty? It is because in the world a separate self and things possessing a separate self do not exist. What are the things that do not have a separate self? Eye, form, and sight do not possess a separate self, nor that which belongs to a separate self. In the same way, ear, nose, tongue, body, thoughts, their objects, and their knowledge do not possess a separate self either, nor that which belongs to a separate self.[46]

When physical and mental aggregates are working together, a sense of self is formed. From the interaction of the five aggregates in the physio-psychological machine, the concept of "I" is created.

Yet this sense of self or "I" as an unchanging substance is an illusion. "Self" is just a convenient term for the whole collection of physical and mental elements (aggregates), which are in a flux of momentary arising and disappearing, and are devoid of a permanent core. There is no permanent entity that carries over from lifetime to lifetime, or even from moment to moment. This is the teaching of the emptiness of the five aggregates.

The Buddha told Shariputra, "Form is simply a name. Likewise, sensation, perception, memory [impulses], and consciousness are simply names. Shariputra, the self is simply a name. There is no self that can ever be found. And it cannot be found because it is empty."[47]

When I was a student of Won Buddhism, I gave a Dharma talk as part of my practicum. While I spoke in the meditation hall, a master entered and stood behind me, listening to my talk. I started to become self-conscious. After finishing the talk, I turned around to see whether the teacher was still there—I was curious about what he had thought. But he was not there. The other students later told me that he had stood behind me for just a few seconds and then left the meditation hall, using the back door. My belief that the master was right behind me listening to my talk made me nervous. Just as my nervousness instantly vanished when I turned around and realized that he was not there, so too the experience of no-self removes all worries, concerns, wandering thoughts, and unwholesome desires, which all arise from our sense of self.

Just as a picture of fire cannot warm us up, the intellectual understanding of no-self is not powerful enough to drastically reduce wandering thoughts and desires. Yet, the deep realization of no-self leads us to be free from unnecessary thoughts and desires. This no-self experience is like severing the root of the tree of suffering. This is why when the Bodhisattva of Great Compassion realized the empty nature of the five aggregates, he became free from all suffering and distress.

The awakening to our empty nature dissolves our sense of self. Because this awakening is the cornerstone of our liberation, many Theravadin Buddhist monasteries chant the following in their services:

> Form is impermanent
> Sensation is impermanent
> Perception is impermanent
> Impulse is impermanent
> Consciousness is impermanent
>
> Form is no-self
> Sensation is no-self
> Perception is no-self
> Impulses is no-self
> Consciousness is no-self

When I was a novice, I worked at the Dongmyung Retreat Center for one year. Behind the retreat center, there were many acacia trees, which caused various problems. Because of their widespread roots, other trees could not grow. We cut the branches and trunks of the acacia trees regularly to destroy them. Yet every year, they grew back again because their roots were still intact. Likewise, as long as there is the root of suffering, i.e. "I" or sense of self, all egoistic desires and wandering thoughts cannot be destroyed. They grow back again and again as long as the root, our ego, is there.

Why do we continue to love or hate someone even though, for instance, that person has hurt us in the past? It is because the seeds of our likes and dislikes, our love and hatred, are rooted in the soil of "I." Since the seeds of our memories continue to be nourished by the soil, the seeds do not die.

Why do some memories or thoughts continue to arise in our minds? Why do thoughts always follow one another in unfolding endless stories, for instance when we are practicing sitting meditation? The seed and the soil are still there. From the ground of "I," the seed continues to take nutrients. The weed (our unwholesome desires) continues to be nourished by the soil, or our sense of self. Just as a seed or weeds sprout and grow when they meet proper conditions, a thought such as a childhood trauma can arise repeatedly under certain conditions.

As long as "I" is there, our worries and agonies will not disappear. Just as weeds cannot take root and grow where there is no longer any soil, the realization of no-self rids us of our desires and unnecessary thoughts. This is the experience of enlightenment, which ultimately leads to the end of suffering.

Modern psychology tries to fix or improve our "self" in order to lessen our worries and anxieties. Yet, as long as there is a "self," we will be unable to completely eradicate our suffering. Only when we are enlightened to the real nature of no-self can we be free from all suffering and distress. The direct antidote and the complete solution to all suffering is supreme enlightenment. This is the path of prajna paramita.

A Zen master said that the moment of his enlightenment felt like the bottom of a jar suddenly disappeared and the water inside the jar immediately flowed out. All his agonies, worries, and distress vanished. This kind of experience can be sudden or gradual, depending on the practitioner or on the technique of his or her practice. However, this is something that we must experience in order to be free from our sense of self.

We are told, "Empty your mind," or "Free your mind from desires," but without being enlightened to the empty nature of ourselves, it is hard to put this advice into practice. Yet when we realize the empty nature of ourselves, everything becomes natural and effortless.

When Master Hui Ko asked his teacher, Bodhidharma, to put his uneasy mind at rest, Bodhidharma did not ask him *why* he suffered. Rather he asked *who* or *what* suffered. He questioned the real nature of Hui Ko's mind. When we clearly realize "who" suffers—that is, we realize the real nature of ourselves—then suffering ends. This is the path of prajna.

Without understanding our true self, our happiness or freedom is conditional, fragile, impermanent, and incomplete. Enlightenment is the only path to perpetual, everlasting, and indestructible happiness. What is more imperative than to realize our true self and to attain enlightenment? That is why in the Diamond Sutra, the Buddha taught that the merits of knowing our true self are vast and immeasurable; he used a diamond as an analogy for our true self, which is indestructible and everlasting.

The great Indian master Aryadeva, in his treatise *Four Hundred Stanzas*, stated that "even if one is not able to gain direct insight into the emptiness of all phenomena, merely by developing some positive doubt about the nature of reality, one creates a state of mind so powerful that it can shatter samsara."[48]

Ego is not a sin; it is a misunderstanding, an illusion in which we are deeply ensnared. The five aggregates are only illusions. Since ego is just misunderstanding, it is not an object to be hated, but an object to investigate. That is why in the Zen tradition, practitioners hold and work, for their whole life, with the koan, "Who am I?" or "What is this?" (*this* refers to the entity called *mind*, which enables us to see, hear, smell, and think).

Ego is darkness and enlightenment is light. When the light is on, the darkness disappears. Even though the darkness has persisted for thousands of years, it disappears in a split second. Just as animals in the zoo are trapped in cages, humans are trapped by the illusion of "self," or "I." The way to liberate our imprisoned mind is to dispel ignorance or darkness through enlightenment.

In *The Sutra of Forty-Two Sections*, section 17, the Buddha said, "Seeing the Way is like going into a dark room holding a torch; the darkness is instantly dissipated, while only light remains. When you study the Way and see the truth, ignorance vanishes and enlightenment abides forever."

THE ORIGIN OF THE IDEA OF SELF

Considering that realizing the empty nature of our self leads us to freedom, it would be helpful to understand the origin of our sense of self. This knowledge will help us break the illusion of self.

Body

People usually identify themselves with their bodies. Bodily shape and appearance frequently determine how people feel about themselves, and appearance is how we distinguish ourselves from others. We say, "I am different from you," meaning that we are physically different from each other.

Our body is made up of sensory organs, and what these organs sense is directly related to how we feel. The more we see, hear, smell, touch, and taste, the more we expose ourselves to sensory experiences, the stronger we come to identify ourselves with our body. When we indulge ourselves with sensory pleasures, the energy of our body is strengthened, and we become further separated from our realization of our true self. In Chinese, the Buddhist concept of our sense objects is *yuk-jin*, which literally means "six kinds of dust," in the sense that they cover our true or authentic self.

To reveal our true nature, we must control our sensory pleasures. This is the foundation of our spiritual practice, through which we may attain enlightenment. Refraining from engaging in sexual misconduct, using intoxicants, wearing jewelry or fancy clothes: these are all basic precepts for controlling our sensory experiences. When a student asked the Buddha, "Who will guide us after you enter nirvana?" the Buddha replied, "The precepts will be your guide."

Without controlling our senses or observing the precepts, enlightenment is impossible.

Mind

Many times we identify ourselves with our mind. Sometimes when we say that we are different from others, we mean that we have different personalities or characteristics, which may cause us to respond to the same situation in different ways. Our personalities and our abilities are related to our self-esteem. The following two factors are the biggest impediments to our enlightenment, keeping us from seeing things as they really are:

Concepts. An anthropologist visited an African village and interviewed many people there. When he saw a beautiful rainbow over the hill, he casually asked a small child how many colors the rainbow had. To his surprise, the boy replied that the rainbow had five colors. When he asked the same question to several other people, they all said the same thing. He later found out that the language which the tribe spoke had never developed words for the colors indigo or violet, and so to the speakers, the rainbow appeared to have only five colors because the concept of "indigo" did not exist for them.

Joseph Goldstein used a wonderful example about how our concepts keep us from seeing things as they are. Westerners, he said, are taught about the constellation called the Big Dipper. Once we have that concept in our minds, it is very hard not to see the Big Dipper in the night sky. As long as we have that concept embedded in our minds, the stars in the Big Dipper appear somewhat separate from the other stars.[49] Our thinking is affected—often distorted—by preexisting concepts.

"Meow" is the English expression for the sound a cat makes. The Korean word for this is "nyaong." Strangely enough, to many

Koreans, when a cat makes sounds, it sounds exactly like "nyaong," whereas to Americans, it sounds like "meow"—though of course, depending on the breed or the age of a cat, it makes different sounds. Depending on the concepts that are embedded in our minds, we hear the same sound in different ways. Just as the image in a mirror is distorted depending on the type of mirror (e.g., convex versus concave, or clean versus dusty), the world that appears in the mirror of our minds looks different depending on what language or concepts we are using.

We think and communicate through our language. The basic building blocks of our language system are concepts. Concepts and language facilitate our daily lives, but there is a cost: our use of concepts and language distort our reality, making us unable to see things as they really are. The French painter Monet said, "To see is to forget the name of what one is seeing."

Since we were children, people have called us by our name. Whenever our name is called, we answer "yes," even though we are not always the same person; our bodies, minds, personalities, and habits are continuously changing. Nevertheless, we identify ourselves with our given name. This has influenced us to have a fixed idea of "I" or "self."

As mentioned previously, it is a naïve assumption, misunderstanding, delusion, or ignorance to think that each name or concept has a corresponding reality. Since concepts block us from seeing the world as it is and pose impediments to our attaining enlightenment, having an excessive amount of knowledge has become taboo in many Buddhist traditions. In the Zen tradition, in order to free our minds from concepts, when the meditation session begins, practitioners are not allowed to read books, including scriptures. Many masters have warned their students against accumulating too much knowledge.

In *The Sutra of Forty-Two Sections*, section 9, the Buddha said, "If you endeavor to embrace the Way through much learning, the Way will be hard to reach. When you guard your mind and cherish the Way, the Way is truly great!"

Thoughts. People in modern times think too much. Most of our jobs are not physically but mentally demanding. Without proper thinking, we cannot succeed in today's world. It has become our tendency or our habit to think without cessation, and because our minds are always occupied with many thoughts, we have the strong tendency to identify ourselves as the thinker behind our many thoughts or judgments.

Our thoughts are patterned by our personalities and our value systems. How our minds relate to or react to certain things or situations is unique, different from another person's reactions just as our appearance is different.

As previously discussed, the fact that we have many thoughts does not mean that there is some thinking entity behind our thoughts. "A thinker" is a concept or idea, not reality. There is no thinker apart from our thoughts or behind our experiences. Just like our emotions and other mental faculties, our thoughts arise depending upon causes and conditions. A continuous thinking process exists without any underlying thinker. Similarly, there is no breather. What really exists is a continuous process of breathing in and breathing out.

Descartes said, "I think, therefore I am," but if we do not think, who are we? Where is the walker when she stops walking? When walking disappears, the walker also vanishes. Likewise, when thinking stops, the thinker vanishes.

Because of our ignorance of our true self as well as our attachment to the idea of an ego entity, we come to have many thoughts and unwholesome desires. The ignorance of our true self is like the wick of an oil lamp. Because of the wick, the flame—our sense of self—burns. Because of the existence of the oil—our unwholesome desires and wandering thoughts—which constantly feeds the wick, the flame continues to burn.

When the wick is removed (when we realize our "self" is empty), the fire is extinguished. Our thoughts and desires constantly strengthen and reinforce our sense of self. Therefore, eliminating our thoughts and desires, which are represented by the lamp's fuel, is a great way to extinguish the flame. This is essential to reaching enlightenment. Just as the moon can be accurately reflected when the ripples disappear from the surface of a pond, in order to reveal prajna, we must free our minds from wandering thoughts. That is why meditation is important for realizing our buddha nature. Without meditation, enlightenment becomes almost impossible.

Verse 282 of the Dhammapada says, "From meditation springs wisdom; without meditation wisdom wanes."

In the Christian tradition, silence also plays an important role.

Be still, and then you will know I am God. (Psalm 46:10)

Meditation is a process of deprogramming. It leads our minds away from wandering thoughts. It liberates our minds, which are deeply conditioned by preexisting concepts and by our language systems.

If Jesus had not been crucified and died, he could not have been resurrected. Without dying in our body (through observing the precepts to guard against sensory desires) and without dying in our minds (through the death of our desires and wandering thoughts via meditation), we cannot be born again as our true selves. When we die in our body, we will be born into a universal body. When we die in our mind, we will be born into the universal mind.

When we are enlightened to the true nature of ourselves, which is neither our body nor our mind, we will become free. This is the moment when a buddha, or a pure consciousness, is born. We will become a universal human, and we will no longer be living in an isolated world. This is the path of prajna paramita.

THE GATELESS GATE OF NONDUALITY 5

A bird sings and the mountain's stillness deepens.

—Zen saying

Here, Shariputra, form does not differ from emptiness, emptiness does not differ from form. Form is emptiness, emptiness is form. The same is true of sensations, perceptions, impulses, consciousness.

...Shariputra...

THE HEART SUTRA is written in the form of a dialogue between Shariputra and Avalokiteshvara Bodhisattva (the Bodhisattva of Great Compassion). Shariputra is one of the most eminent and revered adherents of the Buddha. Said to have been the first enlightened one among the Buddha's many disciples, he is renowned for his wisdom.

Shariputra was born in Upatissa, India. When he was young, he was friends with Maugalyayana, who was born in the neighboring village of Kolita. It is said they were born on the same day. They would one day become two of the Buddha's ten chief disciples.

When they were young, Shariputra and Maugalyayana realized that worldly pleasure was momentary. They wanted to attain deliverance from such transient existence and from suffering, and so they left home to search for the truth.

Their first teacher was Sanjaya, the leader of the sophists, but they were soon disillusioned by the shallowness of his teaching, and therefore they left him. Then they wandered looking for someone who could truly guide them to be free from the sufferings of life and death. They parted from one another, promising that whoever attained the deathless state first should inform the other.

One day, Shariputra happened to meet Assaji, one of the Buddha's disciples, who was making his morning rounds begging in the city. Impressed by his calm, peaceful, yet confident demeanor, Shariputra asked him who his teacher was and what he was teaching. Assaji answered that Shakyamuni was his teacher, and that he taught the dharma of dependent origination.

Assaji recited in verse:

> Of all things that arise from cause
> the Buddha tells how it begins
> and also how it ceases to be
> thus does the Tathagata [Buddha] instruct.

When Shariputra heard the words "dependent origination," he felt like his mind and heart had opened widely, and he wanted to become Shakyamuni's disciple. He immediately searched for his friend Maugalyayana, and said that he had finally found a teacher.

Shariputra and Maugalyayana hurried to the Bamboo Grove Monastery, where the Buddha was teaching. It is said that when the Buddha saw them approaching, he told his disciples that these two would become his two chief disciples and a blessed pair. After they were ordained by Shakyamuni Buddha, both of them reached the final stage of an arhat (a fully enlightened person) within two weeks.

...here, Shariputra...

A Won Buddhist minister asked Daesan, the Third Head Dharma Master of Won Buddhism, "How can I cultivate compassion?" Master Daesan replied, "If you are enlightened, you will become naturally compassionate." Have you ever heard of selfish saints or sages? Master Daesan said that one cannot but love all sentient beings after attaining supreme enlightenment.

When Avalokiteshvara Bodhisattva attained supreme enlightenment, he became compassionate and naturally reached out to help others be free from suffering and distress. This was his original vow (see chapter 2).

When Avalokiteshvara Bodhisattva called out, "Here, Shariputra," it was just like a mother calling out to her only child. Out of compassion, Avalokiteshvara Bodhisattva began to teach the truth of ultimate reality. By calling Shariputra, the Buddha's wisest disciple, the Bodhisattva of Great Compassion awakened prajna in him, the inherent wisdom that dwells in every practitioner.

...here...

"Here" (in Sanskrit, *iha*) is often omitted in English and Chinese translations. However, this word *iha* is significant. The author Red Pine wrote that "the emphatic *iha* (here) is often omitted by translators but is one of the most important words in the sutra. *Iha* is the Zen master's shout, the poke in the ribs, the cup of tea."[50] By saying the word "here," the Bodhisattva of Great Compassion awakens Shariputra as well as all practitioners, so that we can come back to reality, to this very moment. When students asked about the Way, Zen Master Rinzai oftentimes shouted "Ha!" This roaring shout helped many students to be enlightened to their true nature. Zen Master Duksan often hit students with his stick when they asked about the Way. These are all compassionate and expedient means used by masters to bring their students back to reality by helping the students cease their discursive thinking or still their intellectual minds.

In Zen, this kind of teaching is called "direct showing of the truth," or "direct pointing to the mind." Here, the word "direct" refers to experiencing the truth or reality without using any words or concepts.

Just as Rinzai did with his "Ha!" or Duksan did with his stick, by saying "here," the Bodhisattva of Great Compassion guides Shariputra and all practitioners to directly experience reality. Reality is, in fact, nirvana, which exists here and now. By saying "here," the Bodhisattva of Great Compassion teaches that what you hear or see at this very moment is the ultimate reality, and it is right before you. It is like awakening a fish that asks about the existence of water by saying that water is all around it. This *iha* directly awakens the buddhahood within ourselves.

...Form does not differ from emptiness, emptiness does not differ from form. Form is emptiness, emptiness is form...[51]

An ascetic visited the Buddha and asked about the Way. The Buddha did not say anything, but remained silent. After a while, the man smiled and thanked the Buddha profusely and left.

The Buddha's attendant saw this meeting and became puzzled. He asked the Buddha why the man had thanked him even though the Buddha had not said anything. The Buddha answered, "The finest horse will gallop at just the sight of the shadow of the whip."

For practitioners of the highest capacity, the word "here" is enough to awaken them. However, for those of lesser capacity, further teaching is necessary. Out of compassion, Avalokiteshvara Bodhisattva kindly explains the truth in a more detailed manner: "Form does not differ from emptiness, emptiness does not differ from form. Form is emptiness, emptiness is form."

In modern Western logic, form is form, and emptiness is emptiness. Existence is existence. Nothing is nothing. This is common sense.

Form and emptiness appear to be two polar opposites. They cannot be the same.

Yet the Bodhisattva of Great Compassion teaches that form does not differ from emptiness, and emptiness does not differ from form. In his supreme enlightenment, this is what he realized: this is the ultimate reality.

In the logical sense, emptiness is emptiness, not form. But when we take a deeper look at things, this is not reality.

My first experience of this truth happened when I was in elementary school. I saw a rat killed by a car on the street in front of a hardware store. The bloody scene of that big rat with its internal organs bursting out was very upsetting, and nobody dared to remove this road kill. Whenever I passed the hardware store, my eyes instinctively searched for the rat. During the next month, the rat was run over by passing vehicles many times. All the blood and internal organs were dried out and the remains of that rat became smaller and smaller. Eventually, those remains disappeared entirely!

I thought it was very strange that although no one removed the rat, it finally did disappear.

Even though there is no doer, everything in the universe continuously changes. From the stars in the sky to the cells in our bodies, everything is constantly changing. This is reality. There is not a single thing in this world that remains unchanged for even a moment.

Our bones appear solid and constant. Yet in the course of seven years, our bones are completely replaced. When we see the flame of a candle, it appears constant, but each moment, it is a different flame. Form as something fixed or solid is purely an idea or an illusion, not reality.

As discussed in chapter 3, all things arise depending on causes and conditions and disappear continuously. Since everything dependently arises and nothing can exist in and of itself, everything is devoid of self-substance or inherent existence; therefore, in the absolute sense, things do not exist. That is why the reality is, as the Heart Sutra says, "Form does not differ from emptiness... Form is emptiness." This is the truth.

Empty nature is not just inherent in physical things but also in all mental or emotional faculties; they all arise dependently and cease continuously. Since all mental or emotional faculties originate depending on certain causes and conditions, then sensations, perceptions, impulses, and consciousness are also devoid of inherent existence or self-substance. The Heart Sutra acknowledges this, saying, "The same is true of sensations, perceptions, impulses, consciousness."

Whether it is something physical, mental, or emotional, everything has a conditional and momentary existence. Everything arises from nothingness and returns to nothingness. Emptiness is the true description of the ultimate reality of all things.

We can experience the empty nature of all things when we meditate. For instance, in insight meditation, we stay focused by observing our bodily sensations, feelings, or thoughts, which lets us recognize that all these things are constantly arising and ceasing. For example, if we experience and constantly observe that some part of us is itching, we realize that this sensation will eventually disappear. Our bodily sensations, feelings, and thoughts all share the nature of impermanence, and no-self.

EMPTINESS IN SCIENCE

The empty nature of all things is also demonstrated in physics.

I still remember the experiment that was carried out in science class when I was in elementary school. The teacher asked the students to put salt into a cup full of water and to stir it until the salt dissolved. We discovered that the volume of the water remained the same although the salt was absorbed into the water. The teacher told us that this experiment demonstrated the existence of space between water molecules.

Whether it is water or a gold bar, matter appears solid, compact, and continuous. However, huge spaces exist between the molecules. These molecules are pulled toward each other by nuclear forces.

A molecule is made up of atoms. An atom consists of a nucleus and electrons. There is an immense distance between a nucleus and an electron. Using the hydrogen atom as an example, if we say that the nucleus is as big as an apple, then the electrons would have to be 10 kilometers (about 16.1 miles) away from it. When a galaxy is observed from afar, it appears dense and solid, yet most of the galaxy is empty. Likewise, the space between a nucleus and an electron is mostly empty. If we removed all the space between the electrons and nuclei in all the atoms of the earth, our planet would become the size of a basketball.

Why, then, does matter look solid and continuous despite the fact that most of its parts are empty? This is because waves of light are not thin enough to enter into that empty space, and so "our eyes can't see the atomic level, at about one hundredth of a millionth of an inch."[52]

Visible light is made up of waves whose wavelength (the distance from crest to crest) is between four and eight hundred thousandths of a centimeter (1/400,000 cm). Our eyes cannot see structures smaller than this. Bacteria (1/300,000 cm) are the smallest common objects visible with an optical microscope. To probe more deeply, we must use something with a short wavelength. Particles like electrons make waves with wavelengths thousands of times shorter than those of light. So, with an electron microscope, we can see viruses (1/10,000,000 of a meter), the structure of molecules (1/1,000,000,000 of a meter), and the surface of individual atoms. (To see the world smaller than this, physicists use particle accelerators to speed particles up to create even smaller wavelengths.[53])

If our eyes were like x-rays, when we saw a human being, it would appear as a skeleton. In the streets, we would see walking skeletons. If our eyes were like gamma rays, whose waves are shorter than the waves of an x-ray, we could not tell whether a human was there at all.

What is the basic building block of all material things? Finding the answer to this question has been the quest of scientists for millennia. Democritus, a Greek philosopher, called this basic unit an "atom" (*atomos* in Greek means "uncuttable" or "indivisible"). But the atom is composed of smaller parts. An atom's nucleus is made up of positively charged protons and electrically neutral neutrons, which can be further divided into minute particles called quarks.

Quantum physicists have concluded that these minute particles exist without form; their presence is found only through light and vibration. There is no fundamental building block at all. What is observed through super microscopes is not any substance but rather dynamic patterns in a continuous dance of energy. What is ultimately revealed is not any basic building block but rather an interchange of energy. Erwin Schrödinger warned us against such a materialistic view of atoms and their constituents, saying, "It is better not to view a particle as a permanent entity, but rather as an instantaneous event. Sometimes these events link together to create the illusion of permanent entities."[54]

Astrophysicist Trinh Xuan Thuan writes, "According to Bohr and Heisenberg, when we speak of atoms and electrons, we shouldn't see them as real entities, with well-defined properties such as speed and position, tracing out equally well-defined trajectories. The 'atom' concept is simply an image that helps physicists put together diverse observations of the particle world into a coherent and logical scheme."[55]

As revealed by modern physics, form as a fixed entity is purely a concept, not reality. The reality is "forming." Thus quantum physics shows that "form does not differ from emptiness."

In the Diamond Sutra, the Buddha says that the concept or idea of "minute particles" is just a name, not reality:

> Subhuti, what do you think? Would there be many molecules in [the composition of] three thousand galaxies of worlds? Subhuti said: Many indeed, World-honored One! Subhuti, the Tathagata declares that all these molecules are not really such; they are called "molecules." [Furthermore,] the Tathagata declares that a world is not really a world; it is called "a world."[56]

**...Emptiness does not differ from form... emptiness is
form. The same is true of sensations, perceptions, impulses,
consciousness...**

We have already discussed the meaning of "Form does not differ
from emptiness... Form is emptiness," but what does the converse—
"emptiness does not differ from form... emptiness is form"—mean?
Why does emptiness not differ from sensations, perceptions, impulses,
and consciousness?

If we think about the concept of "God," we can more easily understand the relationship between emptiness and the five aggregates
(form, sensations, perceptions, impulses, consciousness).

When I was in college, a Christian evangelist approached me while
I was eating lunch in the dining hall one day. He asked me, "Do you
know God?" I replied, "How do you define God?" He answered,
"God is a creator, the creator of the universe."

He showed me his pen and said, "This pen was made by men. Who
do you think made the stars, the earth, mountains, and all things in
the universe?" I asked, "Who do you think then created God?" He
answered, "God was not created by something else. God exists by
Himself." I said, "If God can exist by Himself, why then cannot all
things exist by themselves?" He did not say anything further and left.

When people define God as creator—"In the beginning God created the heavens and the earth" (Genesis 1:1)—it does not necessarily
mean that God preceded the universe in terms of time. Saying that
God created the world does not mean that God waited for a long
time and one day decided to create the world. Saint Augustine says
that before the world, there is no time. Time is, by definition, the
movement of something; it is measured in terms of a regular motion,
such as the earth's rotation or the vibration of an atom. So it makes no
sense to talk about time before the birth of the universe: Augustine
"thought it ridiculous that God should have waited an infinite length
of time before creating the world. In his opinion, the world and time
arrived together. The world wasn't created *in* time, but along *with*

time."[57] Creator and creation are not separate and sequential things. It is true that God as creator can conceptually precede creation, just as the concept of fruit conceptually precedes a specific kind of fruit, like an orange. In terms of reality, creator and creation exist simultaneously. Creator and creation cannot be separate. Without creation, we cannot think of a creator. Creator and creation are two sides of the same coin (reality).

Let us consider the following concepts—darkness versus light, valley versus peak, and space versus matter. Each appears to be the opposite of its complement. The two are conceptually different. Yet the reality is that they cannot be separate; they are two aspects of one reality. How can we create the peak of a mountain without creating the valley below? How can we think about darkness without the concept of light? Can space exist without matter? Darkness is, by definition, the absence of light. Space is the distance between objects. Without matter, we cannot think of space. Without light, we cannot think about darkness. Without the peak, we cannot think of the valley. One master put it poetically: "A bird sings and the mountain's stillness deepens."

Concepts or words—yin and yang, good and bad, sacred and profane—may seem to be opposites, but they are actually two aspects of one reality. They always exist together. The same is true of the relationship between emptiness and the five aggregates.

When we say that emptiness is the ultimate reality of ourselves (and ourselves comprise the five aggregates), we cannot think of emptiness without the existence of form, sensations, perceptions, impulses, and consciousness. Emptiness means the empty nature *of* something; the five aggregates are empty *of* inherent existence. Emptiness exists and is meaningful only in the context of the aggregates (see chapter 3 for details).

Master Chen-k'o says, "As for seeing that the Five Skandhas are empty, this is not an emptiness separate from the skandhas but the emptiness of the skandhas."[58]

Just as an ocean is not separate from the waves, emptiness cannot exist without form, sensations, perceptions, impulses, and conscious-ness. Emptiness—the ultimate reality—is not separate from the phenomena themselves. Emptiness and phenomena are conceptu-ally different, yet they are two facets of the same reality. From one perspective, we can see the various appearances of phenomena; from another perspective, we can see the empty nature of all phenomena.

Emptiness and the five aggregates cannot be separate. They define each other. This is the meaning of "emptiness does not differ from form [sensations, perceptions, impulses, consciousness], and empti-ness is form."

Regarding this, Master Te-ch'ing said, "The true emptiness of pra-jna is like a huge round mirror, and every illusory form is like an image in the mirror. Once you know that images don't exist apart from the mirror, you know 'emptiness is not separate from form.'"[59] Since all things dependently arise and are therefore empty, they are change-able. For example, clay is soft, and so it can be molded into various forms and transformed into many other shapes. Sotaesan, the found-ing master of Won Buddhism, said, "Even that single straw will mani-fest itself into a hundred million transformations and exhibit various kinds of creations and talents."[60]

Shunyata

The idea of emptiness was theorized and systematically explained by Nagarjuna, an Indian philosopher and master, who lived five hun-dred years after the Buddha. He systematized the philosophy of emp-tiness and developed the philosophy of the Prajna Paramita Sutras. The Madhyamaka school of Mahayana Buddhism, also known as the Middle Way school, was formed based on his teaching.

Nagarjuna says, "The nature of reality *does not depend on something else*, some other thing or circumstance."[61] The idea of emptiness was introduced in order to reveal the ultimate reality of all things. Because emptiness exists in relation with all phenomena, emptiness is also empty of inherent existence. In other words, emptiness is also empty.

Nagarjuna's *Fundamental Treatise* says:

> The Conqueror said that emptiness
> Eradicates all dogmatic views;
> As for those who take a dogmatic view of emptiness
> He said that they are incurable.[62]

Since the ultimate reality is neither real nor unreal, neither existent nor nonexistent, the buddhas and bodhisattvas who see and dwell in the realm of reality have their eyes half-closed and half-open, neither looking inside nor looking outside.

Shunyata, or emptiness, also means "cipher," "zero," "hollow," or "void" in English. *Shunyata* is the noun form of the adjective *shunya*, which means "empty" or "void." In the West, zero means nothing, whereas in Indian usage, *shunyata* means totality, dynamic wholeness, or the possibility of all things. It is not nonbeing, but wondrous being. When Moses first encountered God in the burning bush, he was surprised that it was not consumed. He became very afraid and asked "Who are you?" God said to Moses, "I AM that I AM" (Genesis 3:1–14).

Because the ultimate reality is beyond any conceptual designation, the word "emptiness" is used to indicate that the ultimate reality cannot be defined or grasped. Emptiness is like pure and uncontaminated space that is able to contain all things, the source of everything, the source of life. Emptiness, or the absence of inherent existence, is the final reality, and empty nature, the final mode of all beings, is the characteristic which all phenomena share.

Because the inside of a flute is empty, it can create various sounds. Everything can be manifested because of emptiness. As Nagarjuna said, "because of emptiness, all things are possible."[63]

Prajna is another name for emptiness. A poet wrote that there is no one, yet the creek flows and the flowers bloom. When we plant a seed, it sprouts and grows naturally. From heavenly movements to the rotation of seasons, what is the hidden force that moves all things in the universe? Many things are operating in an orderly manner. The cosmos is a harmonious system. In fact, the word "cosmos" comes from a Greek term meaning "ordered world."

When I was in junior high, I noted with interest that the sex ratio is approximately fifty-fifty in most animal species, which ensures the continuation of the species. According to the chemist James Lovelock, the earth is a harmonious, self-regulating living system that can provide various conditions suitable for life and the maintenance of equilibrium. Lovelock studied many things and made various discoveries. For instance, since life on earth began, the sun's energy has increased, yet the surface temperature of the earth has remained stable. The composition of earth's atmosphere has remained constant as a result of the production or removal of living organisms. The ocean's salinity has remained constant; this stability is an important factor in the existence of most cells. Lovelock refers to this self-regulating living system as Gaia, after the Greek goddess.

The source behind all these phenomena has been called by many names: God, Brahman, Creator, Allah, or Father. In the Judeo-Christian tradition, God has many names: *Elohim* (strong God), *El Shaddai* (God Almighty), *El Elyon* (The Most High God). When Muslims pray with prayer beads, they call the ninety-nine names of Allah, which is the Arabic word for God. In Taoism, instead of personifying the underlying entity as God, it is called Tao, or the Way. In Buddhism, it is called *shunyata*, emptiness, because the ultimate truth is beyond words and speech and cannot be described by any means.

After Shakyamuni Buddha attained supreme enlightenment, he named the ultimate reality prajna. What or where is prajna? Where is God or the universal truth? Does prajna or universal truth exist in Shakyamuni Buddha's teachings, or in the Bible, or in the Koran?

"Form is emptiness, emptiness is form" means that the truth, prajna, or God, exists in all things in the universe. This Dharma teaches that the universe itself is prajna.

One day, after attaining enlightenment, Korean Zen Master Cheon Kang urinated in the temple courtyard. One monk saw him and became very upset and scolded, "You are a monk. How could you urinate in front of the temple, which is the body of the Buddha?" Cheon Kang replied, "Buddha is everywhere. Where, then, should I urinate?"[64]

In Hua-yen Buddhism, emptiness is personified as Vairochana Buddha,[65] or the Buddha of Great Illumination. Vairochana Buddha exists everywhere and in every time. The universe itself is his body. The songs of birds, the colors of flowers, the currents of streams, the figures in clouds—all of these are the sermon of the Buddha.

A monk asked a Zen master, "What is the Way?" The master replied, "It is dried shit." The Buddha, truth, or sacredness is not in the temple, the church, the sutras, or the Bible. The truth exists everywhere, from an ordinary pebble to leftover food.

I saw a picture of a cloud taken in Taiwan. The picture resembled a popular painting of the Bodhisattva of Great Compassion. The person who took the picture interpreted that image as the manifestation of Avalokiteshvara Bodhisattva. Similarly, several months after the passing of Pope John Paul II, one man took a picture of the flame in his campfire. The flame was very similar to the image of the late Pope. The people around the campfire saw this flame and said that the late Pope still protected them.

Yet the Diamond Sutra clearly says:

Who sees Me by form,
Who seeks Me in sound,
Perverted are his footsteps upon the way,
For he cannot perceive the Tathagata [Buddha].[66]

And:

Subhuti, what do you think? Is the Tathagata to be recognized by some physical characteristics? No, World-honored One; the Tathagata cannot be recognized by any physical characteristics. Wherefore? Because the Tathagata has said that physical characteristics are not, in fact, physical characteristics.

Buddha said: Subhuti, wheresoever are physical characteristics there is delusion; but whoso perceives that all characteristics are in fact no-characteristics, perceives the Tathagata.[67]

Some people say that they have heard the voice of God during prayer, or have met a buddha or a bodhisattva in a dream. People impose various meanings on these occurrences; for example, crowds of people wait to see the statue of the Virgin Mary shedding tears.

As the Buddha says, we cannot seek the truth in material characteristics. If we relate these signs to buddhahood or the truth, we are all deluded and walking on the wrong path.

The real buddha or truth is your spouse, your coworkers, or the people around you—whether you like them or not. Your sarcastic boss or your trouble-making children are the true manifestations of buddhahood. If they did not exist, how could you live?

Two Paths to Reach Buddhahood

The realization that Buddha is everywhere has important ramifications for how we should live our lives and for how we can attain buddhahood.

One path to buddhahood is by attaining enlightenment first. Then, once you realize that everything is the manifestation of buddhahood or the truth, deep respect and reverence for all beings will arise in you and you will very naturally respect and treat others as buddhas.

The other path to buddhahood is to respect and treat others as buddhas first. When you continue to practice and treat others in that way, eventually you will attain enlightenment and reach buddhahood.

For laypersons involved in many daily activities, this second approach is very important. In our daily lives we have to live and interact with others. This approach is not only practical but is also a realistic path to enlightenment.

In Won Buddhism, a motto describing this second approach says, "Everywhere a buddha image, every act a buddha offering." This motto implies that we can make a buddha offering at any time, in any place.

Consider this story:

> One day, while the founding master of Won Buddhism was residing at Pongnae Cloister, an old couple was passing by and said that they were on their way to Silsang-sa to make an offering to the Buddha statue in the temple so that their daughter-in-law, ill-natured and extremely unfilial to them, might be changed thereby for the better.
>
> Hearing this, the Master said, "You know that you will be helped if you make an offering to the Buddha statue, but you don't know that you will be better helped by making offerings to a living Buddha."
>
> The couple asked, "Where is the living Buddha?"
>
> The Master said, "Your daughter-in-law in your home is a living Buddha. She is the one who has the authority to be filial or unfilial to you. So, why don't you try to make an offering of worship to her first?"
>
> The couple asked, "What is the way of making an offering of worship to her?"
>
> The Master said, "Buy for her something she might like with the money you would have spent for making an offering of worship to the Buddha statue, for instance. Try to treat her as you would respect the Buddha. Then you will see the results of your making an offering of worship depending on your sincerity."
>
> The couple returned home and did as was advised. Their daughter-in-law changed herself to be very filial to them. So the old couple paid a visit to the Master and expressed heartfelt appreciation.

The Master said to his disciples beside him, "This is an example of the realistic worship of Buddha offered directly to the actual source of misery and blessedness."[68]

Since everything and everyone is a manifestation of the Buddha, even our daily work can be a buddha offering. The true buddha offering is not just offering fruit, money, or prayer in front of a buddha statue. Authentic buddha offerings include washing dishes, taking out the trash, or helping someone in need.

Since we can find the Buddha everywhere, every act is sacred. In doing our daily work in a sacred way, we are engaged in a great task of helping society and we will eventually reach buddhahood.

One morning a monk asked Zen Master Chao-chou, "What is the Way?" Chao-chou replied, "Did you have breakfast?" The monk answered, "Yes, master, I did." Chao-chou replied, "Then wash your bowl." Upon hearing these words, the monk attained enlightenment.

EMPTINESS OF PHENOMENA

All dhammas are without self.

—The Dhammapada

Here, Shariputra, all dharmas are empty.[69]

DHARMAS ARE objects of our minds. When "I," or self, comes into being, the object then arises. These dharmas represent all phenomena.[70]

"All dharmas are empty" means that just as the five aggregates are empty, all phenomena are empty. They are all dependently arising and do not have an inherent existence or intrinsic nature.

A thief entered a temple at night and searched everywhere for something valuable to steal. When he could find nothing precious to take, he became furious and woke up one of the monks.

He asked, "Where are the valuables? Give me something."

The monk replied, "There is nothing valuable in this temple. I am just studying and practicing the Dharma here."

"Where is the Dharma?"

"It is in my heart."

"Then I will have to take that Dharma from your heart," said the thief. But when he drew his knife to cut out the monk's heart, the monk said:

> On the branch
> Where the flowers bloom every year,
> Can you find a flower
> When you cut through the branch?

The thief stopped. His expression transformed and he fell to his knees, begging the monk's forgiveness.

With this poem, the monk taught the dharma of dependent origination. The flowers do not exist by and of themselves. They come into existence only when certain conditions are met.

When a person makes a fire by rubbing two sticks together over a pile of straw, where does the fire come from, the straw, the sticks, or from the air? When we clap our hands, where does the sound come from? Does it come from the right hand, or the left hand? Does it come from the air, the ear, or the mind?

Just as all the elements of our body and mind exist dependent on causes and conditions (see chapter 3), all phenomena are also dependently arising. No phenomena or dharmas can exist in and of themselves.

From books and tables to mountains and stars, from philosophical ideas to political systems, nothing can exist by itself. Since all dharmas dependently arise, devoid of any fixed substance or intrinsic nature, all dharmas are therefore empty[71]—that is, they are empty of inherent or true existence. In other words, in the absolute sense they do not exist.

Regarding the emptiness of all dharmas, Nagarjuna said:

> There is not the slightest thing
> That does not come from a dependent origin.
> And therefore there is not the slightest thing
> That is not emptiness.[72]

The Avatamsaka Sutra says:

> Clearly know that all dharmas
> Are without self-essence at all;
> To understand the nature of dharmas in this way—
> Is to see [the Buddha of Great Illumination] Vairochana.

Understanding the empty nature of all dharmas—that all phenomena arise depending on certain causes and conditions—leads our minds to be understanding and broadly compassionate in our daily lives.

A volunteer at an after-school program for underprivileged children told me this story. This volunteer noticed that whenever the children talked, whether inside or outside of the classroom, they always talked too loudly. He cautioned the children against their behavior many times, to no avail. Irritated, he assumed that they were naturally impolite. However, his judgment disappeared when he visited their homes, which were located in a manufacturing area. They were growing up exposed to loud noises from the nearby factories. As a result, they had all experienced hearing loss, which caused them to speak at a near-shout. When he saw their environment, the volunteer realized his mistake.

Who knows whether the driver who just cut in front of you is rushing to the hospital? Who knows whether your colleague, who you think is not working hard enough, might be experiencing some difficulties of which you are unaware?

The Buddha said that one who sees dependent origination sees the Dharma, and one who sees the Dharma sees dependent origination. When we understand that all things arise from multiple causes and conditions, we become less judgmental and less critical. Our minds can become broader and more compassionate.

The dharma of emptiness teaches us that the objects we crave or are attached to are impermanent and unreal. Like a rainbow, these objects appear to be real, but they merely arise under certain conditions and later dissolve.

The only thing that the Buddha was concerned with was human suffering and the way to end it. According to the Buddha, the cause of human suffering is attachment.

Attachment or craving can be classified into two types: the attachment to self and the attachment to objects. The attachment to self (as subject) includes clinging to our appearance and our health. The attachment to objects includes clinging to material things, like cars and clothes, or nonmaterial things, like our spouse, career, or fame.

The attachment to self and the attachment to objects are two innate forms of grasping. As soon as a baby acquires the sense of "I," the conception of and attachment to "mine" follows. When I was young, whenever I quarreled with my sister, it was usually over an object that both of us wanted at the same time. Nations fighting for territory can be thought of in the same manner.[73]

Master Chandrakirti wrote, "First conceiving an 'I,' we cling to an ego. Then conceiving a 'mind,' we cling to a material world."[74]

Strictly speaking, the attachment to objects can be included in the attachment to "I." All attachments can be found within the five aggregates. Without the basis of "I" or self, attachment to objects cannot arise, just as the weed cannot grow without the soil. However, the average person's life goal is to achieve something external—to acquire material things like money, or nonmaterial things like fame—and many people's happiness or success is defined by how much they have achieved or how much they possess. Therefore, dividing human attachments into these two types makes sense.

In Buddhism, three common traits that all phenomena share are called the "three marks" or the "three characteristics" of existence. First, everything is impermanent; second, everything is suffering; and third, everything is empty or no-self. All Buddhists accept these three characteristics as basic teachings. However, regarding the third characteristic, no-self, interpretations differ. Theravadins interpret no-self to mean selflessness of person (emptiness of self), whereas Mahayana followers (including disciples of the Heart Sutra) further subdivide this characteristic into two types: emptiness of self and emptiness of phenomena. Emptiness of self means the selflessness of the five aggregates or of the person, whereas emptiness of dharmas means the selfless nature of all phenomena. The Heart Sutra shows that as long as the life direction of most people is to search for external objects, it is most practical to divide emptiness into these two categories.

To let go of the grasping of "I," the Buddha taught the selfless nature of the person, i.e., "self" is just a name, not reality. To let go of the grasping of objects, the Buddha taught the emptiness of dharmas, the selfless nature of phenomena.

In a narrower sense, objects represent our possessions. The following example illustrates how our possessions strengthen our ignorance and substantiate our ego.

At graduation ceremonies, there are usually some seats designated for VIPs. Several years ago, the person in charge of a particular graduation ceremony forgot to designate a special seat for one politician. When the politician arrived and discovered that his seat was not prepared on the stage, he got very angry and left the ceremony. The higher one's position is, the bigger one's ego can become. The wealthier a person is, the more arrogant he may become.

Our possessions constantly inflate our ego and reinforce our sense of self. This means that our possessions strengthen ignorance (the root cause of suffering), and so possessions can become a major obstacle to attaining liberation. Therefore, letting go of attachment to possessions is crucial for practitioners who wish to attain enlightenment and have freedom of mind. This is the foundation of all practice because the ultimate solution to suffering is enlightenment, or the complete transformation of ego.

That is why simple and frugal living has been emphasized in all spiritual traditions. That is why monks and nuns take vows of chastity and poverty. These are not just moral beliefs, but vows taken for our own enlightenment and liberation.

The following is a story about a rich man who met Jesus:

Now someone came up to him and said, 'Teacher, what good thing must I do to gain eternal life?' He said to him, 'Why do you ask me about what is good? There is only one who is good. But if you want to enter into life, keep the commandments.' 'Which ones?' he asked. Jesus replied, 'Do not murder, do not commit adultery, do not steal, do not give false testimony, honor your father and mother, and love your neighbor as yourself.' The young man said to him, 'I have wholeheartedly obeyed all these laws. What do I still lack?' Jesus said to him, 'If you wish to be perfect, go sell your possessions and give the money to the poor, and you will have treasure in heaven. Then come, follow me.' But when the young man heard this he went away sorrowful, for he was very rich. Then Jesus said to his disciples, 'I tell you the truth, it will be hard for a rich person to enter the kingdom of heaven! Again I say, it is easier for a camel to go through the eye of a needle than for a rich person to enter into the kingdom of God.' (Matthew 19:16–24)

Jesus said that just as no one can serve two masters, one cannot serve God and money,[75] and that one's mind is where one's possessions are.

To cross a river easily, our boat should be light, not heavy. For us to cross the sea of suffering to nirvana, our minds should be light. That is to say, our minds should not be burdened with our many possessions.

There are six paramitas that can help you to cross over from the suffering world to nirvana. The first paramita, generosity, or the giving up of personal possessions, is a way to lighten the boat. Sotaesan, the founding master of Won Buddhism, said, "Sentient beings seem smart for focusing solely on their own concerns, but ultimately they end up injuring themselves; buddhas and bodhisattvas seem foolish for doing things only for others, but ultimately they end up benefiting themselves."[76]

Generosity practice is the realization of no-self, which is the manifestation of our true self. Generosity is the best way to break our ego, dissolve our sense of self, and cultivate compassion, the foundation of all our practices. By practicing the paramita of generosity—especially when we give up things that we cherish, whether they are material things or ideas—our sense of self, which grips our minds, will be loosened.

For a while, I was concerned that I could not go very deeply into meditation when I practiced. When I thought about why this was so, I compared the Buddha's life with mine and realized one important thing: the Buddha's starting point before practicing was totally different from mine. In the Buddha's case, before he sat for meditation, he had already let go of all his attachments. He had left his loved ones and the palace, his comfortable environment. Before he searched for truth, he went through a complete renunciation. When he sat under the bodhi tree, he was already without any attachments; he was completely ready, and his foundation was solid. His great enlightenment followed his great renunciation.

I discovered that, despite being a minister, my mind was still full of attachments, although they were not material. Just as a ship cannot leave the port if it is anchored, we are not free to go into deep meditation or reach enlightenment if we have many attachments. Practitioners must constantly remind themselves that perfect enlightenment follows perfect renunciation.

You may ask, *If we let go of everything, how can we live in contemporary society?* Letting go of our possessions implies letting go of our attachments to our possessions. It does not mean that we should let go of, or give up, necessary things like our food, our shelter, or our car. It means that our life should not be directed toward the accumulation of material things. One of the precepts in Won Buddhism is not to live your life in pursuit of wealth.[77]

Living in the contemporary world, we may need many things. This is fine as long as we are not attached to these things and are using them for good purposes. In doing so, we are realizing the dharma of no possessions. The Hebrew patriarchs like Abraham and Job were very wealthy men. However, their minds did not dwell on their riches.

Solomon, the son of King David, became king of Israel. One night God appeared to him in a dream and asked what he wanted. Solomon asked God for wisdom and an understanding heart so that he could govern his people wisely. God was very pleased and said to him, "Because you asked for the ability to make wise judicial decisions, and not for long life, or riches, or vengeance on your enemies, I grant your request, and give you a wise and discerning mind superior to that of anyone who has preceded or will succeed you. Furthermore, I am giving you what you did not request—riches and honor so that you will be the greatest king of your generation" (King 3:11–13).

If we are doing the work of God, the work of the truth, the universe will take care of our needs. When a cup is empty, it has the potential to contain all things. When we let go of everything in our mind and our mind is pure and innocent, the universe will become our provider, our helper, and our guide.

In *The Sutra of Forty-Two Sections*, section 22, the Buddha said, "People cling to their worldly possessions and sexual passions so blindly as to sacrifice their own lives. They are like a child who tries to eat a little honey smeared on the edge of a knife. Even though the amount is not enough to appease his appetite, he will lick it and risk cutting his tongue in the process."

A practitioner who searches for enlightenment is supposed to abstain from having an extravagant life, possessing fancy clothes, living in an expensive house, or driving costly cars because these things can taint our minds. Sungchul, a Korean Zen master, said that he does not want to be born into a rich man's home in his next life, because that kind of environment is not conducive to walking a spiritual path. Daesan, the Third Head Dharma Master of Won Buddhism, said that he was fortunate not to live in the Vatican, where people continuously respect and revere holy men.

The luxurious life that many people desire dulls one's spirituality. Material possessions and attributes are obstacles to enlightenment.

Our possessions may make us feel satisfied, but like a drug, they reinforce our ego and strengthen our ignorance. More often than not, they are obstacles to our ultimate enlightenment.

From an individual level to a national level, we should use our possessions sparingly, and let the remainder be used by others. The Buddha said that when one becomes financially stable, he or she should become either a monk or a nun, or a committed practitioner. In the Theravadin tradition, following these words of the Buddha, many people become ordained as monks and nuns following their retirement, or after their children get married. In Western societies, people are encouraged to live and practice in a spiritual community after they retire or whenever their schedules permit.

We cannot be selfish and happy at the same time. We cannot be selfish and become enlightened at the same time. Let us boldly exercise the dharma of few possessions and no attachments, and loosen the powerful grip of our sense of self. This realization of no attachment and few possessions will ultimately break the ignorance that builds up around our false notion of self.

In Korea, there is a special set of clothes called *suwee*, which is used to dress the deceased. *Suwee* is like regular clothing except for one thing: there are no pockets. There is nothing that we can take with us when we leave this world.

> The Founding Master [of Won Buddhism] said, "No matter how much a person might have accumulated grains and money throughout his life, he cannot take anything with him when he dies. How can we call that which we cannot take along with us our eternal possessions? If we want to create eternal possessions, then while we are alive we must work hard for others' benefit in every possible way, but must do so without dwelling on any sign that benefit is conferred so that we may accumulate merit that is free from the outflows. Our true, eternal possession is the vow regarding the right dharma and the power of the mind that

has cultivated it. By devoting ceaseless efforts to this vow and to mind practice, we will become a master of wisdom and merit in the infinite world."[78]

In Dickens's *A Christmas Carol*, Scrooge, an old and bitter miser, sees the ghost of his late business partner on Christmas Eve. His partner had worked himself to death in order to make more money, and he appears with many heavy chains and shackles on his body. He can barely walk because of the heavy chains and the weight of the boxes filled with gold coins. Scrooge sees his own destiny in his partner's appearance.

Next, Scrooge is visited by three spirits: the Ghost of Christmas Past, the Ghost of Christmas Present, and finally, the Ghost of Christmas Yet to Come. He is warned that if he does not change his ways, he will face a dire fate. Horrified and deeply saddened, Scrooge vows to change his life. Weeping bitterly, he suddenly awakes to find that all three spirits had visited in just one night, and that it is now Christmas morning. He is overwhelmed with joy to realize that he has a second chance.

Scrooge symbolizes a contemporary person who is totally egocentric and only interested in his life goal: accumulating material things. In order to achieve his life goal, Scrooge imprisons himself in a small cocoon in which he sometimes felt safe but most often felt miserable. So too do many people in contemporary society live in a small world, which is their separate sense of self, imposing hardship on themselves as well as on others.

After Scrooge became aware of what could happen to him if he continued his present lifestyle, he became free from his own separate sense of self, and he changed overnight into a person of generosity and compassion, filled with joy. Above all, Scrooge became a free and happy person, as he had been in his youth.

Just as Scrooge had a second chance after he awoke on Christmas morning, we all have a second chance to change our way of life every day, every moment.

Neither Appearing Nor Disappearing

Through the cessation of this and that
This and that will not be manifest.
The entire mass of suffering
Indeed thereby completely ceases.

—Nagarjuna[79]

They do not appear or disappear, are not tainted or pure, do not increase or decrease.

WHEN I was in my early twenties, I came to know a man whose girlfriend left him without saying a word. Her "disappearance" depressed him for a long time, but he became a cheerful and happy man again when a new girlfriend "appeared."

A number of years ago, a famous Korean actress committed suicide. She made that choice because she could not endure widespread malicious rumors; she was in deep personal agony because she thought that her "pure" reputation had become "tainted."

There are many people who become very happy when their fortunes or riches "increase" and become sad when their fortunes or riches "decrease."

Whether they are material things (such as a new car, or a big house), or nonmaterial things (including fame, recognition, health, honor, or integrity), when they appear or disappear, increase or decrease, seem pure or tainted, people become happy or unhappy, feel despondent or joyful. This is how our minds and emotions work.

Depending on our environment, which is constantly changing, our mind or mood continuously goes up and down. The Buddha said that the waves in the ocean [mind] are constantly stirred by the passing wind [objects].[80]

Shun, a saintly Chinese Emperor, was a man of humble birth. Before he became emperor, he made his living as a potter, an occupation of the lower class. However, it is said that his mind remained the same whether he was a potter or an emperor.

The life of Jesus was tumultuous and full of hardships. He was falsely accused by Pharisees and persecuted by Roman soldiers. Yet he always said, "Peace be with you... My peace I give to you."[81]

The Buddha explained nirvana as the "unconditioned mind," a mind that is not affected by our environment. The goal of our spiritual practice is to transform our wandering mind (which is constantly affected by our changing environment) into the "unconditioned mind."

Nagarjuna explained nirvana as:

> Unrelinquished, unattained,
> Unannihilated, not permanent,
> Unarisen, unceased:
> This is how nirvana is described.[82]

While nirvana is the state of the Absolute, the world in which we live is the dualistic world of relativity.

> While the Founding Master [of Won Buddhism] was abiding at Pongnae hermitage, the wretched shriek of a wild boar a hunter was slaughtering nearby was so pitiful

that it prompted the Founding Master to say, "One's gain is another's loss."[83]

We may be pleased to find and buy inexpensive clothes that were made in developing countries. These clothes, however, are sometimes inexpensive because they are made by child labor, or because the labor union leader was executed for trying to unionize company employees. When one thing profits, another thing suffers a loss. That is the reality of our lives or this world.

Won Hyo (617–86 C.E.) was a prominent Korean Buddhist master. He left home and became a monk because he was deeply disillusioned and disheartened by this dualistic world. Won Hyo was of noble birth, and when he was young, he joined Wharang, an elite youth corps. He fought in, and won, many battles. One day he lost a battle in which his dearest friend and comrade was killed. Devastated, Won Hyo returned to his camp, crying bitterly over the loss of his dearest friend.

When he was completely exhausted from crying, the thought arose, "What are my enemies doing at this very moment, while I am suffering so badly?" He envisioned a banquet where his enemies were enjoying themselves, drinking toasts to one another, bragging about their exploits and how many enemy soldiers they had killed, and laughing about how stupid the enemy was. As he visualized this, Won Hyo became full of anger and resentment. This image stirred his blood and inflamed his desire for revenge.

Suddenly, he realized that he had done these exact things many times after he had won a battle. Just as he was in agony now, he realized that many people suffered similarly because he had killed someone dear to them. He felt suddenly awakened from a deep dream. He became so disillusioned by this reality that he left society to become a Buddhist monk. He wanted to search for the absolute truth and to live so that all people could benefit at the same time.

The world in which we live is relative and dualistic. In a sports game, both teams cannot win at the same time. The truth about this relative nature of the world is represented in the Heart Sutra in the words "appear or disappear, tainted or pure, increase or decrease."

At a time when the Korean economy was in a severe depression, a man visited my teacher, a Buddhist monk. He was distraught because he had been demoted at work, which caused his salary to be reduced. A younger subordinate, who used to work for him, had taken his job; therefore, he felt ashamed and sorry for himself.

My teacher took him to the temple court. In the late autumn, many flowers were blooming in the garden, from tall chrysanthemums and roses, to many tiny nameless flowers. My teacher asked the depressed man whether the little flowers were as beautiful as the tall chrysanthemums. The man saw that those tiny, nameless flowers were just as beautiful as the larger chrysanthemums and roses. Even though the tall chrysanthemums blocked them, the tiny flowers did their best to absorb the sunlight.

My teacher's point was that the truth does not discriminate. It is our mind that compares, discriminates, and passes judgment. This is the cause of suffering. The sun shines not only on the good person but also on the bad person. The rain falls not only on the holy man but also on the evil man. In the mountains, tall, handsome trees and beautiful flowers grow simultaneously along with all kinds of weeds. Nature does not discriminate. It does not compare. It nurtures all the trees and animals, including poisonous grass and venomous snakes. The truth, or reality, is characterized by nondiscrimination, nonduality.

A doorway is neither an exit nor an entrance. It depends on where you stand. If you are inside the room, it is an exit; if you are outside the room, it is an entrance. The Rocky Mountains are neither in the west nor in the east. If you are in Los Angeles, they are to the east; if you are in New York, they are to the west.

Because of "I," all kinds of discriminative thoughts arise. Our separate, false sense of self creates a dualistic world because many pick and choose: this occupation is good or that occupation is bad, this person is good or that person is disagreeable, either a Republican or a Democrat is better than the other. The reality of the absolute truth, the realm of complete equality, the truth of no discrimination, the nondualistic world—these things are hidden by our dualistic mindset.

Some regions flood while other regions suffer from drought. However, the total amount of water on the earth remains the same. When a candle burns, it becomes shorter; part of it is constantly disappearing, but the total energy remains the same. This demonstrates the First Law of Thermodynamics, which states that things are constantly transformed while the total energy remains the same.

From an individual or local perspective, it seems that things "appear or disappear," or "increase or decrease," yet from the global perspective, nothing is appearing or disappearing, nor increasing or decreasing.

To enlightened ones whose minds are united with the entire universe, nothing appears or disappears; nothing increases or decreases. Images in a mirror can appear or disappear, or become "tainted or pure," depending on what stands before the mirror. The mirror itself, however, remains the same.

The passage in the Heart Sutra that says "they do not appear or disappear, are not tainted or pure, do not increase or decrease," means that our original mind, or the ultimate reality of all phenomena, does not appear or disappear. It is neither tainted nor pure. It does not increase or decrease. It is eternal and everlasting, remaining constant.

As previously discussed, buddhas and bodhisattvas are enlightened to the truth of the empty nature of all things. They become one with the original mind, which is like empty space. Because of its empty nature, when night falls, the empty space becomes dark; when day comes, it becomes light. Things inside that space can appear or disappear, increase or decrease, but the space itself remains the same.

Master Hui-chung said:

> All dharmas are the mind. But the mind has no body or limbs. So how can it be created or destroyed, pure or

impure, whole or incomplete?... If we see dharmas born, then we see dharmas destroyed. But dharmas are not really born, and they are not destroyed. They are like cataracts that appear as flowers in the sky. They are false appearances that obstruct our eye of wisdom. The attachment to individuality of ordinary people is called defilement, and the realization of the emptiness of the individual is what is meant by purity. But if defilement can be eliminated and can then be called purity, then defilement is essentially empty, and in emptiness there is also no purity."[84]

When Won Hyo reached the age of forty-five, he went to China to study more about Buddhism, which was the customary practice for many Korean Buddhist monks at that time. In those days, Korea was divided into three kingdoms: Sila, Kokureo, and Backjae. Won Hyo first tried to walk to China by passing through the northern kingdom of Kokureo, which shared a border with his home kingdom of Sila. But he was caught by soldiers of Kokureo and was imprisoned because they thought that Won Hyo was a spy from Sila. He remained incarcerated for several months until a Buddhist soldier of Kokureo released him.

He next decided to go to China by ship. To reach the sea, he had to cross the border of Backjae, an enemy kingdom located to the west of Sila. Won Hyo met another monk, Eu Sang, who also wanted to go to China to study Buddhism. Together they crossed the Backjae border and proceeded to the port. Because of Won Hyo's previous experience, they walked at night and rested during the day, hiding themselves. One night as they walked in the mountains, the moon was suddenly covered by thick clouds, and the world plunged into darkness. To make matters worse, it began to rain. The night was so dark that they could not even see what was right before them. They felt their way through the darkness to find some shelter for the night. Eventually they discovered a cave, which seemed a perfect place to keep out of the storm. Inside the cave, they quickly fell asleep.

In the middle of the night, Won Hyo awoke and was so thirsty that he fumbled around in the darkness looking for water. He found a bowl that was filled with rainwater and drank deeply, finding it most refreshing. He quickly fell back to sleep. In the morning, when Won Hyo awoke, he was shocked to discover that the cave was a place where nearby villagers had put dead bodies. He saw that the bowl from which he had drunk such refreshing water was actually a skull filled with dirty water and maggots. Sickened, he immediately began to vomit.

After a while, he pulled himself up, and the thought arose in his mind, "Last night, when I was very thirsty, the water that I drank was so sweet and refreshing. Yet when I saw that the water was in a skull, I felt sick and I vomited, even though it was the same water." At that moment, Won Hyo became enlightened and clearly saw the truth that everything is of our own mind's creation. He composed a verse, which says: "When a thought arises, all dharmas arise; when a thought ceases, all dharmas disappear."

Whether it is contained in a toilet or in a golden cup, water is just water. The water of the Ganges River is neither sacred nor profane. To the Hindus, it is holy water; to many tourists, it is unsanitary water because many cremation grounds are located along its banks. Similarly, to Buddhists, seeing the Buddha image in their dreams is auspicious, but to some Christians the same image might be interpreted as a bad omen. But it is just an image in our dreams; it is just a thought, neither auspicious nor inauspicious.

When we realize the truth that everything is of our own mind's creation, we can attain freedom of mind on the individual level. On the global level, social reformation follows because we realize that all forms of discrimination, from racial to sexual, originate in our thoughts, and these thoughts are not the absolute truth. Once we realize this, religious wars over "holy" places will also disappear, because this holiness exists only in our minds.

How can we progress from the dualistic world, the world of suffering, to the world of absolute truth and complete equality?

As long as the dualistic world arises in our thoughts, and the root of these thoughts is our sense of self, then the means of liberating ourselves from the dualistic world is enlightenment, the realization of the empty nature of all things.

Sotaesan, the founding master of Won Buddhism, said that since ancient times, there has never been a practitioner who has aspired to attain the great Way who has not practiced meditation.[85] It is almost impossible to attain enlightenment without meditation and without cultivating wisdom—especially through koan practice. Meditation, koan practice, and scripture study are all important, yet just as important is the practice of dropping our "picking and choosing" attitude. Because of our likes and dislikes and our attachment to preferences, our minds get entangled. We lose freedom of mind, instead continuously strengthening our ignorance. In our daily lives, the mindful practice of letting go of this "picking and choosing" attitude is crucial.

According to Nagarjuna:

> Through the cessation of this and that
> This and that will not be manifest.
> The entire mass of suffering
> Indeed thereby completely ceases.[86]

Seng Tsan, the Third Patriarch of Zen Buddhism, wrote:

> The Great Way is not difficult
> for those who have no preferences.
> When love and hate are both absent
> Everything becomes clear and undisguised.
> Make the smallest distinction, however,
> and heaven and earth are set infinitely apart.
> If you wish to see the truth,
> then hold no opinions for or against anything.
> To set up what you like against what you dislike
> is a disease of the mind.[87]

Especially in the Buddhist tradition, many masters have taught their students to let go of their dualistic thoughts using various methods.

There was a Korean monk who studied and practiced Dharma with his teacher, Zen Master Chung Mae. When the master was very old and near death, the young monk cared for him with great commitment and sincerity. The monk wanted to be with his teacher during his final moments. The master suddenly defecated in his pants, got up, and started to rub the feces on the wall with his hands. The room began to smell terribly. Thinking the master had lost his mind, the young monk started to leave the room. At that moment, the master held him and said, "You need to be present to see the last moment of the realized one," and then he died. The room was immediately filled with the sweet smell of incense.[88] The master, who had great Dharma power, tried to teach this young monk to let go of the picking and choosing attitude and to abandon his preferences.

It is said that when begging for food, Ananda, Buddha's attendant, would visit rich men's houses because he was worried about their future. Due to their conceit and laziness, rich men tend to fall into a lower realm of existence in their next lives. Kashapa, one of the Buddha's ten main disciples, is said to have visited the houses of poor people so that they could create merit by giving alms to him. The Buddha is said to have begged for food from door to door without discrimination. In our daily lives, doing things without "picking and choosing," without discriminative thoughts, is a major component of practice. It is the path of achieving liberation of the mind.

Letting go of discriminative thoughts can also be taught to children at an early age. One Korean elementary school teacher has applied Won Buddhist teachings to help her students understand their minds and attain freedom. From time to time, she asks them to come to school wearing clothes they dislike. Many students claimed to hate a particular style of clothing. Yet when they actually put on the clothing, they soon discovered that it was not so bad. To help her students break the bad habit of an unbalanced diet, she designated a certain day on which students brought a food that they disliked for lunch. Students realized that when they actually ate this food, it was also not as bad as they had expected.

Through these kinds of actual practices, people can have freedom of mind and be liberated from the tendency of likes and dislikes. These practices help us to break various types of bondage, which our minds created, and to free our minds from dualistic thoughts from the constantly fluctuating environment. These practices help us break free from our fixed ideas and preconceived notions.

The following story is from the diary of a young Won Buddhist minister who was in charge of the youth group at a Won Buddhist temple in the United States. He wrote this entry after a regular Sunday evening service when many temple members gathered to celebrate a birthday.

After the birthday candles were blown out, a teenager approached the minister and teasingly asked him to sing a song on stage. All the temple members knew that the young minister was shy, so they were shocked when he got on the stage without any hesitation. He sang a hip-hop song and danced to the music, delighting everyone.

The next week when he gave a Dharma talk on that event, he spoke about how he had felt when he was asked to sing. His talk moved me and many other people. He wrote in his diary:

> There is a Korean saying, "Like a bull heading to the slaughterhouse." This expression is used to describe a situation where someone is doing something that they really, really do not want to do. When I was asked to sing a song in front of many people, I felt the same way. I became very tense. All the temple members were watching me, waiting for my reaction. I was nervous, but I did not want to break the merry atmosphere.
>
> I decided to sacrifice myself for everybody else's amusement. I sang a song and danced as if I were crazy. I used this opportunity as part of my practice.

One interesting discovery was that during my singing and dancing, I felt a huge liberation. I felt like I had become free from some burden that I had been carrying for a long time. I became free from a weight (my own idea of myself) that made me shy and silent.

Originally, I as well as all other people in the world, are neither shy nor bold, neither introverted nor extroverted. It is true that during the twenty odd years of my life, my living circumstances and personality made me shy. I was trapped by that idea. Even though I already learned and understood clearly that my original nature is not shy or bold, I have nevertheless habitually lived like a shy introvert. When I sang and danced, I let go of my ego. At that moment, I was not different from the Second Patriarch who had cut off his arm in front of his teacher, Bodhidharma.

There is a Zen saying: "When you stand on the edge of a cliff, take another step forward." When I took another step toward the unfamiliar world, I felt a great liberation. It was a giant relief.

Let us think about how much we are deluded by our thoughts, which many times are neither reality nor truth.

A minister who used to work with me told me about her experience of how much a person can be deluded by their thoughts. After many years, her long-time dharma friend visited her and they shared her room, which had two beds separated by a partition. She had fun talking with her friend over the partition, even though she could not see her face. Both were in bed and, before falling asleep, her friend said how happy she had become upon hearing that her mother was moving from Korea to Hawaii. Her friend missed her mother very much but could not go back to Korea because of her work. She told the minister how she had been feeling unwell, but after hearing that her mother was coming, she felt great. The minister realized how much humans can be deluded by their thoughts: *Her mother had not yet come to Hawaii, yet she already felt differently.* This is delusion.

We all live in this way. Because of one thought, we suffer; because of another thought, we are joyful. All kinds of emotions: depression, jealousy, anger, envy, frustration, despair, and hopelessness originate in a thought. We are fooled and deluded by that thought, which is not reality. These thoughts drive our minds and dictate the course of our lives. They make us happy or miserable, depressed or joyful, angry or pleased.

Let us maintain the realization that our thoughts are just thoughts, not reality. The world is as it is. Because of our thoughts, which our own minds create, we live in a world of our own making. We are imprisoned there.

A Zen master once said, "We should not fear the arising of thoughts, just fear being slow to notice them."

When a thought arises, let us realize that it is just a thought. Let us not become entangled in more stories, which our false ego writes. Let us be awakened to the truth that thoughts are not reality.

If we commit to meditating on a regular basis, working with koans, studying scriptures, and above all, making an effort in our daily lives to let go of picking and choosing, then the door of enlightenment will open. The amount of freedom that we enjoy at each moment, regardless of our situation, will be greater and greater.

When the Shoes Fit, One Forgets About Them

8

To study the Buddha Way is to study the self.
To study the self is to forget the self.
To forget the self is to be enlightened by all things.
To be enlightened by all things is
to be freed from one's own body
and mind and those of others.
No trace of enlightenment remains
and this traceless enlightenment is continued forever.

—Zen Master Dogen

Therefore in emptiness, no form, no sensations, no perceptions, no impulses, no consciousness. No eyes, no ears, no
nose, no tongue, no body, no mind; no form, no sound,
no smell, no taste, no touch, no object of mind; no realm
of eye, ear, nose, tongue, body, or mind consciousness.

THIS PASSAGE from the Heart Sutra tells us that the perceiving subject, the perceived object, and our perceptions are all
empty.

In the previous chapters, "I" was shown to be the perceiving sub-ject, which is empty—all five aggregates are empty—and that all dharmas are the perceived objects, and are empty.

As this passage shows, not only are the perceiving subject as well as the perceived objects empty, but the perceptions (which arise when our sense organs come into contact with the sense objects) are also empty. Sense organs, sense objects, and our perceptions do not inher-ently exist. They come into being depending on causes and conditions. Since they are dependently arising, they are devoid of true existence.

During the Buddha's time, philosophers and spiritual practitioners, including Buddha's disciples, argued about many philosophical and metaphysical controversies. They argued about whether the universe was eternal or not, whether the universe was finite or not, whether a buddha existed after death or not, and so on.

Regarding these things, the Buddha told this story:

> A man is wounded by a poisoned arrow, and his friends and relatives bring him to a surgeon. Suppose the man should then say: "I will not let this arrow be taken out until I know who shot me; whether he is a Ksatriya (of the war-rior caste) or a Brahmana (of the priestly caste) or a Vaisya (of the trading and agricultural caste) or a Sudra (of the low caste); what his name and family may be; whether he is tall, short, or of medium stature; whether his complex-ion is black, brown, or golden; from which village, town or city he comes. I will not let this arrow be taken out until I know the kind of bow with which I was shot; the kind of bowstring used; the type of arrow; what sort of feather was used on the arrow and with what kind of material the point of the arrow was made.[89]

Using this analogy, the Buddha said that the person who just loves to think about and discuss unnecessary metaphysical or philosophi-cal questions is like the person who was wounded by an arrow, yet refused to get treatment for the wound. The one and only thing the Buddha taught was how to end human suffering. The essence of the Buddhadharma is to help people to be free from suffering.

So what is the source of human suffering? The root of our suffering is always "I," or the self. All aspects of suffering arise from the six kinds of consciousness: seeing, hearing, smelling, tasting, touching, and thinking. For instance, when I see my boss, resentment may arise. When I hear the news that I failed an exam, I become very upset.

If these perceptions of consciousness do not arise, then our suffering does not arise because our suffering loses its foothold. *The Sutra of Forty-Two Sections*, section 7, says:

> Once a man came to see the Buddha, and denounced him because the Buddha was observing the Way and practicing great loving-kindness. The Buddha kept silent and did not reply. When the denunciation ceased, the Buddha asked, "If you are courteous to people and they do not accept your courtesy, the courtesy returns to you, does it not?" "It does," the man replied. The Buddha said, "Now you are denouncing me, but I do not receive it, so the misfortune returns to you and must remain with you. It is as inevitable as an echo that follows a sound, or as a shadow that follows a form. In the end, you cannot avoid it. Therefore, be mindful, and cease from doing evil."

Highly enlightened minds are not influenced by what they see, hear, smell, sense, or think, although they are clearly aware of these sensations and thoughts. Just as the wind cannot blow away space or light, sensory experience does not move the enlightened mind. There is a Zen saying that "the sun sets on the ocean but it does not get wet." This describes the state of the enlightened mind, or our original mind. Zen Master Dogen said, "When someone has spiritually awakened, he resembles the moon's 'residing' in water: the moon does not get wet nor is the water shattered."[90]

The sutra of *Hsiu-Hsiu-An Discourse on Tso-ch'an* says, "When seeing, there is no seeing; when hearing, there is no hearing." This describes the state of the enlightened mind.

The six kinds of consciousness are made up of five kinds of sensory consciousness (visual, auditory, olfactory, gustatory, tactile) plus mental consciousness. In order to understand the empty nature of the six kinds of consciousness, let us think about how our consciousness arises.

Consciousness arises when our six sense organs, as perceiving subjects, come in contact with the six sense objects, as perceived objects. When our eyes (or ears, nose, tongue, body, or mind) meet visual form or light (or sound, smell, taste, touch, idea, or object of mind[91]), visual (or auditory, olfactory, gustatory, tactile, or mental) consciousness arises.

Depending on the object—e.g., eating chocolate or drinking spoiled milk, or seeing my boss or my love—our perceptions or consciousness can be pleasant, unpleasant, or neutral. We often direct our life toward trying to avoid unpleasant objects and to hold on to pleasant objects.

The six perceiving subjects and the six perceived objects are all together called the twelve bases. Together, these twelve bases and six kinds of consciousness are called the "eighteen elements" or "eighteen fields." Buddha said this world is eighteen elements.[92]

To comprehend the empty nature of the eighteen elements, let us consider the following. Because the six sense organs are the basis of the objective world, they are called the six roots. If we have no sense organs, can we see, hear, smell, taste, touch, or think? Of course not. Even though there are six sense objects, without the six sense organs, no perceptions or consciousness can arise.

Even if we have sense organs, perceptions or consciousness cannot arise without sense objects. Imagine that you were born and lived in a completely dark cave your entire life. Even if you have eyes, if there is no light you cannot see, and visual consciousness cannot arise. Similarly, even if you have ears, if there is no sound, hearing or auditory consciousness cannot arise.

Seeing is seeing something. Hearing is hearing something. Thinking is thinking something. In order for seeing (hearing, smelling, tasting, touching, thinking) to occur, not only sense organs but also sense objects are necessary.

Let us consider a dead person. Even though he or she has sense organs (eyes, ears, nose, tongue, body) and is surrounded by sensory stimulants like light, sound, smell, and so on, the dead person cannot experience these sensations, so perceptions cannot arise.

For visual consciousness to arise, the existence of eyes and light are not enough. Consciousness is a prerequisite for visual consciousness to occur. For auditory consciousness to arise—for seeing, hearing, smelling, or thinking to arise—not only are ears and sound necessary, but consciousness is also necessary. It is just like taking a picture. The camera (which works like an eye) and an object (that which is being photographed) are not enough. A photographer is required, who works like the consciousness.

Consciousness is therefore an indispensable factor in the arising of our experience. Only when sense organs, sense objects, and consciousness work together can various kinds of consciousness arise. For example, in order for an image to be reflected in a mirror, we need three things: the mirror, an object, and light. The Buddha used this analogy: "Three cut reeds can stand only by leaning on one another. If you take one away, the other two will fall."[93]

This book has discussed in detail that emptiness means the absence of inherent existence (see especially chapter 4). Since the eighteen elements dependently arise—that is, they only arise when a perceiving subject, the perceived objects, and consciousness work together—therefore the eighteen elements are empty. Since the eighteen elements cannot exist in and of themselves, in the absolute sense they do not exist. So the Heart Sutra says:

Therefore in emptiness, no form, no sensations, no perceptions, no impulses, no consciousness. No eyes, no ears, no nose, no tongue, no body, no mind; no form, no sound, no smell, no taste, no touch, no object of mind; no realm of eye, ear, nose, tongue, body, or mind consciousness.

No form, no sensations, no perceptions, no impulses, no consciousness means that the five aggregates are empty (see chapters 3 and 4 for details). *No eyes, no ears, no nose, no tongue, no body, no mind* refers to the emptiness of the perceiving subject. The person who is experiencing or perceiving is empty. *No form, no sound, no smell, no taste, no touch, no object of mind* refers to the emptiness of the perceived object. The object or the phenomenon that is experienced or perceived is also empty. *No realm of eye, ear, nose, tongue, body, or mind consciousness* means that all perceptions or consciousness are also empty. The observer, the observed, and the perceptions or consciousness are all empty because they cannot exist on their own.

Zen Master Seung Sahn once pounded his staff on the ground and asked, "Is this staff, the sound, and your mind one or two?" A student said that it was one, another said that it was two. Instead of answering them, Seung Sahn pounded his staff on the ground again, implying that neither is a good answer, because both of these answers are merely intellectual concepts. He tried to demonstrate that sound, like everything in the world, comes into existence dependent on other conditions.

Seng Tsan, the Third Patriarch of Zen Buddhism, said:

> When no discriminating thoughts arise, the old mind ceases
>   to exist.
> When thought objects vanish, the thinking subject vanishes,
> as when the mind vanishes, objects vanish.
> Things are objects because there is a subject (mind);
> the mind (subject) is such because of things (objects).
> Understand the relativity of these two

and the basic reality: the unity of emptiness.
In this Emptiness the two are indistinguishable,
and each contains in itself the whole world...

In this world of Suchness
there is neither self nor other-than-self.
To come directly into harmony with this reality
just simply say when doubt arises, "Not two."
In this "not two" nothing is separate,
nothing is excluded.
No matter when or where,
enlightenment means entering this truth.[94]

Master Hui-chung said, "People misapprehend their own mind and see form as something outside their mind. They don't know that form exists because of their mind. And where could form come from, if not from their mind? Thus, it says, 'Form is not separate from emptiness.'"[95]

The oneness, or inseparability, of our minds and sense objects has been proved scientifically by quantum physics (see chapter 5 for more discussion). Erwin Schrödinger, one of the founders of quantum physics wrote, "Subject and objects are only one. The barrier between them cannot be said to have been broken down as a result of recent experience in the physical sciences, for this barrier does not exist."[96] Jules Henri Poincaré, the French mathematician, said, "It is impossible that there is a reality totally independent of the mind that conceives it, sees it, or senses it. Even if it did exist, such a world would be utterly inaccessible to us."[97] Eugene Wigner, one of the pioneers of quantum mechanics, said that without entering someone's consciousness, quantum results are not fixed. He said, "It is not possible to formulate the laws in a fully consistent way without reference to consciousness."[98]

Where does the valley end and the peak begin? Where does the peak end and the valley begin? Where is the division between downtown and the suburbs? Where is the division between east and west, or the division between the Pacific and Atlantic oceans? They are all conceptually different and have different names, but they are only different aspects of the one reality.

Pacific and Atlantic oceans, peak and valley, east and west, are conceptual distinctions, not factual divisions. Likewise, perceiving organs, perceived objects, and perceptions are only conceptual divisions. They are different aspects of the one reality. As a matter of truth, they cannot be divided or separated. Think of a bar magnet, which cannot be divided to get only a north pole or only a south pole. Perceiving organs, perceived objects, and perceptions are not independent or separate entities.

Let us consider the distinctions of the six sense organs. Where does the tongue end and the body begin? Where does the nose end and the body begin? Eyes, ears, nose, tongue, body, and mind are human distinctions. The division is entirely arbitrary. They are convenient designations, mental constructs that have nothing to do with reality. In reality, these sense organs exist as one entity. In terms of the Dharma, we should not consider these six to be separate or independent entities.

One can say that it is our eyes that see, but without our mind, brain, or nervous system (which is a part of the body), how can our eyes see? One can say that it is our tongue that tastes, but without our mind or consciousness, or without the help of our eyes, hands, or brain, how can our tongue taste? One can say that our mind thinks, but without the faculties of seeing, hearing, smelling, tasting, or touching, how can thinking be possible? In order to solve a mathematical problem, we have to see the problem with our eyes and use our hands to write.[99]

Other Buddhist masters have had much to say about these interdependencies. Zen Master Tung-shan said, "When you hear the sound with your eyes, then you will know..." Zen Master Dogen said, "In mustering the whole body and mind and seeing forms, in mustering the whole body and mind and hearing sound, they are intimately perceived..."[100]

As the above passage from the Heart Sutra explains, in an absolute sense, the distinctions between the eighteen fields cannot exist. Just as eyes, ears, and so on belong to one body—although they have different names—and just as body and mind belong to one human being, the eighteen elements do not exist independently. They belong to one ultimate reality that has many labels: Mind, One life, God, Dharmakaya Buddha, and so on. The eighteen elements or all phenomena are the creation of our mind.[101] All the Buddha's teachings can be condensed into this one sentence: All things are born from mind.[102]

Zen Master Tung-shan attained enlightenment after seeing his reflection in a stream. The emptiness of ourselves, or the Dharma that everything is of our mind's creation, is the enlightenment that we should experience.

We can get a glimpse of the empty nature of all things on a daily basis. For instance, depending upon our state of mind, or how hungry we are, or whom we dine with, the same food can have a different taste. Depending upon your particular situation (e.g., you just got promoted or laid off), the same news can sound very different. If you are absorbed in something, you might not even hear that news at all.

This shows us the empty nature of all things and that all things are of our minds' own creation. When a monk asked Chao-chou, the Chinese Zen master, "Does a dog have buddha nature?" Chao-chou answered, "No." This is not the logical answer. Buddha taught that all sentient beings have buddha nature. Chao-chou's "No" is a well-known koan. When a Korean monk held this koan in mind, and worked with it for a long time, his entire mind became "no." His mind became so focused and clear that all wandering and dualistic thoughts vanished. Eventually when the question itself also disappeared, he became enlightened. Working with this koan enabled him to realize the true meaning of "no," or the absolute truth.

When Zen Master Tung-shan was very young, he read the Heart Sutra. When he encountered the passage "No eyes, no ears, no nose, no tongue, no body, no mind," he was very surprised and touched his eyes and ears to make sure they were there. When koans remove all the distinctions detected by the eyes, ears, nose, tongue, body, and mind—that is to say, when our minds become free from seeing, hearing, smelling, tasting, touching, and thinking—then we can be awakened to the empty nature of all things, including the eighteen elements. When our eyes, ears, nose, tongue, body, and mind disappear, our whole being and all things in the universe will become our sense organs.[103] At that time we can truly understand and become one with this "no" in the Heart Sutra.

The poet Rilke indirectly expressed this truth in a poem:

> Extinguish my eyes, I'll go on seeing you.
> Seal my ears, I'll go on hearing you.
> And without feet I can make my way to you,
> Without a mouth I can swear your name.

When people begin to practice meditation and study the dharma of emptiness more deeply, they identify themselves less and less as physical or mental beings. For instance, when you practice meditation and observe your bodily sensations, thoughts, or feelings (which are constantly arising and ceasing) in order to stay focused, you can easily observe the empty nature of these physical and mental elements and begin to move away from identifying yourself with your body and mind. Many practitioners then begin to identify the observing consciousness that watches the arising and ceasing of bodily sensations or thoughts as their true self, believing that this true self is unchanging. They tend to think that this primal awareness or universal consciousness is their core nature, their unchanging substance.

However, you must remember that our consciousness is also dependently arising and is empty, just like all the elements of our being. As discussed before, without sense organs and sense objects, consciousness itself cannot exist.

Seng Tsan, the Third Patriarch of Zen Buddhism, said, "Although all dualities come from the One, do not be attached even to this One."[104] When practice deepens, practitioners sometimes experience the disappearance of themselves. When they are deeply absorbed in meditation with no thoughts or bodily sensations, they sometimes experience the disappearance of their body and become startled. Some practitioners touch their head or hands to make sure they are there. This kind of experience can be frightening, like losing the ground under your feet. Joseph Goldstein likened this experience to freefalling from an airplane.[105] People can panic, thinking that they will hit the ground. But when we attain prajna, or the realization of the emptiness of self and phenomena, instead of being afraid, we can enjoy the falling. When we know clearly that there is no one to fall (emptiness of self) and there is no ground to hit (emptiness of phenomena), then we can enjoy the freefalling just as we enjoy the thrill of a rollercoaster.

When you realize that there is no one to shackle and your body is just an illusion, you will be completely free and can enjoy each moment of life. This is the prajna experience and the way to ultimate liberation.

THE TWELVE LINKS OF DEPENDENT ORIGINATION

9

If we observe the lives of all sentient beings and the process of their rebirth, we can discover that the occupations of humans as well as their ways of living are immensely diverse.

However, we can divide them into two types.

One is the world of attachment; the other is the world of liberation.

In the first world, humans are driven by greed, anger, and delusion. They do not think about tomorrow but live for the pleasures of today. In this world they darken their spirits and scatter their minds, which are originally pure and perfect, and lead their lives creating many transgressions.

In the latter or second world, humans are guided by concentration, wisdom, and mindful action, and live their lives illuminating their minds, gathering their thoughts, and collecting their spirits. They live to create many blessings for tomorrow even if today is not pleasant.

—Daesan, the Third Head Dharma Master
of Won Buddhism

BUDDHIST TEXTS—especially those of the Theravadin tradition—often describe how the Buddha awakened to the ideas of dependent origination and the Four Noble Truths. Just as Newton came to understand the law of gravity and thereby explained all phenomena of the universe based on that law, the Buddha found the truth of dependent origination and explained by that truth the workings of the world, the universe, and our minds. The dharma of dependent origination is so essential that the Buddha said, "Anyone who is able to see the nature of Interdependent Co-Arising is able to see the Buddha."[106] The Buddha also said that one who sees dependent origination sees the Dharma, and one who sees the Dharma sees dependent origination.

"Dependent origination" or "dependent co-arising" is the translation of the Sanskrit *pratityasamutpada*, which literally means "interdependent origination."[107] Dependent origination means that all things in the universe, whether sentient or nonsentient beings, whether physical, mental, or emotional entities, arise dependent on all others; or in other words, all phenomena arise together in a mutually interdependent web of cause and effect.

The Buddha says:

> When this exists, that comes to be;
> with the arising of this, that arises.
> When this does not exist,
> that does not come to be;
> with the cessation of this, that ceases.[108]

Dependent origination teaches that nothing can exist by itself. All things come into being because of a number of factors, called conditions, and are transformed into other factors, which constantly condition still more factors in an ever-continuous manner.

Think about how a tree comes to exist. It begins as a seed, and with the help of many conditions, such as sunshine, rain, and fertile soil, it sprouts and grows. Consider how anger and resentment arise: from some thought or memory, such as when you hear something that upsets you, or when you see something that disturbs you. Everything—from our personality to physical phenomena, from our thoughts to any kind of emotional state—arises depending on other conditions. Every existence is conditional. Nothing exists that is not subject to dependent origination.

When the Buddha was twelve years old, before he became enlightened, he had his first glimpse of the dharma of dependent origination. While the young Siddhartha sat under a tree, he saw a farmer plowing a field. Since Siddhartha was raised inside the palace and sheltered from anything unpleasant,[109] the sight of this backbreaking labor was quite surprising to him. While feeling sorry for the farmer, he noticed a worm emerge from the soil. All of a sudden, a bird appeared and ate the worm. While the bird was eating the worm, an eagle swooped down from the sky and took the smaller bird away.

This was the young Siddhartha's first glimpse of dukkha, the unsatisfactory aspect of all life, and he became sad and pensive. He thought to himself, "If the farmer had not plowed, the worm would not have come to the surface. If the small bird had not happened to be near the field, the worm would not have lost its life. If the small bird were not absorbed in eating the worm, the bird could have escaped the eagle, and so on." This was Siddhartha's first experience of the dharma of dependent origination.

After the Buddha attained supreme enlightenment, he completely realized the truth of dependent origination, and he specifically explained the cyclic condition of samsara, by means of the dharma of the twelve links.

The dharma of the twelve links is the detailed description of how humans are born, suffer, and die, in twelve causal stages. Since this dharma explains the cyclic existence of the human condition, through understanding this dharma, we can attain that wisdom which frees us from cyclic existence, and we can travel the path free from samsara.

All kinds of human suffering—whether illness or death, departing from loved ones, or not being able to obtain what we want—originate from birth, from the fact that we have human life. What the Buddha realized is that due to our karma, which originates from ignorance, humans are driven into successive rebirths and subsequent suffering. Therefore, to explain the endless cycle of human birth and death, the Buddha used the teaching of the twelve links. The first link we must understand is ignorance.

THE TWELVE LINKS

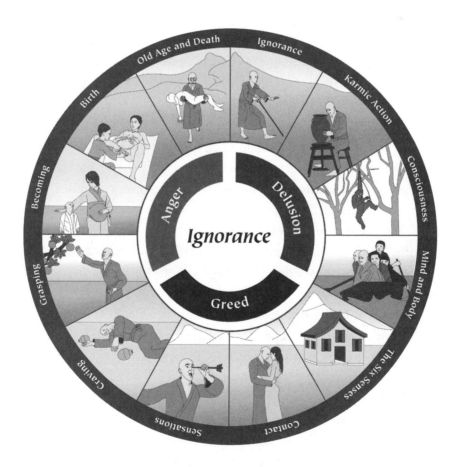

The Wheel of Life

Ignorance. Ignorance, or *avidya*, is the root cause of human rebirth and subsequent suffering. *Avidya* means the lack of understanding, lack of wisdom: *vidya* means "seeing," or "understanding," while *a* means "not," or "without." The Chinese translated *avidya* as *mu-myeong*, which literally means "ignorance," or "no light"; *mu* means "nothing" or "without," and *myeong* means "brightness."

One of the most gruesome battles fought by the Roman army was against the Huns, who often invaded Roman territory and were never easily defeated. One particular battle continued into the night. They fought under the moon, and when the moon disappeared suddenly, the battlefield became pitch black. Since no soldier on either side could tell whether any of the men around him was friend or foe, soldiers killed anyone near them. In the morning, both armies realized that they had killed many of their own soldiers.

Humans live just like the soldiers in that battle. Since most humans are not enlightened and are therefore not able to see things as they truly are, we continue to act in our lives the same way the Roman soldiers did. Fueled by desire or habits, and not seeing the consequences of our actions, we at times create wholesome karma, at other times unwholesome karma. Just as the absence of light caused the Roman soldiers to commit actions that caused them misery, *avidya* (darkness or ignorance) drives us to participate in all kinds of karmic actions. In the end we reap the result of suffering.

Ignorance here refers to our ignorance of reality, which is the empty nature of all things (ourselves and all phenomena). This ignorance gives rise to grasping. The twelve links are represented by the twelve images on the Wheel of Life, a traditional graphic representation of the samsaric cycle of existence. Ignorance is symbolized by a blind person groping his way with a cane, wandering in samsara, often falling down and succumbing to suffering because he does not know what is before him or where he is going.

Regarding the origin of ignorance, Chongsan, the Second Head Dharma Master of Won Buddhism, said:

Although the empty sky is originally clear, winds arise as energy moves, and clouds arise accordingly, causing darkness under heaven. Although our nature is originally pure, ignorance arises in accordance with the motion and quietude of the mind. When the mind calms down, its purity and brightness are restored; when the mind is agitated, ignorance arises. However, if the mind functions without disturbance, it keeps calmness in motion, maintaining its brightness; and if the mind moves in disturbance, ignorance comes into existence, causing darkness in the mind.[110]

Volitional or Karmic Action. The second link is *samskara*, which is volitional or karmic action. Driven by habitual energy and impulses caused by ignorance, people create various karmic actions. As long as there is ignorance, there arises the formation of karma: positive, negative, or neutral. This second link is symbolized by a potter shaping a vase on a wheel. Just as a clay pot is fashioned into many different sizes and shapes, people mold their karma through actions of body, speech, and mind.

Consciousness. Karmic actions, which we create with our body, speech, and mind, plant their latent seeds upon our consciousness or mindstream, or *vijnana*, which carries the imprints of all our wholesome and unwholesome karmic actions. When these karmic imprints are activated, they precipitate all the other links and ultimately lead to our rebirth in the various realms of existence. These karmic imprints on our consciousness join past to present and present to future.

This third link is symbolized by a monkey restlessly swinging from tree to tree. The monkey represents our deluded consciousness, driven by karmic energy. Just as a monkey mindlessly jumps from this branch to that branch, upon our death our deluded consciousness causes us to be born again as some type of sentient being in one of the various realms of existence.

Mind and Body, or Name and Form. The mental element of our being is referred to as *nama*, or name, and the physical element is referred to as *rupa*, or form. Our deluded consciousness causes us to be linked to a womb, and thereby develop a body (*rupa*) and a mind (*nama*); the third link gives rise to the fourth.

This fourth link of mind and body is symbolized by five men in a boat. These men represent the five aggregates that make up our sense of self: a physical body and the four mental elements, namely sensations, perception, impulses, and consciousness (see chapter 3).

The Six Senses. When the body and mind are formed, the six sense organs—eyes, ears, nose, tongue, body, and mind—then develop inside the womb. These are called the *adayatana*.

This fifth link is symbolized by an empty house with five windows and a door, which represent the six senses through which the outer world is perceived. From afar, the house looks as though it were lived in, even though it is empty. In the same way, humans are just the five aggregates of mind and body. There is no master or invisible entity called soul or *atman* where our mind and body reside.

Contact. When a baby is born, its sense organs come into contact, or *sparsha*, for the first time with the sense objects: contact between the eye and form, between the ear and sound, between the nose and smell, between the tongue and taste, between the body and touch, and between the mind and thoughts or ideas. Thus, the sixth link arises from the fifth.

This contact is symbolized by a man and a woman embracing one another. This represents the meeting of the sense organs with their objects of perception. The contact of the sense organs and sense objects leads to the experience of sensation, which is the next link.

Sensations or Feelings. When eyes, ears, nose, tongue, body, and mind come into contact with form, sound, smell, taste, touch, and thought, eye consciousness arises, as well as ear, nose, tongue, body, and mind consciousness. This consciousness is sometimes pleasant, sometimes unpleasant, and sometimes neutral, and is referred to as *vedana*, or sensations.

For humans, most information comes from what we see. Among the various sensations, the visual ones affect the human mind the most. For instance, if a young man is attracted to a woman, he is attracted most by her appearance, or the visual sensation caused by her form. Therefore, sensation, the seventh link, is represented by a person whose eye is pierced by an arrow, symbolizing visual contact and its corresponding sensation. Sensations condition craving, which is the eighth link.

Craving or Desire. Sensations give rise to desire, or *trishna*, which is the cause of all human suffering. When a sensation is pleasant (like the taste of delicious food or the thought of a new lover), there arises the craving or the desire not to be separated from that object. When sensations are unpleasant (like the sight of a horrible accident, or a painful thought from the past), a desire to be free from that painful sensation arises.

In relation to objects, there are six types of desire: craving for forms, craving for sounds, craving for smells, craving for tastes, craving for tangible objects, and craving for mental objects.

The eighth link is symbolized by a man drinking wine. Just as one becomes drunk or deluded by wine, one becomes deluded by desire. Just as thirst will never be satisfied by wine, humans cannot be satisfied by the things they desire, and therefore they crave sensations even more.

Grasping or Clinging. The desire not to be separated from, or the desire to be free from, some object gives rise to grasping or clinging, which can be defined as actively striving to hold on to what is pleasant and to push away what is unpleasant. Clinging, or *upadana*, is an attachment to some object. We have the desire to keep an object and to possess it permanently. However, all phenomena are impermanent. Therefore, we inevitably become discontented and frustrated, experiencing dukkha or suffering. Grasping or clinging is the condition that leads to becoming, which is the next link.

Grasping is symbolized by a man picking fruit from a tree. Just as Adam and Eve were forced to leave paradise because they picked and ate the forbidden fruit, which "was attractive to the eye, and was desirable for making one wise" (Genesis 3:6), grasping is the cause of suffering.

Becoming. Grasping or clinging gives rise to becoming, or *bhava.* Through grasping, we act with our bodies, speech, and minds, creating karma. Even after we die, the energy of clinging continues, driving us to search for another body. Being powerfully attracted toward our future parents, we take birth or "become" once again. The cessation of becoming is nirvana.[111] This tenth link is symbolized by a pregnant woman.

Birth. Through the power of becoming, we are reborn in some realm of existence whenever the necessary conditions are met. Birth, or *jati,* inevitably leads to the next link, which is old age and death. The eleventh link is symbolized by a woman giving birth.

Old Age and Death. As soon as humans are born, they start to grow old and eventually die when the aggregates cease. This is referred to as *jaramarana,* or old age and death. Good health simply means the slowing down of the process of death. Everything that is born will die. This twelfth link is symbolized by a corpse bearer.

Traditionally, there are many interpretations of the dharma of the twelve links of dependent origination. This chapter discusses the sequential interpretation, examining the twelve links of dependent origination over a period of three lifetimes: past, present, and future.

Link one, ignorance, and link two, karmic formation, belong to the past life and represent the conditions that are responsible for the occurrence of the present life. The third through tenth links (consciousness, name and form, the six senses, contact, feeling, craving, clinging, and becoming) constitute the process of evolution within the present life. The eleventh and twelfth links, birth and old age and death, belong to the future life. Karmic actions, currently performed by our deluded consciousness in this present life, result in a future life. Ultimately, ignorance and its resulting karmic formations cause the repeated emergence of the lives of sentient beings. This is samsara, characterized by dukkha.

Describing the twelve links as a process, which unfolds over three consecutive lifetimes, is a traditional way of explaining them. Actually these links are happening in each moment of our daily lives, whenever a thought arises. We do not have to understand the twelve links in a linear way. For example, not only does ignorance (the first link) give rise to volitional actions (the second link), but volitional actions also reinforce our ignorance, and ignorance also affects human consciousness (the third link). Other interpretations present different numbers of links. For example, in the *Mahanidana Sutta*, the Buddha lists only nine links. At other times, the Buddha taught ten links, omitting ignorance and volitional actions.[112]

The dharma of twelve links does not have to begin with ignorance, the "first" link. For instance, we can start from the eleventh link, birth. These links are cyclic phenomena, like the stages of a tree's life cycle, which proceeds from seed to sprout, from trunk to fruit, which again produces seeds. There is no beginning or ending. Each link is both a cause and an effect. However, just as it is convenient to describe a tree's life starting with the seed, using ignorance as the first link is a convenient and a customary practice.

The Awakening of Faith states, "As the result of the winds of ignorance, Mind which is intrinsically pure becomes agitated and forms waves." All sentient beings are led by ignorance because they do not realize the empty nature of themselves and all phenomena. This causes us to crave things, visible and invisible. It is this craving that causes suffering and the conditions for endless future rebirths.

We desire, and try to hold on to, many things. However, all cravings are fundamentally the graspings of our five aggregates. For instance, someone who is addicted to gambling becomes addicted through the sensation or feeling of excitement rather than the gambling itself. We can love and become attached to another person, e.g., a new girl-friend. However, we are really attached to the image of her created by our own mind, rather than to that person herself. In other words, the craving, attachment, and clinging, which are the causes of suffering, always arise within the five aggregates.

Ahimsaka was born into a Brahmin family in the kingdom of Kosala, India. When he was young, he was sent to a prominent Brahmin guru to study. Ahimsaka was intelligent and diligent, and so he excelled beyond the other students and quickly became his teacher's favorite. He enjoyed many privileges in his teacher's house, which made the other students jealous.

One day the students falsely accused Ahimsaka of seducing their teacher's wife and having an affair with her. At first, the teacher did not believe their accusation, but after hearing it over and over, he believed them and vowed to take revenge on Ahimsaka. Because Ahimsaka was too strong for him to attack physically, the teacher asked him to kill a thousand human beings and to bring one finger from each as payment for his teaching. He said that this would complete Ahimsaka's training. The teacher thought that in the course of killing people, Ahimsaka himself would certainly be killed.

Committed to earning his teacher's approval, the obedient Ahimsaka trusted his teacher and unquestioningly left his teacher's house in order to find people to kill. He became a highway murderer, at first keeping count of the number of people that he had killed by hanging the fingers of his victims on a tree. However, because birds subsequently ate some of the fingers, he started to wear his trophies around his neck as a garland. He quickly came to be known as Angulimala, which means "garland of fingers."

The king of Kosala heard of his ruthless killing and vowed to hunt him down. When Ahimsaka's mother heard about the king's intent, she set out for the forest in order to find her son and warn him of the king's intent. By that time, Angulimala had collected 999 fingers and was very anxious to find his last victim.

The Buddha knew that if he did not intervene, Angulimala might kill his own mother because of his desperate need for his teacher's approval. So the Buddha also set out for the forest to find Angulimala. When Angulimala saw a woman in the forest, he approached intending to kill her, but discovered that she was his mother. At the same time, he also saw a monk approaching. He decided to kill the wandering monk instead, and so he immediately ran toward the Buddha, drawing his sword.

But strangely, he could not catch up with the slow-walking Buddha.

The frustrated Angulimala finally cried out, "You there, monk, stop!" To this the Buddha replied, "I have stopped. It is you who have not stopped."

Angulimala did not catch the significance of these words, so he again shouted, "Monk! Why do you say that you have stopped while I have not?" The Buddha said, "I have stopped ignorance, desires, and harming living beings, but you have not stopped desires, anger, or killing. So it is you who has not stopped."

These words deeply moved Angulimala, and he thought that the monk was not only very brave but also highly enlightened. Throwing away his sword, he changed his ways and joined the Buddhist order.

Prior to becoming Buddhist, Angulimala thought about how to find and kill people every single morning when he awoke. Likewise, each day many people repeat the same bad habits, or repeat their anger and resentment against a person or a situation, or think about unwholesome ways to achieve their goals. Are we that different from Angulimala?

Repeating something again and again—that is samsara, the endless cycle of suffering. When a deluded thought arises, the samsaric world is unfolding; when a deluded thought fades, samsara ceases. *Samsara* literally means "movement," whereas nirvana is stillness—where the flame of desire caused by ignorance is extinguished. Only when ignorance stops do the twelve links, or the endless cycle of birth and death, disappear.

The person who conquers ignorance and is thereby liberated from the cycle of birth and death is called an *arhat*, which in Sanskrit means "foe destroyer" or "vanquisher of enemies." In this case, the enemy is our ignorance. The temple where Shakyamuni Buddha is enshrined is called *dae-woong-chun* in Chinese, which means "hall of a great hero." Buddhas, who are completely enlightened beings, are called heroes because they have conquered their enemy, which is ignorance.

Since all humans wish to end suffering permanently, what can be more imperative than breaking the shackles of ignorance and restoring prajna? That is why studying the Prajna Paramita Sutras are so meritorious: they are the path to revealing prajna.

When I first learned about the twelve links of dependent origination, it was as though I had discovered the treasure of all the mysteries of life and death. When I considered how few people on this earth know of this Dharma, I became very grateful for the opportunity to know it. I came to understand deeply that the one and only thing that liberates us from the endless cycle of rebirth is conquering ignorance, i.e., enlightenment. For this reason, I came to practice meditation more diligently. Nagarjuna said, "The cessation of ignorance occurs through meditation and wisdom."[113] Grasping or attachment arises because of ignorance, but our attachment or grasping also constantly reinforces our ignorance, thus strengthening our sense of self, just as fuel constantly feeds a flame. Attachment, especially when we are dying, is very serious and poses a grave impediment to our deliverance to a more wholesome realm of existence.

Sotaesan, the founding master of Won Buddhism, said:

> When a person's numinous consciousness departs from the physical body, it first follows its attachments, subsequently receives a body in accordance with its karma, and so continues to transmigrate in this boundless world. The only way to become free from this transmigration is to sunder all attachments and transcend karma.[114]

There is a Won Buddhist minister who used to work at a charitable organization. Since she worked indoors during the day, she began to play tennis outdoors to refresh herself and to improve her health. Several months after learning and practicing tennis, she really began to enjoy the game. Whenever she had free time, she went out to the tennis court to play.

One morning, she went to a nearby mountain with her friends. While crossing a brook, her foot slipped off the stepping-stone and she had a bad fall. She hit her head on a rock and immediately lost consciousness. Her friends panicked and dragged her out of the stream. They laid her on the ground and shook her to try to restore her consciousness.

In her hazy state, she heard her friends' voices and saw herself on the tennis court; she was sitting on the bench watching a tennis game. Even though she was not conscious, she realized that this vision arose because of her attachment to tennis, and that attachment was not good for her. She made up her mind to leave the court and tried to stand up from the bench. She later said that standing up from the bench was extremely difficult. It was as if her whole body were attached to the bench with a strong adhesive. As she struggled to leave the bench, her friends finally succeeded in waking her up. She now clearly understood how dreadful an attachment can be, especially when considering eternal lives. She came to be a more sincere practitioner.

Letting go of our attachments is something that we should practice mindfully in our daily lives. Otherwise we cannot maintain a calm and clear mind at the last moment of our lives.

Several years ago, the wife of a Won Buddhist minister developed cancer. After successful surgery and medical treatment, she enjoyed good health for several years. However, the cancer recurred and spread throughout her body. Recovery became difficult and her condition deteriorated. At first, whenever her sons visited her in the hospital, she welcomed them wholeheartedly and tried to talk cheerfully with them while holding their hands. After the doctor delivered the news that there was little chance of recovery, she decided that it was time for her to let go and prepare for her next life. She did not let her sons hold her hands in the hospital. This was a practice she used in order to let go of her attachments.

When a tree is cut and falls, it comes down on the heavier side, on the side that has many branches. Since the departed spirit usually follows its attachments, the practice of nonattachment is very important when one is dying because it prevents rebirth in a lower realm of existence. Consider the following anecdote:

> The Founding Master [of Won Buddhism] addressed the congregation at a meditation hall, "Do you know what the kingdom of Yama [the lord of death] and its messengers are? The kingdom of Yama is nowhere other than inside the wall of your own house; the messengers of Yama are none other than your family members. This is because ordinary people's spirits, being entangled in deep affection toward their own family members in this life, do not rise far when the body dies... The buddhas and enlightened masters from ancient times emphasized the importance of departing without attachments and acting without attachments, because only in this way can one avoid falling into unwholesome destinies."[115]

In order to remove ticks after walking in the forest, we should first carefully observe our bodies and clothes. Likewise, in order to practice nonattachment, we should first observe our minds carefully and understand clearly what kind of attachments we have.

Consider again Dickens' *A Christmas Carol*, which is discussed in chapter 6. On Christmas Eve Scrooge sees the ghost of his late partner, who worked himself to death in order to make more money. His friend could barely walk because of the heavy chains and the weight of the boxes filled with gold coins shackled around his body. He said to Scrooge that he was in chains because of his greed for money.

Is the state of his friend's spirit very different from ours? When our lives are looked at from a spiritual perspective, are we bound with chains? How many chains and shackles do you think you have?

However big a ship is, if it is tied to an anchor, it cannot embark on the vast ocean. Attaining freedom of mind and freeing ourselves from samsara begins with the mindful practice of nonattachment.

We can conclude our chapter with a statement from Master Sotaesan:

> The spirit that is bound by greed, hatred, and delusion will be bound to its attached mind at the time of death, and thus will not be able to come and go freely. Cloaked by the karmic power of ignorance, the spirit only finds light where its mind is attached and ends up being dragged to that place...
>
> On the other hand, because the spirit that has subjugated greed, hatred, and delusion is not bound to its attachments at the time of its death, it is able to come and go freely, to see and think correctly, and since it distinguishes between appropriate and inappropriate places, it is not bound by its karma. When it receives a new body, this occurs as is appropriate, with perfect composure. Also, when it enters the womb, it plants itself in consideration of its grateful love for its new parents.
>
> Whatever vows one has made will be realized in both great and small matters as the karmic rewards of one's resolution. Thus, the spirit is free in birth and death, and it moves about without ever being dragged around by transmigration within the six destinies, turning at will the twelvefold chain of causal conditioning.[116]

Let us watch our minds and realize what kind of attachments we have, and then remove them one by one by practicing mindfulness.

The root of cyclic existence is action.
Therefore, the wise one does not act.

—Nagarjuna[117]

**No ignorance, nor extinction of ignorance, no old age
and death, nor extinction of them.**

THE TEACHING of the twelve links of dependent origination
explains the process of human rebirth, or the cyclic nature of
the human condition in its causal relationships. According to
the teaching, human ignorance leads to grasping and consequently
suffering in human life. When ignorance, which is the first link and
the root cause of all human suffering, is broken, then the second link
of karmic formation disappears. The third link (consciousness) also
disappears and so forth. Eventually, the twelfth link, the link of old
age and death, is broken.

However, the above passage from the Heart Sutra seems to contra-
dict the teaching of the twelve links. While this may appear conflict-
ing, this passage simply means that the twelve links are also "empty."
That is to say, in the absolute sense, they do not exist. Note that for

the sake of brevity, the ten links between ignorance (the first link) and old age and death (the twelfth link) are omitted.

In chapters 3 and 4, the empty nature of "I" was explained: the five aggregates and the eighteen fields are empty. If the five aggregates are what make up human beings, then the twelve links are the actions of human beings. Since "I" is empty, then our actions, which are the twelve links, cannot have substance. The emptiness of the five aggregates consequentially leads to the empty nature of human activity, the twelve links.

Since each link is caused by another, which is to say that each and every link is dependently arising, they are not inherently existent. They are all empty of true existence.[118] Whatever the link, each is only a conditional existence and momentary phenomenon. They are all constantly arising and ceasing, and they do not have their own independent self-existence.

After the Buddha attained supreme enlightenment, he was amazed to realize, "All sentient beings are already buddhas who are whole, perfect, and complete, lacking nothing." Enlightenment is the realization that there is no ego to destroy. Our sense of self is an illusion, a mental construct. Since we are all already buddhas who lack nothing, and there is originally no ignorance, then "extinction of ignorance" becomes meaningless. Therefore, any effort to extinguish ignorance—which we call practice—becomes empty. That is why the Heart Sutra says, "No ignorance, nor extinction of ignorance..." How can we extinguish something that does not exist? The extinction of ignorance presupposes the existence of ignorance. Since there is no ignorance, from the absolute point of view, then in the enlightened mind, ignorance and the extinction of ignorance disappear at the same time.

The same can be said of "old age and death and the extinction of them." Since "old age and death" are empty, then their extinction becomes meaningless.[119]

Master Hui-chung says, "If the dust and domains of sensation exist, they can end. But because they don't really exist, what is there that ends? 'End' means 'death.' If the twelve links of causation arise, then life and death can end. But because causation does not arise, there is no end of life and death."[120]

One winter day, three monks decided to practice meditation for one week without talking. Late in the afternoon, one monk said, "This hall is too cold to practice meditation." The monk seated next to him said, "We promised not to talk this week. Why are you speaking?" Upon hearing that, the third monk burst into laughter and said, "I am the only person who did not speak." If ignorance, or old age and death, disappears, then the extinction of ignorance, or the extinction of old age and death, also disappears. If there remains a thought in the mind of the practitioner that he or she has finally attained great enlightenment and conquered ignorance and old age and death, then he or she is not truly enlightened.

To the enlightened one, the twelve links as well as the extinction of them do not exist. An enlightened mind is like a pure space that does not change, just as space itself is not changed by light or darkness.

The Diamond Sutra says:

> Subhuti, what do you think? Does a holy one say within himself: I have obtained Perfective Enlightenment? Subhuti said: No, World-honored One. Wherefore? Because there is no such condition as that called "Perfective Enlightenment." World-honored one, if a holy one of Perfective Enlightenment said to himself "such am I," he would necessarily partake of the idea of an ego-entity, a personality, a being, or a separated individuality.[121]

When there is a speck of dust in our eye, the whole world appears blurred. Because of our sense of self, we cannot see the truth or the world as it is. When we put a staff in water, it appears crooked. When we take it out of the water, it appears straight again. Likewise because of our notion of self, we cannot see the world as it truly is.

Master Won Hyo said, "When a thought arises, all dharmas arise.

When a thought ceases, all dharmas disappear." When the sense of self disappears, the twelve links as well as their extinctions vanish.

The Buddha said that the three worlds are nothing but mind. The world that we live in is *manomaya*, or our mind's illusion.[122] Nagarjuna said, "If you understand your mind, you understand all things." A Buddhist master said, "When a thought is deluded, one becomes ignorant; when a thought is enlightened, one becomes a Buddha." The twelve links, the dharmas, and the distinction between buddhas and ignorant beings all depend on one's mind.

Master Chen-k'o said:

> Once the Five Skandhas are seen as empty, the light of the mind shines alone. When all the clouds are gone, the full moon fills the sky. Thus, birth and destruction, purity and defilement, completeness and deficiency are all snowflakes on a red-hot stove. Once you realize true emptiness, how could the Five Skandhas alone be empty? The Twelve Abodes of Sensation, the Eighteen Elements of Perception, the Twelve Links of Dependent Origination, and the Four Noble Truths are all tortoise fur and rabbit horn. Ice doesn't melt by itself. It disappears when the sun comes out. Dharmas such as the Five Skandhas and Eighteen Elements of Perceptions and Twelve Links of Dependent Origination are like ice, and the illumination of prajna is like the sun.[123]

The Diamond Sutra also says:

> Subhuti, if anyone should say that the Tathagata [Buddha] comes or goes or sits or reclines, he fails to understand my teaching. Why? Because Tathagata has neither whence nor whither, therefore is He called 'Tathagata.'[124]

When a thought that arises from our sense of self disappears, our past, present, and future lives vanish at the same time.

One day a Buddhist monk happened to see a beautiful woman who had come to the temple to pray. At that time, he felt no progress in his spiritual practice and the life of a celibate monk seemed boring. No matter how hard he tried, he could not forget her, and he eventually left the priesthood to marry her. He became a farmer and sold his crops to make a living. The life of a farmer seemed difficult to him, and married life was not as romantic as he had expected. On his sixtieth birthday, his wife and sons prepared a lavish dinner for him, and when the meal was finished, he was left alone. He looked back over all his married years, and the memories that arose in his mind reflected a hard life of toil and tribulation in order to support his family. He felt lonely and came to regret his decision to leave the monastery and abandon the chance to become enlightened and help many people. Bitter tears of regret fell from his eyes as he thought, "I should have remained a monk. I should never have left the temple." As he wept, he heard the sound of a temple gong. He was so surprised that he immediately woke up only to realize that it had all been a dream! He had fallen asleep while prostrating on the cushion in front of the Buddha image. During his short snooze, he had lived for almost forty years.

Enlightenment is awakening. It is waking up from a dream. *Kyedah* literally means "awakening" in Korean, but it usually is translated as "enlightenment." "Buddha" means "the awakened one." Buddhist masters say that our lives are just a dream because average people live holding on to the illusion of a self as though it were real. An average person's life revolves around the concept "I," which, like a dream, is just an illusion.

Let us think about why we dream. We dream because we have a sense of self and because our thoughts continuously arise based on the notion of self. From the idea of self come all kinds of desires and thoughts, which are transformed and visualized while dreaming. When we dream, the "I" sometimes appears on the stage, and sometimes it is behind the scenes, but it is always the leading actor.

Whether we are dreaming at night or whether we are living our lives during the day, as long as our thoughts or lives are unfolding based on the notion of self, they are all dreams. Only after we are enlightened to the empty nature of our selves and realize that our idea of an ego entity is an illusion or a mental construct will our dream stop, along with the endless cycles of birth and death.

Zen Master Yung Chia said in *The Song of Enlightenment*:

> Have you not seen one whose study has ended,
> Who does nothing, who abides in the Way at ease?
> He does not banish deluded thought. He does not seek the
>   truth,
> To him the true nature of ignorance is buddha nature;
> This illusory empty body is the Dharma Body...
>
> In a dream, there are six vivid realms of existence;
> After enlightenment, completely empty,
> Not a single thing can be found...
>
> Do not seek the truth, do not despise the false,
> Realize that both are empty;
> They have no characteristics.
> Without characteristics, there is no emptiness
> And no nonemptiness.
> That is the Tathagata's [Buddha's] genuine form.

Average practitioners say that the world is illusion, so let us renounce the world. The enlightened one says that since the world is an illusion, why bother to renounce it? After enlightenment, everything comes home.

Whether one lives in a gold or iron prison, one is still imprisoned. Whether the dream is sweet or nightmarish, it is still not reality.

As long as we do not know the reality of our mind, we cannot be completely free. Only when we are awakened can the light of prajna shine through and that invisible prison called "I" vanishes.

Every one of us has a dream, but the greatest and most important goal for all humanity is to awaken from the bottomless dream that continues to darken and delude our minds.

This is the path to freedom, the path to complete liberation. This is prajna paramita.

THE FOUR NOBLE TRUTHS

*The one and only thing that I teach is
human suffering and the way to end it.*

—Buddha

*Whoever sees dependent arising
also sees suffering,
and its arising,
and its cessation as well as the path.*

—Nagarjuna

THE FOUR NOBLE TRUTHS were the subject of the Buddha's first discourse after his enlightenment. This is the most fundamental teaching of the Buddha.

The Buddha is said to have sat for seven weeks under a bodhi tree after attaining supreme enlightenment. In a deep *samadhi* state, he could clearly see all the samsaric worlds where people are born, suffer, and die. He could also see the path that leads to the end of suffering and cyclic existence. At the end of the seventh week, in a complete state of peace and freedom, he walked to Deer Park, where he proclaimed the Four Noble Truths to the five ascetics with whom he had first practiced extreme austerities. This was the first turn of the Wheel of Dharma, or the first teaching of Shakyamuni Buddha after his complete enlightenment.

The Four Noble Truths are the truth of suffering; the truth of the cause of suffering; the truth of the cessation of suffering; and the truth of the path leading to the cessation of suffering.

"The Four Noble Truths" is the translation of the Sanskrit *Catur Arya Satya. Catur* means "four" and *arya* means "preeminent" or "most excellent." Although *satya* is usually translated as "truth," its fuller meaning is "facts" or "reality," the way things truly are. So *arya satya* means "preeminent reality," or "the reality or facts that stand out."

The Four Noble Truths explain a sober reality; they are teachings so straightforward that even a child can understand them. They contain nothing radical or complicated, but their implications and usefulness are both rich and profound.

Much of the Buddha's Dharma is based on these teachings, and by contemplating this Dharma we can apply it to our lives and practice.

In the Testament Sutra, the Buddha says, "The moon can turn hot, and the sun can turn cold, but the Four [Noble] Truths are not subject to change."[125]

THE FIRST NOBLE TRUTH: SUFFERING

The first noble truth says that life is *dukkha*. Although usually translated in English as "suffering," *dukkha* (Pali; in Sanskrit, it is *duhkha*) has a broader and more profound meaning. It refers to dissatisfaction, dis-ease, insecurity, and incompleteness.

Dukkha need not be some kind of acute pain, misery, or distress, such as what people experience in a war-torn country or in refugee camps. It may not be extreme rage, like one might feel upon discovering that a spouse has been unfaithful. Dukkha may be everyday stress and irritation, boredom, or even just a leg that aches while sitting on the meditation cushion.

When we are tired, we rest. When we are hungry, we eat. When we cannot stand our boss or our spouse anymore, we get a new job or get divorced. In other words, our life can be a constant series of reactions to the dukkha that we experience, but it is never exactly as we would like it to be. Even though we are exhausted, we still have to go to work. Even if we find out that our spouse is not faithful, in many cases we have to live with him or her anyway. There are millions of people in the world who are starving and have nothing to eat. We have to live with unavoidable dukkha in our everyday lives.

The Buddha taught that there are eight kinds of dukkha, which can be outlined as the following: birth is suffering, aging is suffering, illness is suffering, death is suffering, dissociation from the pleasant is suffering, association with the unpleasant is suffering, not obtaining what we seek is suffering, and the scorching blaze of the five aggregates is suffering.

Birth Is Suffering. Have you ever seen a baby who is smiling during birth? Even when the Buddha was born, he came into this world crying. Many women say that labor is the greatest pain they have ever experienced.

All our life's suffering—including anger, disappointment, depression, jealousy, and sadness—begins with birth.

Aging Is Suffering. However powerful, smart, and successful we are, we cannot avoid aging. As we grow older, we become unable to physically, mentally, or emotionally enjoy many things. In old age, we all tend to encounter unsatisfactory situations, such as being ignored and being lonely. We also experience decreased mental, visual, and auditory capacity, as well as decreased ability to process information and recollect events. This is all unavoidable and is suffering.

Illness Is Suffering. I have seen many people in the terminal stages of cancer and I know how painful that is. I know one young boy who lost his hearing because a simple fever was not treated in time. In less privileged countries, many people still die because of the lack of simple medicines. Illness is definitely suffering.

Death Is Suffering. I still remember the tears my mother shed for almost half a year after my grandmother passed away. One time, I saw a lady wailing at her late husband's funeral. She embraced his coffin and cried, "Why? Why, God? Why my husband?" Her husband had been killed in a car accident two days before his graduation from a Christian seminary.

Some people meet a very painful death. The uncertainty, the fear, the anxiety before death—all of this is suffering.

The Buddha said, "Some people die in their mother's womb, and some die as soon as they are born; some die when they are crawling and some while walking; some are young, and some are old. Everyone disappears like the fruit that falls to the earth."

Dissociation from the Pleasant Is Suffering. We may think that the greatest stress we can experience is being parted from our loved ones, but the objects of our love need not necessarily be a person. Losing our attractive appearance, our popularity, or our job can also be dukkha. I recall the story of a woman who became obsessed with plastic surgery after she got divorced. She thought her husband had been having affairs with other women because she had lost her charm. Despite many operations, she could not become as attractive as she had hoped. She eventually needed psychiatric treatment and was sent to a mental hospital.

However much we cherish something, we will eventually lose it. Reflect for a moment on what you cherish most. Impermanence is the nature of all things.

Association with the Unpleasant Is Suffering. There are things that we dislike but have to encounter every day or every week. These could be a family member, a particular odor, or our job.

Even if we hate our jobs and are very tired, we still have to go to work in the morning. Even if we dislike our roommate, in many cases, we still may have to live with him or her.

Many situations exist that make us suffer but that we cannot avoid.

Not Obtaining What We Seek Is Suffering. My mother developed colon cancer when she was in her early sixties. Despite all her efforts, ranging from strict diet and exercise to prayer and meditation, she could not restore her health, and the cancer spread to all of her internal organs. In spite of working very hard, many people cannot earn enough money to make ends meet. Contrarily, many prosperous people are also dissatisfied in spite of their wealth. The inability to attain what we want is suffering. We may perceive this in terms of being unemployed, or having a poor appearance, or poor health, a lack of money, or the loss of fame. This is the nature of life.

The Scorching Blaze of the Five Aggregates Is Suffering. The Buddha said the world is on fire; human minds are ablaze. We suffer from uncontrollable jealousy, anger, inner conflicts, bad memories, and regrets. Like a moth that is so attracted to the light of a flame that it flies into the fire, we humans destroy our freedom and happiness because of mental and physical desires.

These eight types of suffering have been described here in a personal way, but suffering on a global level is also boundless: trillions of dollars are spent on many wars, and millions of children die because they cannot get clean water or simple medicine. The list is endless. The Buddha said that if all the tears that humans shed could be gathered, they would fill a vast ocean.

Why did the Buddha speak of these various kinds of suffering in such a specific way? He did so to convince us that the reality of suffering in our lives is unavoidable and inevitable. Dukkha is an inherent part of our world. If there is a common bond for all humanity, it is dukkha. If there is one universal factor in every nation, in each civilization, it is dukkha. We all live in the same nation, called the Republic of Dukkha.

Yet sometimes we experience pleasure and enjoy the experiences in our lives. So why did the Buddha say that life is dukkha? It is because everything is temporary; a beautiful flower withers, hair eventually turns gray. Everything that pleases us will eventually pass away. This is why the Buddha said, "Whatever is impermanent is dukkha."[126] Even if everything seems perfect, the happiness that comes from our environment—that conditional happiness—is insecure, fragile, and fleeting. Only in fairy tales can one live happily ever after.

I know a person who suffers from mental illness but since he does not think that he needs help, he will not go to the hospital for treatment and so keeps experiencing the same symptoms. If we do not face our lives directly, if we fail to recognize this sober reality clearly, then we will remain tangled in our problems, and we will not devote the time and effort necessary to free ourselves from dukkha.

Suffering is not noble, but our recognition of suffering is noble. Our solution emerges from this recognition. In Korea, families are sometimes given bad medical news before the person suffering from illness is told. When my mother began to feel sick because of her colon cancer, we knew the cause before she did and so someone in our family had to tell her, "Mom, you have cancer." All of my family members were reluctant to play that role. As a minister, I candidly told my mother what the doctor had said. She was very grateful for my unadorned remarks because I had given her the opportunity to prepare for her next life. I am grateful for the Buddha's straightforward discussion regarding the inevitability of suffering. Because he taught this reality clearly, we can face our lives directly and thereby redirect our minds so that we can be free from samsara.

To be free from suffering, accepting the first noble truth (life is suffering) is the price we have to pay. Just as our eyes cannot see themselves, we tend to forget this solemn truth, which is so simple and obvious that it easily goes unnoticed. Even if we have heard it, we do not always take it seriously. Instead of putting our heads in the sand like the ostrich, let us face this truth courageously and directly.

When some misfortune happens, we should not say, "Why me?" We do not suffer alone: in reality, no matter what their situation, everyone experiences suffering. There is a person I know whose daughter is somewhat mentally handicapped. When the woman first discovered this, she agonized over it and had trouble accepting it. She visited many prominent doctors and did everything she could to improve her daughter's condition, but with little effect. Once she accepted her daughter's condition, however, her inner peace was restored. Subsequently, because of her own stable and peaceful state of mind, her daughter's condition began to improve.

When I was in the second grade, several nurses visited our class to inoculate us for influenza. A couple of my classmates left the classroom when they saw the syringe, fearing the pain that might come from the shot. I realized that even though they'd left, they would just have to get the shot later. When I calmly accepted the situation and received the injection, I found that it wasn't as painful as I had feared.

Let us accept life as it is. Many times our interpretation of a difficult situation can cause us unnecessary suffering. For instance, when pain arises in the legs while practicing sitting meditation, our unnecessary struggle against the pain, which springs from our interpretation, anticipation, and expectations about it, will make us suffer more. If we just relax, and without any resistance observe the pain as it is, we find that the pain gradually disappears. We can relate to that pain in a completely different way, and as a result our suffering subsides.

An elderly Won Buddhist practitioner, while on her deathbed, was disturbed by many attachments and a fear of death. She did not want to die, and her distress made the situation extremely difficult for her family. Soothing words from her loved ones did not help. Her husband finally asked a well-respected Won Buddhist minister to visit her. Upon arrival, the minister very calmly said to her, "Mrs. Lee, it's time to go." Those simple words completely changed Mrs. Lee's perspective and helped her to accept the situation calmly.

In the Won Buddhist scriptures, Master Sotaesan speaks on the wisdom of acceptance:

> The Founding Master was explaining the meaning of "being content with poverty and rejoicing in the Way": Generally speaking, poverty refers to an insufficiency of some sort. If one's facial appearance falls short, it is poverty of the face; if one's learning falls short, it is poverty of learning; if one's property falls short, it is poverty of material assets.
>
> The saying "being content with one's lot" means to be comfortable with one's given portion in whatever aspect. If one is not content with one's existing poverty and struggles to avoid it unreasonably, then one will only become more anxious and increase one's suffering instead. If poverty is unavoidable, accept it with equanimity and take pleasure in preparing for future wisdom and merit.
>
> The reason, however, that a practitioner who is content with one's lot comes to rejoice in the Way is because one understands that whatever poverty and suffering one receives now will change into merit and happiness in the future; furthermore, one derives pleasure from the fact that the functioning of one's mind never digresses from the truth and one's power of cultivation is able to enter the genuine realm that transcends suffering and happiness. Since ancient times, sages and philosophers have all understood this principle and applied such a state of mind in their actual lives; and thus, while living in poverty, they lived an unparalleled life of rejoicing in the Way.[127]

There are many situations that we cannot change, but if we realize the truth of dukkha, or the inevitability of unsatisfactory aspects of our lives, then we can change our perspective, and we can relate to difficult situations in a very different way. If we realize the first noble truth clearly, nirvana can unfold and exist in our daily lives.

Although my mother had cancer—the doctor said she was not expected to live more than six months—she lived her remaining days fully and joyfully up until her last moment, which did not come until seven years later.

Zen Master Dogen said in the Shobogenzo:

> When you find your place exactly where you are, practice occurs, actualizing the fundamental truth. When you find your way in this very moment, practice occurs, again actualizing the fundamental truth; for the place and the way are neither large nor small, neither yours nor others'. The place and the way are not carried over from the past, and are not merely arising now.

People who know or display an interest in Buddhism find its ideas to be fresh, universal, and sensible. However, in order to put those teachings into practice, in order to actualize the Dharma, some incentive is required. Suffering has played a significant role in transforming some people into great practitioners. For example, Hyo Bong was a judge in the twentieth century when Korea was under Japanese rule. He sentenced to death a Korean who had fought for the independence of Korea. Shortly afterward, he felt great remorse and left home to become a monk. His regret was a motivating force that drove him to practice with great zeal and determination. He later became the first patriarch of modern Korean Zen Buddhism.

For many people, the impetus to move from a mere knowledge of Buddhism on an intellectual level to the actual practice of Buddhism has come through suffering. Actualizing practice begins for many people when they hit rock bottom and keenly feel suffering. From that moment on, many people begin to seriously reflect on their lives. Like a lotus flower that blooms in the mud, people may awaken and enter the path because of their suffering.

When we are alert and mindful, then suffering can be transformed into blessing, a steppingstone toward maturity and spiritual progress. Many times suffering causes us to reflect on and helps us to realize what the most important thing in our life is. This realization helps us to redirect our lives and thereby leads us to walk on the spiritual path.

THE SECOND NOBLE TRUTH: THE CAUSE OF SUFFERING

People hate suffering but love its cause.

—Traditional aphorism

The second noble truth, *samudaya*, follows naturally from the first noble truth; if there is suffering, then there must be a cause.

> Buddha said the cause of suffering is "grasping" or "craving."
> This is the noble truth of the origin of suffering. It is this craving which produces repeated existence, is bound up with delight and lust, and seeks pleasure here and there, namely, craving for sense pleasures, craving for existence, and craving for nonexistence.[128]

The Pali word *tanha*, which Buddha identified as the cause of suffering, is usually translated as "grasping," "craving," or "clinging." *Tanha* literally means "thirst." Just as we thirst when our body needs water, people thirst for money, power, sex, knowledge, recognition, and approval. *Tanha* or thirst is driven-ness, grasping, compulsion, clinging, or craving. From this thirst, all forms of suffering arise. The Buddha said, "The world lacks and desires, and is enslaved to 'thirst.'" As long as there is this thirst to be and to become, as we discussed in chapter 9, the cycle of birth and death continues. It can only cease when its driving force, this thirst, is cut off through wisdom, which is attained when we see the ultimate reality.

In our daily lives, we blame many factors for the cause of suffering, ranging from a lack of money to a lack of good health or to stressful relationships. Difficult financial situations might make us suffer, but there are many people in the world who live very happy lives even though they are poor. There are many rich people who live miserable and stressful lives. It is telling that in most developed countries, the suicide rate is higher than in developing countries, and the market for antidepressants is enormous.

I remember a friend who became very upset when he began to lose his hair; contrast him with another friend who did not pay any attention to his baldness at all, especially after he got married.

Material things, appearance, and academic achievement, among other objects, are not the ultimate cause of suffering. The root cause is one thing: attachment, or clinging. Just as a tree has a root and many branches, suffering has one cause and many symptoms.

People cling to material things (a new car, jewelry, or favorite shoes), persons (a child or spouse), and cravings for sensual pleasures. People also cling to intangibles such as fame, position, approval, and views or opinions, such as conservative or liberal ideologies. When the Soviet Union fell, some Korean college students who were involved in the student movement became disappointed and depressed—at that time their ideology was rooted in socialism. Today, as yesterday, attachments to different religious ideas and beliefs cause many of the conflicts in the world. Our attachments are sometimes obvious and sometimes very subtle.

I recall a story that exemplifies this sentiment. A poor man earned his living by making baskets from reeds by the river. One day he received three gold coins because a rich man was impressed by his cheerful, optimistic mood. The poor man had never received such a large sum. He started to worry about where to hide the money and how to spend it. Being anxious and worried, he could no longer sleep or sing cheerfully. When he gave the money to a less fortunate friend of his, he could sleep soundly again.

Dharma is just this simple. The more attachments we have, the more we suffer; to the extent we crave, to that extent we suffer.

Daebong, a Buddhist who was studying psychology in the United States, one day asked Korean Zen Master Seung Sahn, "What is sane and what is insane, from the Buddhist perspective?" The master replied, "If you are much attached to something, you are insane. If you are slightly attached, you are slightly insane. If you are not attached, you are sane." Daebong thought to himself, "The master's answer is better than my ten years of studying psychology. He should be my teacher." Daebong became a Zen monk and a disciple of Master Seung Sahn.

From grasping arises frustration, aggression, and despair. As long as grasping exists, there will be suffering.

One day, the Buddha was asked, "Why are some people liberated and others not?" He replied, "Whosoever clings to the objects perceived by the senses cannot gain liberation. Whosoever stops clinging will be liberated."[129]

Many Korean children living by the seashore catch crabs by piercing fish heads or tails with a wire that is then bent into a "U" shape. They then place this bait between rocks on the beach. The next day, when they pull the wire out from the rocks, the children find crabs dangling with their claws firmly holding the fish. If only the crabs would open their claws, they would drop into the water and escape. The crabs, however, never release their claws and therefore are captured by the children.

At the end of ninth grade, our class had pictures taken for our graduation album. When the photographer developed the film and displayed our pictures, I discovered that my picture had not turned out well. I was embarrassed and upset, thinking that it was something that could not be changed, and that many girls would see it and talk about it. I wanted to have another picture taken. I tried to call the photographer many times, but he did not answer. I was distressed all week, waiting for the album with my ugly picture to arrive. But I found out later that nobody cared how my picture looked in the album.

From small and insignificant attachments to serious ones, clinging destroys our happiness and limits our scope of the freedom that enriches our lives. The Buddha described human life well when he said, "Men hate suffering but love its cause."

One disciple asked the Buddha, "What is your teaching in one sentence?" The Buddha replied, "Nothing whatsoever should be clung to."

In our daily lives, we can and should love and take care of many things, like our children, and our careers, but we should not cling to them. The extent that we cling is also the extent to which we suffer.

THE THIRD NOBLE TRUTH: THE CESSATION OF SUFFERING

When drifting through life on a boat or
Climbing toward old age leading a horse, each
Day is a journey and the journey itself is home.

—Basho[130]

The first noble truth is that life is suffering. The second noble truth is that there is a cause of suffering, which is grasping or attachment. The third noble truth is the cessation of suffering, *nirodha*; when the cause of suffering is removed, suffering ceases.

We can empower, calm, and focus our minds through regular meditation, which lessens our clinging and changes perverse states of mind into wholesome states of mind. Meditation reveals our true nature and the light of our original nature shines.

These are some of the benefits of meditation. If you regularly meditate with sincerity and commitment, you will find that you become far less attached to many things, even though you did not make a direct effort to do so.

One Chinese army general loved to drink green tea in a quiet place. He especially cherished a certain porcelain teacup, which he had received as a gift. One day while he was pouring tea, he almost dropped the cup from the table. Although few things in the world could frighten him, his heart froze with terror. Holding the cup in his hand, he thought to himself, "While I've been on many battlefields, I have never been so frightened. So what made my heart jump?" After pondering this, he threw down the cup and broke it. Meditation is important when attempting to break the chains of attachment, but just as important is practicing mindfulness in our daily lives. Our decision to let go of attachments is like the general throwing away his cherished cup.

In order to practice detachment, Chögyam Trungpa, a Tibetan Buddhist teacher, intentionally made his environment a little inconvenient. For example, he would put his TV remote control a little out of reach. Likewise, many Catholic and Buddhist monks shave their heads in order to practice detachment from their appearance.

A ship embarking on a long journey should first haul up its anchor. To attain buddhahood, we must first let go of attachment. This is a fundamental step. In the Buddha's case, great enlightenment followed great renunciation.

Let us reflect on how many chains and shackles we have. Let us think about what sort of attachments we have, and how to be free from them.

Consider this story:

> The Founding Master [of Won Buddhism] said, "It is often the case that people's major transgressions start with minor faults. Therefore, you must occasionally examine your own conduct, and if you discover even a minor fault, do not procrastinate, but work hard to correct it.
>
> "There is an animal in the south called an orangutan that is so strong and quick that humans can't capture it by force. But they say that these animals like alcohol, so people leave a large bowl full of liquor along the roadside, so

that an orangutan will see it as it walks by. At first the animal laughs at it and walks away, but then it comes back and drinks a little, then returns again to drink more, repeating this action several times until without even being aware it has drunk all the liquor. Finally it passes out drunk and people come out to capture it. The liquor that the animal initially intended only to sip is eventually completely finished, until it finally is either killed or captured alive.

"Human beings are just the same. If minor faults keep accumulating because they were not corrected in the beginning, people will commit major transgressions and badly ruin their future. How can one not be careful about this?"[131]

Since the cause of suffering is grasping or thirst, when it is removed, suffering falls away. This is nirvana, emancipation, or liberation. Therefore nirvana is also called the "extinction of thirst." The Buddha says, "It is the complete cessation of that very 'thirst' (*tanha*), giving up, renouncing it, emancipation from it, detachment from it."[132]

One may ask from where grasping or attachments originate. Just as a tree grows from the ground, our grasping and attachment emanates from our sense of self, which is the ego. The evangelist Billy Graham once said that at the center of the words *sin, pride*, and *Lucifer*, there is "I." All of our cravings, attachments, desires, and angers originate from that ground called "I." The center of all of our problems is always "I."

Since the realization of our true self, which is no-self, leads us to see into the groundlessness of our desires, attachments, graspings, and wandering thoughts, then enlightenment leads to the cessation of suffering. If our desires or graspings are like weeds, how can they grow or take root when there is no ground to grow in? Therefore the ultimate solution to all suffering is enlightenment. As the Heart Sutra says, "The Bodhisattva of Great Compassion, when deeply practicing prajna paramita, realized that all five aggregates are empty and became free from all suffering and distress."

Since nirvana (the cessation of suffering) can be achieved by enlightenment, enlightenment is nirvana, and nirvana is enlightenment.

The Buddha indicated that grasping, the cause of suffering, can be classified in two ways:

The Grasping of Existence. Whether it is a person, a material thing, or a concept, the desire to possess something permanently, or the desire to not be separated from it, is the grasping of existence.

An example is the desire to live forever with a loved one. I remember watching a television program where a woman on TV who was so attached to her dog that after the dog died, she kept her beloved pet's body in her bedroom for a long time. One might want to hold on to a youthful appearance; one might wish to hold on to a job or relationship forever. These are common grasping feelings that we cling to.

The Grasping of Nonexistence. This is the desire to push an object, experience, or person away from us. We might want to push away an enemy, a spouse, a mean boss, a pain, an annoying sound, a fear, an anxiety, dirt in the kitchen, or a restless feeling during sitting meditation. It could be anything that we would like to remove.

Whether it is the grasping of existence or the grasping of nonexistence, this grasping or thirst is the desire that things should be changed in one way or another because we are never satisfied with things as they are. These graspings are part of the mindset that things are supposed to be what we wish them to be.

I should become richer, more popular, healthier, or leaner. My spouse should become more romantic, more talented, and more successful. My parents should become wealthier and more understanding, and my children should be smarter, and more respectful. My meditation practice should be deeper. My meditation cushion should be at least this high or this comfortable.

This obsession or desire to "become"[133] is the source of dissatisfaction and discontentment, which is dukkha.

This "should/become" can take many forms, but whatever form it takes, it creates discontent and makes everything unsatisfactory. Our lives are characterized and shackled by this "should/become."

We live in an invisible prison. Our minds are enslaved by this "should/become" attitude, which means we are not living or enjoying the present moment fully, but instead, constantly postponing our happiness or contentment to a future that will never arrive.

A man once received a high-quality bottle of wine from a friend in celebration of his engagement. All the time he was engaged, he was tempted to open that wine. But he kept thinking, "It's such a good wine to waste even on this occasion. Let me save it for a more special occasion." Then when he was married, he had the same thought. When his first baby was born, he still did not open that wine and continued to save it for an even more special occasion. Finally, that wine was opened at his funeral.

The way to live freely and richly is to live in the present moment, to be faithful to this moment. If we lose this present moment, we lose our life. We do not have to, nor should we, postpone enjoying our lives until the weekend or until work is finished or until all our problems are solved. If we lose this very moment, we lose the richness of our lives. Life is a continuum of the present moment.

A piece of music is not played for the sake of hearing its finale. It is the playing itself that is the point. If music is being played for its ending, then the faster it is played, the better. Just as we enjoy every movement of a symphony, so we should learn to enjoy each and every moment and aspect of our lives.

This is not to say that we should indulge ourselves in sensory pleasures, not considering the future. Sensory pleasure is related to our body, which is constantly decaying. It has a past, a present, and a future, unlike our original mind, which is neither being born nor dying. Thoughts are like images in a mirror. They can come and go, constantly changing. But the mirror, like our original nature, remains the same. Staying in the present moment means dwelling in our original mind.

When a disciple asked the Buddha, "What is the path leading to nirvana?" the Buddha replied, "The path leading to nirvana is present moment awareness."

Zen Master Dogen profoundly said, "Sitting is enlightenment, and enlightenment is sitting."

An American woman went to Vietnam to join the Thich Nhat Hanh Meditation Retreat. Along with all of the other participants, she did a lot of walking and sitting meditation. One day when she came out of the Buddha Hall, she discovered that her shoes were missing, and it was time to join the walking meditation group. Since the temple was located in a rural area, she did not have time to buy replacement shoes. Therefore, she decided to walk barefoot. When she walked on the grassy field, she really enjoyed the soft, moist sensation under her feet. It was a fun and refreshing experience.

When the group reached the bus station, an old Vietnamese woman who was standing with her grandson pointed to her feet and said, "Where are your shoes?" Unable to communicate with the Vietnamese woman in her language, the American woman just shrugged. A Vietnamese monk in the group explained what had happened. The old lady said to her grandson, "Why don't you give her your shoes? I can buy you new shoes in the market today." The boy gave the American woman his shoes, and she walked with those shoes on from the bus station.

Enjoying the present moment in any situation, and being happy and content regardless of our environment, is our birthright. By returning ourselves to the present moment, we can enjoy every aspect of our lives. This is enlightenment. This is awakening.

Nirvana or enlightenment is not necessarily some state or destination that we can achieve after lengthy practice. Enlightenment is a moment-by-moment experience that occurs when we are fully awake. By bringing our attention back to the present moment, and by faithfully living in the present, we can experience enlightenment in our daily lives.

Once I heard about a man who had collapsed because of the strain of several sleepless nights. He had recently started a new business and could not afford time away from it. His friends were worried when they heard that he had to be hospitalized for several weeks. When they visited him in the hospital, they expected him to be anxious, but they were surprised to hear a lot of laughter inside his room. They discovered that he was with his wife, children, and several relatives, all of whom were cheerful. When they asked if he was worried about his business, he replied, "If I were not sick and hospitalized, how could I have this much time to spend with my family? I feel very sorry that I do not spend enough time with my loved ones, so these moments are very precious to me."

Just like this ill man, or the shoeless woman on her walking meditation, when we return to the present moment and stay with it fully, we can enjoy nirvana in any situation, and we can turn an unfavorable situation into a favorable one.

Life is a journey, a process. Like mountain climbing, every step is meaningful and we should enjoy each moment of the process. We do not have to rush to the peak of the mountain to get the best view. Many times the clouds obscure our view from the peak anyway.

Climbing itself is the journey. Climbing itself is the goal. A Zen master said, "Each day is a journey and the journey itself is home." Similarly, Zen Master Yun Men spoke the mystery of the universal truth when he said, "Every day is a good day."

If we know the truth and the meaning of the present moment, our lives will be far freer and filled with abundance.

Many times we refuse to let the ebb and flow of life be what it is. We continually tie our existence to some fixed idea of how this or that should be. This "picking and choosing" attitude deprives us of freedom, and because of this attitude, the scope of our freedom becomes much more limited. This "picking and choosing" attitude shackles us, and it becomes an obstacle to our liberation.

Seng Tsan, the Third Patriarch of Zen Buddhism, wrote:

> The Great Way is not difficult
> for those who have no preferences.

When love and hatred are both absent
Everything becomes clear and undisguised.
Make the smallest distinction however
and heaven and earth are set infinitely apart.
If you wish to see the truth,
then hold no opinions for or against anything.
To set up what you like against what you dislike
is a disease of the mind.[134]

We should not struggle against situations that we cannot change. "Not struggling" does not mean accepting things passively or doing nothing to improve our situation. "Not struggling" means breaking the barrier of dualistic thoughts, freeing ourselves from fixed ideas or expectations, and coming back to reality.

There are many situations that are difficult to accept as they are, and we can make a great effort to change or improve these situations. However, we should learn to enjoy each moment until the final goal is reached. This is the way of living in reality. This is the path to enjoyment of the present moment.

When a cow grazes in the field, it is not constantly pondering, "Where is the best grass?" It grazes naturally just as the grass grows naturally. It lives its life as freely as the wind.

This way of living is called "nondoing" in Taoism. Taoist masters teach us to "live as the grass grows in the field." This is how children live. They cry when asking for something, but then moments later, they can laugh.

Jesus said:

I tell you the truth, unless you turn around and become like little children, you will never enter the kingdom of heaven! (Matthew 18:3)

Children live in the present moment; they are always faithful to the present. Living moment by moment is living fully in the present, which is eternity. It is the path to complete freedom. This is what our practice is all about. All the mystery and richness of our lives exist in this present moment.

How do we deal with distracting thoughts when we practice sitting meditation? How can we stay at peace and remain free from the whirlwind of wishes for the future and memories of the past? What is the past? It is an idea. It exists only in our memory. It is a thought. What, then, is the future? It too is an idea, which exists only in our minds; it will never come. When wandering thoughts arise in our minds while we are meditating, we bring our attention back to our breath or to our bodily sensations. This enables us to free ourselves from those wandering thoughts and keeps us centered. *Thoughts are not reality!* They are merely the creations of our minds. Bringing our awareness back to our breath or our bodily sensations is a method for returning to reality. This technique empowers and calms our minds.

We can apply this technique in our daily activities. If we clearly understand the importance of the present moment, then we can apply this Dharma to all aspects of our lives. When we lose our job, instead of being depressed or feeling sorry for ourselves, we can think of it as a precious opportunity to reflect and practice in preparation for greater things. When we are alone at home, instead of feeling lonely, we can use that time to practice meditation, or to study Dharma. When our child or our spouse comes home, instead of complaining that now it is too noisy to practice meditation, we can consider this situation as an opportunity to create blessings by helping them or to practice the Dharma of nonattachment and patience. In my case, when I experience back pain and I cannot practice meditation, I devote that time to my studies, service to others, and personal fitness.

Just as oil is inherent in sesame and butter is inherent in milk, joy and contentment are inherent in our lives. If we know the mystery of the present moment and we are fully awake, then we can extract joy and contentment from any situation. We can realize nirvana everywhere in every moment. Happiness is our choice.

Every day Master Jui-yen used to call to himself, "Master!" and would answer, "Yes!" Again, he would call, "Thoroughly awake! Thoroughly awake!" and he would answer, "Yes! Yes!" "Don't be deceived by others, any day or any time." "No! No!"[135]

THE FOURTH NOBLE TRUTH: THE PATH

Whatever is dependently co-arisen
That is explained to be emptiness.
That, being a dependent designation,
Is itself the middle way.

—Nagarjuna[136]

The fourth noble truth is the path (*marga*) leading to the cessation of dukkha. It is known as the "Middle Path" because it avoids two extremes—one being the search for happiness through sensual indulgence, the other being the search for happiness through self-mortification or extreme asceticism. This path is neither self-indulgence nor self-denial, so it is called the "Middle Path."

Siddhartha Gautama, who became Shakyamuni Buddha, was born in the sixth century B.C.E., a prince of the city Kapilavastu, which is in present-day Nepal. For the young prince, life was carefree and rich in sensory pleasures, and he grew up sheltered from the knowledge of suffering as an aspect of the human condition. This changed when on a trip outside the palace, he saw the harsh conditions that people endured and acutely felt the inevitability of dukkha. At the age of twenty-nine, he left the palace to search for the truth. He rigorously engaged in all kinds of ascetic practices to the point of becoming emaciated and endangering his life. However, these practices failed to bring about supreme enlightenment. He then concluded that extreme ascetic practice was not the way to attain liberation.

Not long after this, Siddhartha had two experiences that helped him find the way. The first was a spontaneous memory of a childhood experience when he was not wrapped in the desires of the body but rather lived very naturally and freely, and his mind was calm and peaceful. The second came when he happened to hear a nearby sitar player saying to his student, "If the string is too tight, it will snap when you pluck it; if it is too loose, it will not play. Somewhere in the middle lies harmony."

Siddhartha thought, "Probably by following the middle way, one could best be led to attain great enlightenment." While he reflected on this, a young farm girl happened to be passing by and offered him some rice milk. He accepted the offering, and having nourished his body he retreated to the countryside now called Bodh Gaya. With great determination, he sat down under a bodhi tree and made a vow: "Even if this flesh decays and the bones fall apart, I will never leave this place until I achieve enlightenment." After entering a deep *samadhi* and overcoming all temptations (physical, mental, and emotional) and obstacles, he finally attained the supreme enlightenment. After that he became known by the name Shakyamuni, the Sage of the Shakya Clan.

The Buddha reached supreme enlightenment by following the Middle Path, the way of moderation between the extremes of sensual indulgence and ascetic practice. We should also reflect on whether our own practice is well balanced or not, whether we just practice meditation without the guidance and foundation of Dharma study, or whether we study and discuss Dharma without any actual practice.

What then does the Middle Path specifically mean in our practice? How can we realize it in our daily life?

In teaching the Middle Path, or the fourth noble truth, the Buddha specified eight practices to follow for well-being and the cessation of suffering. This is why the fourth noble truth is also called the "Noble Eightfold Path."

The *Nagara Sutta* says:

In the same way I saw an ancient path, an ancient road, traveled by the Rightly Self-awakened Ones of former times. And what is that ancient path, that ancient road, traveled by the Rightly Self-awakened Ones of former times? Just this noble eightfold path: right view, right aspiration, right speech, right action, right livelihood, right effort, right mindfulness, right concentration... I followed that path. Following it, I came to direct knowledge of aging and death, direct knowledge of the origination of aging and death, direct knowledge of the cessation of aging and death, direct knowledge of the path leading to the cessation of aging and death... Knowing that directly, I have revealed it to monks, nuns, male lay followers and female lay followers.

The Eightfold Path is composed of:

1. Right View or Understanding (*Samyak Drishti*)
2. Right Thought or Intention (*Samyak Samkalpa*)
3. Right Speech (*Samyak Vaca*)
4. Right Action or Conduct (*Samyak Kammanta*)
5. Right Livelihood (*Samyak Ajiva*)
6. Right Effort or Diligence (*Samyak Vayama*)
7. Right Concentration (*Samyak Samadhi*)
8. Right Mindfulness or Awareness (*Samyak Smriti*)

Every step in this path is preceded by the Sanskrit word *samyak*, which is usually translated as "right," but also has a much broader connotation meaning "sound, wholesome, complete, skillful, and appropriate." Although here the conventional translation of *samyak* has been kept, it is important to note that *samyak*, or "right," is not used here in the sense in which it is opposed to "wrong." "Right" here means the Middle Path between two extremes.

In terms of its contents, the Eightfold Path has three divisions:

1. wisdom, or prajna: right view and right thought
2. ethical conduct, or *sila*: right speech, right action, and right livelihood
3. meditation, or *samadhi*: right effort, right concentration, and right mindfulness

These three divisions are called the "Threefold Practice," and they are the three essentials in Buddhist training that open our minds and hearts and ultimately lead to enlightenment.

The elements of the Threefold Practice are closely related and complement each other like the three legs of a tripod; without one, the others cannot stand. Master Sotaesan emphasized the interdependence of the three trainings, using the analogy of the three prongs of a pitchfork:

> The Threefold Learnings [Practice] in our scripture are explained by different names respectively, but in actual practice the Threefold Learnings [Practice] are interrelated inseparably... For practicing the Cultivation of Spiritual Stability, both the Study of Facts and Principles and the Selection of Right Conduct are indispensable assistants. For practicing the Study of Facts and Principles, both the Cultivation of Spiritual Stability and the Selection of Right Conduct must accompany it. For practicing the Selection of Right Conduct, both Cultivation of Spiritual Stability and the Study of Facts and Principles also must accompany it. Therefore, the reason that we practice the Threefold Learnings [Practice] together is to use the integrated power in order to make the most rapid progress in our study. In studying at a monastery, the exchange of various opinions on study is designed to increase, without any harder discipline, necessary understanding for us to attain great wisdom.[137]

Meditation or spiritual cultivation (*samadhi*) is like weeding the ground in order to cultivate a crop. Honing our wisdom (*prajna*) is like planting a seed. Ethical Conduct (*sila*) is like watering and nurturing the plant so that it can bear fruit and we can harvest the crop.

The Threefold Practice (or the Eightfold Path) does not teach practitioners to follow its steps in a sequential manner. They are closely interrelated, and each one is the basis for the others. Just as the United States is guarded by the army, the air force, and the navy, so too our mind is guarded and cultivated by the Threefold Practice.

The Threefold Practice is the path to purify our mind (*samadhi*), to brighten our mind (*prajna*), and to use our mind correctly (*sila*). The Threefold Practice (or the Eightfold Path) constitutes the essential path for our mind in restoring its original nature. There may seem to be eight separate paths, but really there is only one path with eight components. That is why the fourth noble truth is called the Eightfold Path, not the eight paths.

Right View or Understanding. Right view is seeing things as they truly are. This sounds like an easy task, but it is not as simple as it sounds. The following story tells how much our views are frequently distorted by our notion of self.

In a Won Buddhist temple in Korea, there were two men who had been close friends since they were small children. Kim started a business and as it prospered, he had to move his main office to Seoul, where he stayed and worked most of the time. Since he could not take care of the business in his hometown, he asked his friend Lee to oversee that branch office. As Kim's business grew, he became busier and busier and did not take care of his family as he had done before. Eventually, Kim and his wife divorced, and although he had done well financially, he felt lonely much of the time. So he often came to his hometown to see his childhood friend. Since Kim was the boss, he also audited the financial records of the branch office. Lee grew resentful because he was working under Kim for little money, and eventually he surmised that his boss was visiting not to meet with him, but rather to check the books because he thought that Kim was suspicious of him. Kim was terribly embarrassed when, indirectly, he heard about this. Although he made an honest effort to comfort his friend, they nevertheless became estranged, and Lee finally left his job.

When we carefully observe our minds, we can see that we all have the same tendencies and have made similar kind of mistakes. Our sense of self can really block us from seeing things as they are.

The earth appears flat as long as we are on the earth. Only after we view the earth from a great distance do we see it objectively and observe its roundness. As long as there is a sense of self in our minds, we cannot see things clearly or objectively. Ego, or the separate sense of self, is the fundamental source of ignorance. Only after we are free from this will we see things as they truly are, and then we will have right view.

Imagine that we are walking toward the top of a mountain, the peak of which is buddhahood. For a successful journey, we should climb the mountain on the correct trail with our eyes open. If our eyes are closed and we do not follow the proper path, we will not reach our destination.

Before we drive somewhere, first we need to know the directions. Likewise, to attain buddhahood or to live successfully, right view is the foundation that guides us to realization. In truth, a practitioner can have a perfected right view only after becoming completely enlightened. However, by relying on the Dharma, or the words of enlightened masters, practitioners can walk on the proper path to nirvana. Their teachings are a map showing us the way to our true selves. In other words, even when we do not know the path, or we have never been to a place before, if we have a good map or proper directions to follow, we can successfully reach our destination.

In contemporary society, there are many things that we need to know, from how to use a computer to the state of the world economy. We are constantly bombarded with so much information, not all of which is important. The most important knowledge or information is that which leads us to unconditional happiness and freedom. The

Buddha said that this knowledge or information is the correct under-standing of the Four Noble Truths, and this understanding is what he meant by right view.[138]

Master Sotaesan said that the most urgent thing is being aware of, and realizing, the truth of no birth and no death, and the principle of cause and effect, rather than teaching people numerous scriptures or encouraging goodness.[139] Once I realized the truth of no birth and no death, knowing that death is not the end, and that there are countless lives unfolding before me, my view of life totally changed. Death was no longer something to be feared. My life became directed toward attaining something everlasting. This altered value system played a big role in my decision to practice and finally become a Won Bud-dhist minister.

Having the clear goal of liberation, I found that my desire for worldly things lessened so naturally that my life became calm and centered. This tranquil state of mind came from my changed value system, rather than from my practice.

Understanding the principle of cause and effect also changed my life and my behavior. I first accepted this truth when I was a Christian before I began Buddhist practice. The Bible emphasized that God is all-knowing and that He rewards us exactly according to our deeds. In other words, "a person will reap what he sows" (Galatians 6:7). This is another way of stating the principle of cause and effect. This principle made me act in an honest and generous manner, and I became a far more sincere person.

The Buddha said, "There is no single factor so responsible for the suf-fering of living beings as wrong view, and no factor so potent in pro-moting the good of living beings as right view."[140]

Hitler's wrong view of race brought this world to the brink of disas-ter. Pol Pot, the leader of the Cambodian Communist movement, had all the Buddhist monks killed in Cambodia after the communist takeover. Extremist Muslim suicide bombers believe that they will immediately go to heaven after they die, as a reward for their sacrifice.

From personal conflict on the individual level to world wars on the global level, much misfortune has arisen from wrong views. However big a ship is, it only moves in the direction in which it is steered. Our life is unfolding based on our view of life.

There is one kind of African antelope whose herding instinct is so strong that if the leader of the herd reaches the edge of a cliff, many of the antelope in the front of the herd fall off the cliff and die because they are being pushed by the antelope behind. Most of the time our view is shaped by our social value system, and we many times mindlessly follow others in a manner similar to those antelope, imitating what the majority of people are doing and thinking. Today, materialism dominates our society. We consciously and unconsciously let this affect our minds, our values, and our lives. It is hard to swim against the current. Just like the antelope that fall from the cliff and die, if we mindlessly follow the majority, the place that we are led to ultimately is not the realm of happiness and freedom. In any society, in any age, the number of enlightened minds is few. Imitating the lives of others and following the currents of society may make our lives seem easier, but this behavior will keep us living in the mundane world, which is characterized by dukkha.

That is why the Buddha said, "Swim against the stream," and Jesus said, "You are in this world, but you are not of this world."

The Buddha, Sotaesan, Jesus, and other saints and sages are the ones who found the path—the way to unconditional happiness and freedom. Our value system and our lives should be directed by their Dharma words. That is why we need to study the Dharma and read scripture regularly, so that our practice and life will be properly guided. The perspective of the enlightened mind is ultimately right view.

Master Sotaesan often said, "I did not even graduate from elementary school. I do not have much knowledge, but one thing I know for sure: I know how to make you a buddha." If our practice and lives are based on the teaching of enlightened masters, our practice, as well as our lives, will not falter.

Right Thought or Right Intention. The next part of the path, *samyak samkalpa*, is usually translated as "right thought." Since *samkalpa* also has the English meaning of "intention," *samyak samkalpa* is sometimes translated as "right intention." *Intention* is "the purposeful aspect of our activity."

Life is a succession of choices that we make on a daily basis. Our success or failure in our jobs, relationships, and in our spiritual practice (e.g., what kind of meditation technique we follow) depends on our choices, which are based on the thoughts that arise in our minds. Therefore, if we can control our thoughts, then we can control our lives, and we can be successful in our practice.

Right view is closely related to right thought. When we have right view, we have a clear life goal and a wholesome value system. Consequently, many of our wandering thoughts and worldly desires begin to subside, and we become less tempted by worldly things. We become far more peaceful and calm, so we stay focused in our daily activities. In that calm and peaceful state of mind, right thought will arise naturally.

There is a traditional Korean children's story about two brothers, Heung-bu and Nol-bu, who lived in a rural area. The younger brother, Heung-bu, was a kind and generous person but also impoverished. The older brother, Nol-bu, was jealous and greedy, and he took all the money that their parents had left to them both.

One day Heung-bu, while out in his yard, found a swallow on the ground with a broken leg. He felt sorry for the injured bird and bandaged her injury. Feeling better, the swallow happily flew away. The next spring, the swallow returned to Heung-bu's house with her babies and dropped a pumpkin seed in front of him. He planted the seed in his yard. In the autumn, many huge pumpkins grew. When Heung-bu and his wife cut them open, they found treasures inside. Suddenly Heung-bu was very rich, and he moved to a big, fancy house.

Nol-bu heard that his brother had become wealthy and had helped many poor people. When Nol-bu paid a visit to Heung-bu, he was surprised that his brother was living in a palatial home. Growing jealous, Nol-bu asked how his younger brother had become so rich. Heung-bu told the story about the swallow.

As soon as Nol-bu left his brother's house, he began searching for a swallow with a broken leg, but he could not find any. When Nol-bu told his brother's story to his wife, she was also jealous, and she immediately joined him in looking for an injured bird. Despite searching desperately for one week, they could not find any injured birds. Nol-bu finally caught a swallow, broke its leg, put a bandage on the swallow, and let it fly away.

The next spring the same swallow came back to Nol-bu's house and dropped a pumpkin seed in his yard. Excited, Nol-bu planted it. He built a high fence around it so that nobody could see or take his pumpkins. When fall arrived, the pumpkins grew very large. Nol-bu and his wife cut one of the pumpkins open, and to their surprise, instead of treasures, fecal matter burst forth, which filled his whole house with a terrible stench. They almost passed out. When they recovered, Nol-bu and his wife cut open another pumpkin still expecting something good. With a burst of smoke, ghosts came out of that pumpkin and chased them all day long. With each and every pumpkin, more misfortunes plagued Nol-bu and his wife, and Nol-bu wound up losing his entire fortune.

Both Heung-bu and Nol-bu had bandaged the broken leg of a swallow, but their intentions had been very different. As their intentions were different, so were the consequences.

Doctors can inadvertently kill a person during an operation, but that death is different from the killing on a battlefield. Even in war, killing people to protect oneself or to protect one's country is very different from killing people for one's own interest.

Based on our thoughts, we constantly make choices and perform actions. Those choices and those actions lead us to be happy or unhappy, free or imprisoned. Let us always be mindful of what kind of consequences will result from the actions and choices that we make based on our thoughts.

Let us also reflect on the intentions behind our actions—whether our intentions are wholesome or unwholesome, selfish or altruistic. For example, the founding master of the Ten Thousand Buddhas' City, a Buddhist monastery in California, began eating only one meal a day when he was young because he discovered that most of the Chinese people during World War II were too poor to eat three meals. He practiced *bodhichitta* to become one with those people and help them. This is quite different from an overweight person eating one meal a day to lose weight.

When Shakyamuni Buddha left his father's palace to search for truth, it meant that he would not become a king, as one ascetic had prophesized. The prophecy said that if he followed in his father's footsteps and became a king, he would become a great ruler who united all the small kingdoms of India and would help many people. However, when the Buddha left the palace, he made two vows: "I will not come back to the palace until I realize the ultimate reality, and after I attain enlightenment, I will save all sentient beings." So with those vows, when the Buddha sat, he sat with all beings.

The best way to help others is by helping them to attain buddhahood for their unconditional happiness and freedom. So ultimately the thought or intention of attaining buddhahood for ourselves and others is right thought or intention. That is why the Buddha explained right intention as the intention of renunciation, the intention of good will, and the intention of harmlessness.[141]

Right Speech. Chongsan, the Second Head Dharma Master of Won Buddhism, said, "There is a saying, 'Mouth is the gate of calamity'; in fact, however, the mouth is the gate of both calamity and blessings."[142]

Let us reflect on how many good relationships have been broken by the spoken word or groundless rumors, or how many mistakes we have made because we could not control our tongues.

> The Founding Master [of Won Buddhism] said, "By saying even one thing or writing even one line, a person can give

others either hope and peace, or despair and turmoil. Thus, a person does not always commit transgressions because he is fundamentally bad, but will often commit transgressions without realizing it because he does not understand the principle of what creates transgressions and blessings."[143]

We can dislike someone in our mind, but that is different from saying something nasty or abusive to or about that person. By our thoughts and words, we constantly create karma. The energy that impacts the other person through our speech is far more powerful than the energy created by our thoughts.

Some simple words, such as those of parents spoken thoughtlessly to their children, may impact their minds for the rest of their lives, hurting them and others. Our words are like spilled milk: once they are spoken, they cannot be taken back.

Since we create much of our karma by using our tongues, many Buddhist precepts are related to controlling our tongues through right speech. For example, in Won Buddhism, we have the following directives:

> Do not use harsh speech.
> Do not speak about the faults of others.
> Do not talk while someone else is talking.
> Do not speak flowery and ingratiating words.
> Do not be double-tongued.
> Do not make impertinent remarks.[144]

Right speech helps others and opens others' hearts and minds. Right speech is compassionate, wise, and encouraging. Ultimately, right speech is that speech that calms, purifies, and motivates our minds, as well as the minds of others, so that all can reach buddhahood.

One day when the Buddha walked in the forest with his disciples, he picked up a fallen branch and asked his disciples, "How many leaves are on this branch?" "Many," said one disciple. The Buddha asked,

"How many leaves are there in this forest?" The disciple replied, "They are countless." The Buddha said, "My teaching through words is like the number of leaves on this branch. My teaching through silence is like the number of leaves in the forest."

As long as we talk much, we are apt to make mistakes. One teacher said that the reason we have one mouth and two ears is that we should listen to others' words twice as much as we speak.

Lao Tzu said, "The one who knows does not speak. The one who speaks does not know." Saints and sages do not talk much. Their words are strengthened and empowered by silence. The words of Jesus, "Love your neighbor as yourself" (Matthew 22:39), or the words of Confucius, "Is it not delightful to have friends coming from distant quarters?" sound very plain and ordinary. But they are words so powerful that they have changed the world and our civilizations. Written on the wall in a meditation hall of a Korean Buddhist monastery are the words, "If you talk more than five minutes, your practice that day is of no avail."

As our practice matures, we tend to speak less. Talking less is an important part of our practice. Some people dislike being alone, but a solitary environment helps our practice. In the quiet and solitary environment, our practice goes deeper and we can encounter our authentic selves, just as Moses met God in the wilderness after leaving the pharaoh's court and spending many years as a lonely shepherd.

When I studied to become a Won Buddhist minister, all preministers in our dormitory were obliged to do some physical labor once a week. When the preministers worked together, gathering in one spot, they tended to talk a lot. So I chose intentionally to work alone in order to keep silent while working.

As long as we live in modern society and interact with others constantly, we cannot live without speaking. However, it cannot be emphasized enough not to speak too much and to speak mindfully for the sake of our practice and for the sake of society.

Right Action or Conduct. The Buddha says: "Beings are the owner of their actions, the heirs of their actions; they spring from their actions, are bound to their actions, and are supported by their actions. Whatever deeds they do, good or bad, of those they shall be heirs."[145]

More powerful than our thoughts and our words are our actions. Hurting or hitting someone physically is different in its severity from saying something hurtful to that person.

It is said that we are what we do; we are defined by our deeds. Right action is wise and compassionate action. Right action not only benefits oneself but also benefits society. Right action is the action that helps oneself and also helps others.

The greatest way to help others is through opening their minds and hearts and guiding them on the spiritual path to enlightenment. Ultimately this is right action. But in our daily lives, we encounter many unclear situations, and we may not be sure which action is the right one. There are many situations in which we do not know what the consequences will be.

Because we unawakened beings cannot always trust our own judgments, decisions, or thoughts, the Buddha suggested codes of conduct that are specified in the precepts. These codes specify the most fundamental and basic actions that guide us away from creating unwholesome karma.

The most fundamental precepts are the following five, and these are related to right action:

1. Do not kill without due cause.
2. Do not steal.
3. Do not commit sexual misconduct.
4. Do not consume narcotics and liquors without due cause.
5. Do not use false speech.

When the Buddha was on his deathbed, a disciple asked, "What will guide us after your passing when we cannot hear your words?" The Buddha replied, "The precepts will be your guide."

Since right action, or observing the precepts, is the foundation of our practice, So San, a Korean Zen master, said:

> Practicing Zen meditation while remaining immersed in sexual concerns is like cooking sand for a meal. Practicing Zen meditation while yet not avoiding killing any living thing is like a person who plugs their own ears and then shouts something important to himself. Practicing Zen meditation with a mind that would steal is like trying to fill a leaky bowl. And a liar who practices Zen meditation is a person who would try to use feces for incense. Even for the one who has much wisdom, such failings can only lead you to the way of demons.[146]

Once I was driving in a desert area in California, and I saw a barbed wire fence along a freeway. I asked my friend why someone would spend so much money to build something so unsightly. He said that the fence was to prevent desert animals from jumping into the path of oncoming vehicles. At night these animals are attracted by the head-lights and will jump toward the vehicles, which costs many animals, as well as some people, their lives. Just as desert animals destroy their lives because they are attracted to bright lights, so people are unknow-ingly attracted to situations that will lead to suffering.

The precepts are the path to perpetual happiness. By observing the precepts, we can be free from all seemingly attractive obstacles and in so doing be led to enlightenment.

The precepts are not commandments given by some higher being, like the Ten Commandments in Judaism, which were dictated to Moses by God. The precepts are the path to liberation, the teaching based on right view or universal truth, i.e., the principle of cause and effect: when we plant an apple seed, we harvest apples, and when we plant an orange seed, we harvest oranges.

Master Sotaesan said:

Since plants grow by setting roots in the earth, once a seed or a root is planted in the soil, a new shoot will sprout in accordance with the causes and conditions of the season. Since animals live by setting roots in heaven, thinking one thought, committing one action, or saying one word plants a karmic cause in the dharma realm of empty space and its karmic retribution appears in accordance with each and every one of its wholesome or unwholesome conditions. How can one then possibly deceive other human beings or deceive heaven?[147]

For every action, there is a consequence. Let us reflect on the consequences of killing, sexual misconduct, lying, and stealing. If you harm or hurt others, you will be hurt or harmed. If you steal something, something that you cherish will be stolen. This is the karmic principle of cause and effect. The person who knows this truth will not engage in dishonest activity, nor will he or she indulge in actions that bring temporary excitement, such as using narcotics or drinking too much alcohol.

One morning while I practiced meditation in the Philadelphia Won Buddhist Temple, a sparrow flew into the meditation hall. Because the ceiling was very high, the helpless bird was not able to find the windows and get out of the meditation hall. One minister brought a butterfly net and tried to catch the bird in order to release it outside, but because the sparrow was so afraid of the minister and the net, it constantly flew away from him.

The precepts are the path to liberating ourselves from suffering. They may look like the butterfly net, but they are the means to emancipate ourselves and find unconditional happiness.

Right Livelihood. Modern people spend most of their time at work. They realize their dreams or life goals through their occupations. Many people judge their entire life as a success or failure based on what they accomplish at work. So what we do to make a living is especially important, and having a wholesome livelihood or right livelihood is essential.

One day, when the Buddha was walking down a country road, one of his disciples picked up a bit of straw and sniffed it. Buddha asked, "How does it smell?" The disciple replied, "It smells like incense. I think it was used to tie bundles of incense." When they walked further, the disciple saw another bit of straw and picked it up. The Buddha asked, "How does it smell?" The disciple replied, "It smells like fish. I think it was used to tie fish." The Buddha said, "Just as straw is permeated with the smell of what it is near, so, too, people are affected by their environment."

Humans are creatures of their environment. Our value systems, ways of thinking, and lifestyles are influenced by our environment. Hyenas are fierce and bad-tempered animals in the wild, but I once watched a documentary about hyenas that were docile and obedient because they were raised by people with love and care. Similarly, I noticed in my friends that their personalities had been affected by their occupations. Lawyers, journalists, or ministers all gradually form their own personalities with occupational traits. Our minds are affected by our environment, especially by our occupations.

We should be very mindful of what kind of job we have, or will have. What we do for a living not only affects our minds but the whole of society. So what is a good occupation or right livelihood? It is one that helps to purify our minds as well as the minds of others. Selling alcoholic beverages or narcotics to make a living is different from teaching meditation or curing patients of illness.

Master Sotaesan said:

> Among people's occupations, there are those that create merit and those that create transgressions. Occupations that create merit are those that, through pursuing that occupation, bring benefit to all of society and naturally make my own mind wholesome as well. Occupations that create transgressions are those that, through pursuing that

occupation, damage and poison all of society and naturally make my own mind unwholesome as well. Therefore, a person must be discriminating in the choice of an occupation. Of all occupations, the best is the Buddha's enterprise of correctly guiding the minds of all sentient beings and delivering them from the sea of suffering to paradise.[148]

Ultimately, right livelihood is that occupation that creates blessings and cultivates wisdom, which will eventually lead to enlightenment. If one's occupation is directly or indirectly destroying lives, like the job of a butcher, a manufacturer of weapons, or a seller or maker of alcoholic beverages, drugs, or tobacco—all of which dull one's spirit and destroy one's mind—one should seriously think about one's karmic consequences.

Master Chongsan said that slaughterhouses, meatpacking plants, breweries, and the like should be managed by governments to help profit-seeking individuals avoid karmic consequences.

Master Sotaesan said:

When the Founding Master was visiting the Pusan region, a few followers paid a visit and said, "We have the utmost respect for the Great Master's dharma, but since we make our livelihood by fishing, we are constantly breaking the first precept. We are ashamed and discouraged about this." The Founding Master replied, "Don't worry! A person's occupation is difficult to change overnight. Even if you break one precept out of thirty but earnestly keep the other twenty-nine, you will still be able to contribute immeasurable merit to society through your twenty-nine good deeds. Just because you are unable to observe one, why would you have yourself fall into the abyss of transgression and suffering by not observing the other twenty-nine that you could keep? Moreover, if you are able to observe the twenty-nine precepts well, then a way for you to observe the remaining one will naturally appear. With such faith, keep going with your practice without being discouraged.[149]

One must be particularly mindful of one's occupation if one has children; a child is particularly prone to influence from his or her environment.

When Mencius, a Chinese philosopher and sage, was very young, he lived next to a cemetery. He would imitate funeral ceremonies and burial services by digging in the ground and putting dirt on top of coffins. His mother thought that this was not a proper place for her son and moved to a house beside a marketplace. There Mencius mimicked shopkeepers' calls. His mother once again thought that this place was not good for Mencius. She moved again to a house next to a school, where Mencius took lessons in manners and studied books. His mother said, "This place is indeed the best for upbringing." This story is called, "*Mang-mo sam-chun*," which literally means, "Mencius' mother moves three times."

Right Effort. There is a Korean saying: "Salt, even on the kitchen table, has to be added before it can give its flavor."

Even though right speech, right action, and right livelihood are important, without effort, they will not bear fruit. Simply knowing about the Eightfold Path does not lead us to nirvana; we actually have to walk on that path. There are many mountaineers who know the path to Mount Everest's peak, but only a few have stood on that peak. Without our effort, nothing will be achieved. Whether it is our practice or occupation, without sweating and enduring hardship, we will not reap our harvest. The more significant the work is, the more effort we have to make. The more meaningful the work, the more challenging the obstacles we tend to encounter. Since we have to make an effort in whatever we do, right effort is the foundation of the Eightfold Path.

Right effort is ultimately the effort that leads us to buddhahood. Many people in this world work very hard to achieve things like money or fame. Many people are workaholics and achieve some success, but all of us need to reflect on whether our efforts eventually lead us to unconditional freedom.

History tells us that many dictators and people who drove society into disaster were hard-working and intelligent people. Bank robbers also make an effort in executing and carrying out a plan; we should reflect seriously on where our efforts lead us, what the direction of our efforts are, and where we are going in life. We need to know the direction before we can drive toward our destination. Jesus said, "For what benefit is it if a person gains the whole world, yet loses his soul?" (Mark 8:36).

If we just make money for the sake of money, or if we just write books or papers for the sake of fame, ultimately these efforts will not bring happiness to us or to society. The efforts people make in the hope of gaining something to show off, for approval, or for obtaining something that pleases their senses, is not right effort.

As long as right effort is the effort that leads us to unconditional and perpetual happiness, right effort is related to our practice. Since all practice is to control our mind, the Buddha explained right effort from the perspective of mental discipline or meditation.

> Right effort is the energetic will (1) to prevent evil and
> unwholesome states of mind from arising, (2) to get rid of
> such evil and unwholesome states that have already arisen
> within a man, (3) to produce, to cause to arise, good and
> wholesome states of mind that have not yet arisen, and (4)
> to develop and bring to perfection the good and whole-
> some states of mind already present in a man.[150]

Right Concentration. Right concentration and right mindfulness form the path of meditation or mental discipline. When we have right view, the direction of our life is set. When we know the truth and walk on a spiritual path to liberation, we try to think (right thought), speak (right speech), and act (right action and right livelihood) properly.

We actualize this by pouring our time and energy into attaining unconditional happiness, and this is called right effort. To attain buddhahood, we should first try to control our deeds and speech. The last task is to conquer our mind.

In Won Buddhism, certain precepts are given according to the Dharma level of the practitioner: the first ten precepts are for beginning practitioners, another ten precepts are for intermediate practitioners, and the last ten are for the more advanced practitioners. The last three of these thirty precepts are:

1. Refrain from being greedy.
2. Refrain from being angry or harboring hatred.
3. Refrain from being deluded.

These three precepts address controlling the mind. These are the most difficult of all the precepts. Fundamentally speaking, our practice is working with our mind, and controlling our mind is the foundation of all practices. Wisdom arises when our mind settles down. We tend to act inappropriately when we lose our tranquillity and calmness. Right concentration and right mindfulness, which comprise the path of meditation and mental discipline, are therefore the foundation and the culmination of our practice.

There is a Chinese saying that the saddest thing is the scattering of our mind and energy. When our mind is scattered and uncentered, we not only become tired and unhappy, we also tend to make poor decisions and are driven to failure. Without right concentration, we cannot achieve anything in life. A focused mind is a powerful, happy, and wise mind.

The mind usually races in all directions. Therefore, in the Zen, Sufi, and Hindu traditions, this is called "monkey mind." This monkey mind restlessly jumps around from tree to tree or from thought to thought. We can see this when we observe our minds during meditation. Without discipline our mind is hard to settle and control. This monkey mind should be tamed and trained. Our society does not allow us to be still. We have to think and know about so many things, and our jobs are usually mentally, if not also physically, demanding.

Students do not get into schools like Harvard, just as people do not become successful at work, because they are moral or have philanthropic life goals. Rather, it is because of their power to think and make judgments. We live in a society that constantly bombards us with copious information. Since our jobs and our society constantly force us to think, which scatters our mind and drains our energy, we need some serene setting or time to collect our minds and calm down our thoughts. Think about what we do to rest or refresh our minds. Many people read magazines, watch TV, go to a movie, or chat with others. We are constantly consuming our energy, which tires us and dulls our wisdom and spirituality. We need a real and deep mental vacation.

Several months ago, when I visited a friend's house, I parked my car and left the lights on. When I left his house, I could not start the engine because the battery had drained. Why do modern people get so easily upset and have such short tempers? It is because they lack energy, which they have already consumed and scattered in so many things—usually unnecessary things—and they are simply tired. We need a way to conserve our energy and a technique to concentrate our minds, and the time to practice it. Without training our minds, without the practice of meditation, it is hard to maintain a calm and peaceful state of mind while remaining focused.

Last year a child sat next to me on an airplane. When he realized that he had forgotten to bring his iPod and laptop, he became agitated. He was upset and restless for the duration of the flight. In this way, our minds are continuously chasing after so many things: a sound, an image, a smell, a taste, a thought. In order to put our minds at rest, we need to sit regularly on the meditation cushion. To tame our monkey mind, to make our mind focused, sitting meditation is crucial. However, we can concentrate our minds when we are involved in daily activities as well.

Since most people don't meditate more than a couple of hours a day, it is important to maintain or cultivate the peaceful and focused mind while we are performing our regular activities.

Master Sotaesan said:

> The quickest expedients for practitioners to attain the power of Cultivation in both action and rest are as follows. First, in all your actions, do nothing that will disturb or devastate your spirit and avoid such sensory conditions. Second, do not entertain craving or greed in responding to any matter but, instead, habituate yourself to having a dispassionate attitude. Third, when you are doing one thing, don't be distracted by something else, so that you concentrate only on the task at hand. Fourth, in your spare time, pay attention to reciting the Buddha's name or sitting in meditation.[151]

Right Mindfulness or Right Awareness. The final part of the path is *samyak smriti.* The Sanskrit word *smriti* means "recollection, memory, present-mindedness, remembrance." The Chinese translate *samyak smriti* as *jung-ryum* (正念), where *jung* (正) means "right" or "correct." The Chinese character *ryum* (念) is composed of two parts. The upper part (今) means "now" or "the present moment," and the lower part (心) means "mind," "heart," or "awareness." So *ryum* implies the awareness of the present moment, or remembering to come back to the present moment. Right mindfulness or right awareness is the return to the present moment. It is coming back to reality.

Many people live shackled by past memories or thoughts, like childhood abuse, regrets, or even thoughts of what they said yesterday. The past is gone; it exists only in our memory. Similarly, people are often anxious about the future, for example future plans and concerns, or possibilities about what could happen tomorrow. This stems from a fear of the unknown. However, these plans and concerns are only in our thoughts, and the future will never come. Life is a continuation of "this present moment." This becomes obvious when we practice sitting meditation and observe our minds, noticing how much our minds are unnecessarily occupied with regrets or resentments about the past and worries about the future. It is not an easy thing to stay fully in the present moment; however, returning to the present moment is coming back to reality.

Why are we taught to focus our minds on our breath or bodily sensations when practicing sitting meditation? It is not only to calm our minds and concentrate our thoughts, but it is also a technique for staying in the present moment, or in reality. Our breath and physical sensations are what is really happening right here and right now, and this present "now" moment is the only thing that really exists. When we are consumed with past regrets or future concerns, we cannot live our lives fully, because we are unaware of this present moment. Jesus said, "Therefore, do not worry about tomorrow, for tomorrow will worry about itself. Each day has enough trouble of its own" (Matthew 6:34).

Life is a continuum of this present moment. Nothing else. If we miss this present moment, we miss our lives. We often think things like, "only after I pay all my debts, after I get married, or after all my children graduate from school will I be happy." But that perfect moment will never come. Even when you think it has come, it will last only for a brief moment. We must learn to stay in and enjoy the present moment. We should enjoy each and every step when climbing a mountain, instead of enjoying only the moment when we stand at the peak—for after standing at the peak for a while, we must then come back down.

When we stay in the present moment, we become one with nature, with other sentient beings, and with the whole universe. Our scope of freedom is greatly increased. Our life will become richer, enabling us to smile like a child at the bright sun, the beautiful trees, the fresh air, and the sky. Our minds will become much more compassionate, and we will enjoy others' happiness while sympathizing deeply with others' suffering.

Since so many worries and plans distract our minds and limit our lives, we must train our minds, using the techniques of spiritual cultivation. We need to calm our thoughts and concentrate our minds by means of sitting meditation. Since this way of practice is the most fundamental and efficient, the Buddha taught right mindfulness in the context of sitting meditation. Regarding sitting meditation, the Buddha recommended four subjects of right mindfulness:

1. Mindful contemplation of the body
2. Mindful contemplation of feelings
3. Mindful contemplation of the mind
4. Mindful contemplation of mental objects

Through this training method, we can settle our thoughts and purify our minds.

People are so busily involved in many things, from household affairs to work matters, that the time we spend in seated meditation is very limited. That is why it is so important to maintain mindfulness while we are involved in the mundane activities of our daily lives. Practicing "mindfulness in action" is as important as being alert and mindful while practicing sitting meditation.

Many forest fires, which have consumed whole mountains and destroyed homes, are caused by people who have carelessly or mindlessly discarded lit cigarette butts. Think about how much bad habits, which have accumulated over a long time, have affected our lives in negative ways.

When I first took tennis lessons, the coach told me not to hold the tennis racket so tightly. He told me my grip should be firm only at the moment when I hit the ball. Similarly, being mindful in each and every thing we do is difficult. If we try to practice mindfulness with many things at the same time, it will exhaust us and will not lead to a successful practice. We should focus and practice right mindfulness on that which is most essential, most needed, and most important, like breaking some bad habit or some unwholesome tendency of mind. Master Sotaesan recommended that his students pick just a few things to focus on, anything from the precepts (e.g., do not speak about the faults of others; do not consume intoxicants excessively) to something that one personally chooses (e.g., do not spend more than one hour a day surfing the Internet; do not miss the Sunday service; practice sitting meditation regularly for more than thirty minutes each day).

The Buddha said that the world is on fire, and our mind is ablaze; it is burning with desire, anger, and delusion. If our minds are like the boiling water in a cauldron, then extinguishing the fire beneath the cauldron can be compared to the practice of sitting meditation. Ladling out some of the boiling water and pouring in some cold water is like practicing mindfulness in action. Both of these are essential in cooling down the water in the cauldron.

CONCLUSION

The Eightfold Path is like a simple, practical manual for the direct approach to ending suffering. The first noble truth tells us that we humans are suffering. The second noble truth tells us that the cause of our suffering is our grasping mind. The third noble truth is the cessation of suffering, which is nirvana or enlightenment. The fourth noble truth is the path to reach nirvana or enlightenment, which is the Eightfold Path.

The Eightfold Path is a prescription with eight kinds of medicine to cure our suffering. I know of many people who see good doctors yet do not follow the doctors' advice or take their prescriptions properly. I also know many people who register at fitness clubs but rarely go. The Buddha called himself the Great Physician. Even if you see the best doctor, if you do not follow his prescription, you will not get well.

Knowing the Eightfold Path is not enough; we have to actually walk the path. There is an Eastern saying that it is the teacher who shows the door, but it is the student who enters. Neither the Buddha, nor our parents, our teachers, our dharma friends, and our loved ones can walk on that path for us.

Through trial and error, the Buddha discovered the Eightfold Path after he left his father's palace and went through all kinds of ascetic practices. But the Eightfold Path, or the Middle Path, that he teaches is the path that we can walk on in our daily lives, whether at work or at home.

It is, therefore, a great blessing to encounter the Buddhadharma. We are very fortunate that all we need to do is follow the path that our teachers have already discovered:

> The Founding Master [of Won Buddhism] suffered from coughing every winter and each time he delivered a dharma talk his coughing would disrupt it.
>
> On that account, he said to the congregation, "Killyong-ni, where I grew up, as you all know, is a place of severe poverty and backwardness. Thanks to the habituation of my past lives, I fortunately had a spiritual aspiration since I was young and sincerely sought the Way. However, I had no opportunity to ask questions or to receive guidance. I had a spiritual inspiration all on my own, and there was not an act of asceticism and hardship that I did not perform. Sometimes I would go into the mountains and spend the night; sometimes I would spend the whole day sitting on a road; sometimes I would stay up all night with my eyes open; sometimes I would bathe in icy water; sometimes I would fast; sometimes I would stay in a cold room. I finally entered a condition in which I lost all consciousness, and while ultimately my questioning was resolved, the root of my physical illness was already so deep that as my physical energy has weakened, my illness has grown increasingly worse. Because I did not know the road, there was nothing I could do at the time.
>
> "Fortunately, even without performing ascetic and difficult practices, you have directly learned the well-rounded dharma of Mahayana practice by benefiting from my

experiences. This is your great blessing. Generally speaking, the practice of timeless *Son* [Zen] and placeless *Son* [Zen] is the fast lane to Mahayana practice. If you practice in this manner, you will get twice the results with half the work and will succeed without getting ill. I beseech you all not to fall into the error of harming your body by recognizing the uselessness of the ascetic practices I performed before I found the road."[152]

The Path is already known. It's time for us to actually walk that path.

EMPTINESS OF THE FOUR NOBLE TRUTHS

A monk asked Master Tung-shan, "When cold and heat come, how can we avoid them?"

Tung-shan answered, "Why not go to where there is no cold or heat?"

The monk continued, "Where is the place where there is no cold or heat?"

Tung-shan said, "When it is cold, let it be so cold that it kills you. When hot, let it be so hot that it kills you."

—The Blue Cliff Record, Case 43

No suffering, no cause of suffering, no cessation of suffering, no path; no wisdom, no attainment with nothing to attain.

...No suffering, no cause of suffering, no cessation of suffering, no path...

THE PASSAGE "No suffering, no cause of suffering, no cessation of suffering, no path" means that the Four Noble Truths are empty just as the five aggregates, the eighteen fields, and the twelve links are empty, as was explained in previous chapters—that all these essential teachings, taught by the Buddha for many years, are empty. This passage means that from the perspective of absolute truth, the Four Noble Truths do not exist.

Enlightenment is the realization that there is no "I"; i.e., our separate sense of self is an illusion, a mental construct. When "I" or the sense of self disappears, the following links—the cause of suffering, the cessation of suffering, the path to end suffering—disappear simultaneously.

The empty nature of suffering, the cause of suffering, the cessation of suffering, and the path are what we experience on a daily basis. When a thought arises from the notion of self, the world of the Four Noble Truths is unfolding, but when one becomes enlightened, i.e., becomes united with "no mind" or universal mind, then the world of the Four Noble Truths also disappears.

When Bomun, a Korean Zen master (1906–56), had an operation, he asked the doctor to perform the surgery without using anesthetic. The doctor said that since he had to cut open his abdomen and remove several ribs, performing surgery without anesthesia was impossible. However, the monk insisted, and when the doctor operated, Bomun became absorbed in a koan and entered *samadhi*.[153]

Whether it is suffering or a cause of suffering (e.g., an operation, or all the reasons that can create suffering), if it has substance, the pain or suffering will always be felt. But since its nature is empty, that is to say, it is just our own mind's creation, it is felt differently in each and every situation. That is why, at different times depending on our state of mind, the same food can taste very different (see chapter 8).

As Nagarjuna said:

> If suffering had an essence,
> Its cessation would not exist.
> So if an essence is posited,
> One denies cessation.

If the path had an essence,
Cultivation would not be appropriate.
If this path is indeed cultivated,
It cannot have an essence.

If suffering, arising, and
Ceasing are nonexistent,
By what path could one seek
To obtain the cessation of suffering?[154]

After the Buddha's supreme enlightenment, he considered entering nirvana instead of teaching the Dharma, because he thought that no one would believe what he had discovered. It is said that heavenly beings asked the Buddha repeatedly to have mercy on sentient beings and to teach them, saying that some people were mature enough to receive the Buddha's teachings. Complying with these repeated requests, and observing the spiritual and intellectual level of human beings, the Buddha first decided to teach his Dharma and then set out to teach it step by step. In the first stage, since the people's ignorance was so pervasive, their egos so strong, and their feelings of suffering so real, he began to teach no more than the Four Noble Truths. Only after he taught many foundational dharmas such as the Four Noble Truths, the karmic principle of cause and effect, the merits of practice, and the importance of observing precepts did he begin to directly teach the ultimate reality—the empty nature of all things. The Buddha taught the Prajna Paramita Sutras for more than twenty years, starting when he was in his midfifties.

Saints and sages in the Christian tradition have also taught their students according to their level of spiritual readiness:

For though you should in fact be teachers by this time, you need someone to teach you the beginning elements of God's utterances. You have gone back to needing milk, not solid food. For everyone who lives on milk is inexperienced in the message of righteousness, because he is an infant. But solid food is for the mature, whose perceptions are trained by practice to discern both good and evil. (Hebrews 5:12–14)

The following story is an example of a teacher's expedient means.

When a man was on his way home one night, he saw a ghost near a cemetery. Terrified, his entire life became full of suffering and misery. After this incident he could not sleep well, fearing that the ghost might attack him. Since he knew that the only way to sleep soundly and restore peace in his life was to ward off the ghost, he visited a prominent Taoist master. After listening to the man's concerns, the master gave him a talisman and taught him a chant to ward off the evil spirit. From that day on, he slept soundly again and led a peaceful life. Whenever fear of the ghost arose, he took out the talisman and chanted its phrase. Several years passed, and one day a thought arose in his mind: "That master is very old. What if he dies? What if I lose the talisman? The ghost might attack me again!" From that day on, he once again had trouble sleeping. When he next visited the Taoist temple and told his worries to the master, the master replied, "May I tell you a secret?" The master asked him to come closer, and very quietly whispered into his ear, "There is no such thing as a ghost."

The Buddha called himself the Great Physician. His primary interest was in curing the illness of people's minds, rather than teaching the Dharma logically like a professor at a university. Depending on the level of a person's intelligence and/or spirituality, he gave different "prescriptions," or dharmas. The Taoist master first gave a talisman and a chant to the man who feared the ghost. When the man practiced chanting for several years and became seasoned, ready to receive the master's words, the master told him the truth, "There is no ghost." In the same way, when a student was not mature enough, the Buddha first taught the Four Noble Truths. Only when the student was ready would the Buddha reveal the ultimate reality of emptiness—that the five aggregates, all dharmas, the eighteen elements, the twelve links, and the Four Noble Truths are all empty and do not exist in the absolute sense. They only exist within our minds.[155]

According to Nagarjuna:

> If all of this is empty,
> Neither arising nor ceasing,
> Then for you, it follows that
> The Four Noble Truths do not exist.[156]

Since we are already Buddha (whole, perfect, complete, and lacking nothing), the path to attain buddhahood or enlightenment is meaningless. As long as what we seek, this so-called "buddhahood," is what we already have within ourselves, the path to reach nirvana is meaningless. In fact, we are already there, as the Heart Sutra explained with the words "no path."

...no wisdom, no attainment with nothing to attain...

Nagarjuna said:

> If the Four Noble Truths do not exist
> Then knowledge, abandonment,
> Meditation, and manifestation
> Will be completely impossible.[157]

When Confucius met the hermit sage Lao Tzu, Confucius first asked him, "What is morality?" Lao Tzu replied, "When one is immoral, one thinks about morality." As the conversation continued, Confucius grew embarrassed and began to lose his composure, which his attendant had never seen before.

When there is ignorance, then there also exists the wisdom or the knowledge to attain enlightenment. When ignorance disappears, so too does that wisdom ("no wisdom"). When there is no illness, there is no need for medicine. Just as the concept of innocence does not exist in the mind of the innocent child, the idea of wisdom or non-wisdom does not exist in the mind of an enlightened individual.

One day, I began looking for my eyeglasses. It took quite a while before I realized that I was wearing them. In the same way, as long as what we seek is buddhahood, it cannot be attained or lost because it is our very nature.

One Zen master said, "If you try to seek it, you will miss it." Similarly, the Lankavatara Sutra says, "The Buddha mind is the basis, and gateless is the dharma gate... He who seeks after dharma will certainly attain nothing. Outside mind there is no Buddha; outside Buddha there is no mind."

"Attaining enlightenment" is just an expression. In order to explain the Dharma to average people, masters have had to use expressions like "attaining buddhahood or enlightenment." The truth, however, is that there is nothing to attain ("no attainment with nothing to attain"). Korean Zen Master Kyongbong said, "The truth is that there is neither coming nor going, neither wisdom nor ignorance. One has to say something in order to teach, just as to save a drowning person one has to enter the water and get wet."[158]

Concerning this, Chuang Tzu said:

> The bait is the means to get the fish where you want it; catch the fish and you forget the bait. The snare is the means to get the rabbit where you want it; catch the rabbit and forget the snare. Words are the means to get the idea where you want it; catch on to the idea and you forget about the words. Where can I find a man who has forgotten all words? Please take me to him; I would like to have a word with him.

Enlightenment is like the light being turned on. With the light on, we can see what is already there—nothing is added or subtracted. Enlightenment shows us that we are what we seek.

Attainment or gaining always presupposes "I" as the subject that gains something. It also presupposes that there is something that the "I" gains. Since "I" as well as "dharmas" are empty, attainment and nonattainment disappear.

Master Fa-tsang said, "Not only are none of the precious dharmas found in emptiness, the one who knows the knowledge of emptiness cannot be found either. Thus [the Heart Sutra] says, 'no knowledge.' At the same time, neither can this knowledge of emptiness that one knows be found. Thus it says, 'no attainment.'"[159]

Master Deva said, "What can see is knowledge. What is seen is attainment. Because suffering and happiness are forgotten, the mind that knows does not arise. This is called attaining what is not attained. This is complete attainment. It is not the same as mundane attainment. To counter the idea that bodhisattvas attain anything, it says 'no knowledge and no attainment.'"[160]

When "I" exists, the world of duality comes into being. This is the world of discrimination, the world where craving, desire, and suffering prevail. The world where "I" disappears is the world of freedom, the world of the absolute, the world where all enlightened beings dwell.

Before enlightenment, practitioners work hard and endure all kinds of hardships. When one is enlightened, all illusions disappear. All dharmas and the universe become "I." Since "I" is not different from the universe itself, how could anything be attained or lost? Our mind is not different from the dharmas, and all dharmas are our mind—"no attainment with nothing to attain."

There are some mathematical equations that appear complicated but become simple and clear when one variable is omitted. Similarly, when "I" disappears, all of the seeming contradictions found in the Heart Sutra—for example, "No suffering, no cause of suffering, no cessation of suffering, no path; no wisdom, no attainment with nothing to attain"—become clear and everything starts to make perfect sense.

When I first read the Diamond Sutra, I found it puzzling and so paradoxical that nothing made sense to me. But after I studied it and practiced more, nothing could have made more sense.

As long as ego exists in our minds, everything seems confusing and contradictory. When ego vanishes, everything becomes clear and everything comes home. This reminds me of a story of a man who was woken from sleep by screams and gunfire all around. He became frightened because he thought a war had broken out. When he opened his eyes, he realized that it was just the TV. Similarly, unawakened beings suffer and agonize in this world, but when they become awakened, they realize that all things are empty; they realize that although things exist, they exist as a mirage or an illusion.

In the last chapter of the Diamond Sutra, Buddha imparts a four-line verse to his disciples:

> Thus shall ye think of all this fleeting world:
> A star at dawn, a bubble in a stream,
> A flash of lightning in a summer cloud,
> A flickering lamp, a phantom, and a dream.[161]

Imagine you are dreaming. In your dream, you are being chased by a ghost (representing the suffering world and the first and second noble truths). You try everything to escape from it (the third noble truth), and finally, you meet a bodhisattva, and you are able to save your life by faithfully following his words (representing the path to end suffering, the fourth noble truth). But when you wake up you realize that it was just a dream, and then everything (the sufferer, the cause of suffering, the bodhisattva, the path to escape from the ghost) becomes meaningless. The fear of the ghost and your gratitude toward the bodhisattva suddenly vanish.

A Persian king wanted to know about all the human knowledge in the world and ordered his scholars to write about this knowledge. For twenty years they gathered and wrote dozens of books on everything from history and geography to math and science. When they brought those books to the king, he was surprised to discover that there were so many books, and each of them was very thick. So the busy king ordered the scholars to summarize all the books into one volume.

Another twenty years passed while the scholars tried to condense all the knowledge into one book. When they had finished their work and showed the book to the king, he had become too old and sick to read the whole book. So the king told them, "I might die very soon. Tell me in one sentence the essence of this book." One wise scholar replied, "When I studied all the human knowledge of the world, this is what I discovered: men are born, suffer, and die."

The old king gazed at his son, a young prince who had caused the king much concern because of his extravagant lifestyle. The king asked this same wise man, "Will you give some practical advice to the prince? He will succeed to the throne and rule over this kingdom." The wise man replied, "No pain, no gain."

For the average person, "no pain, no gain" can be a practical lesson. In order to cut off the root of suffering, people should do spiritual practice. This is the lesson of the Four Noble Truths (the Eightfold Path is the way to end suffering). But the Heart Sutra says that neither pain nor gain is truly existent ("no suffering... no attainment"). This is the essence of the prajna paramita literature, the absolute truth.

If "no pain, no gain" is the teaching of the Four Noble Truths and the flesh of Buddha's teaching, then "no pain *and* no gain," or emptiness (the ultimate reality), is the marrow of Buddha's teaching.

SUDDEN ENLIGHTENMENT AND GRADUAL CULTIVATION

A flying goose does not leave any trace upon the water.

—Zen saying

The Bodhisattva relies on prajna paramita, therefore the mind has no hindrance; without any hindrance, no fears exist; free from delusion, one dwells in nirvana. All buddhas of the past, present, and future rely on prajna paramita and attain supreme enlightenment.

HUI NENG AND ENLIGHTENMENT

HUI NENG was born into the Lu family in 638 C.E. in the town of Xing in Kwangtung province. His father died when Hui Neng was young, leaving him and his mother very poor. As a consequence, he did not have the chance to learn to read or write. He gathered and sold firewood in the marketplace to make ends meet.

One day, while he was leaving a shop after delivering firewood, he happened to hear a man reciting a sutra. When he heard the phrase "give rise to a mind that does not dwell anywhere," he became fully awake. Hui Neng asked the man about the sutra and where he had come from. The man told Hui Neng that it was the Diamond Sutra and that he came from Tung Chan Monastery in the Huang Mei District of Chi Chou, and the abbot of the monastery was Hung Yen, the Fifth Patriarch of Zen Buddhism.

The man gave him ten *taels* of silver to provide for Hui Neng's mother. Hui Neng arranged for friends to look after his mother and left for the monastery in the north to meet the Fifth Patriarch. It took thirty days to reach the monastery by foot.

When Hui Neng met the patriarch, he introduced himself and said, "I am a commoner from Kwangtung. I have traveled far to pay you respect and I ask for nothing but buddhahood." The patriarch replied, "You are a native of Kwangtung, a barbarian! How can you expect to become a buddha?" Hui Neng replied, "Although there are northern men and southern men, north and south make no difference to their buddha nature. A barbarian is physically different from Your Holiness, but there is no difference in our buddha nature." The patriarch replied, "This barbarian is too bright! Go to the stable and speak no more."

The patriarch realized that Hui Neng was enlightened and tried to hide Hui Neng to prevent certain jealous monks from harming him. Hui Neng withdrew himself and did chores in the rice mill. He chopped wood and pounded rice for eight months.

One day, the patriarch assembled all his disciples and told them, "The matter of life and death, the endless cycle of rebirth, is a grave matter of concern. Since I am old, I would like to transmit the Dharma lineage and give the robe and bowl—the symbol of the patriarchate— to the person who realizes the Essence of Mind. Go and write a poem so that I can tell who has realized the truth. Whoever understands the Essence of Mind will become the Sixth Patriarch."

The disciples, however, did not bother to write any poems, thinking that the head monk, Shen Hsiu, would become the Sixth Patriarch. Shen Hsiu, the most respected disciple, composed his poem after receiving this instruction. But because he was not sure of his own awakening, he did not have the courage to submit his poem to the patriarch; instead he wrote the poem anonymously in the middle of the night, on the wall of the corridor where the patriarch could see it.

The poem read:

> Our body is a bodhi tree
> Our mind a mirror bright.
> Polish it diligently time and again
> And let no dust alight.

When monks saw the poem, they were amazed by it, all exclaiming, "Well done!"

When the patriarch saw the poem, he told his disciples, "If you practice according to this poem, then you will not fall into the unwholesome realms of existence. Recite it diligently and you will receive many great benefits."

The patriarch privately said to Shen Hsiu, "You have reached the door of enlightenment but have not yet entered it." He asked him to compose and submit another poem that would really illustrate that he had entered the door of enlightenment. Shen Hsiu tried hard, but he could not come up with another verse.

A couple of days later, Hui Neng happened to pass by the corridor and saw the poem. Hui Neng asked a young novice, "Whose poem is this?" The novice replied, "You barbarian, don't you know about it? Our patriarch told us to compose a poem to select the next patriarch. He said that he would like to transmit the robe and bowl to the one who composed a poem that shows a clear understanding of the Essence of Mind. Elder Shen Hsiu wrote this poem and our patriarch told us to recite it."

Hui Neng asked the boy to read it for him because he was illiterate. When he heard the poem, Hui Neng immediately realized that the composer had not yet been awakened. Hui Neng asked a district officer there to write his verse for him, which read:

There is no bodhi tree
Nor stand of mirror bright.
Originally there's not a single thing
Where could the dust alight?

When the man had written the verse, all the people present were greatly surprised.

Hui Neng then went back to rice pounding. However, his poem created a great stir; everyone was saying, "Amazing! You cannot judge a person by his looks! Maybe he will become the Sixth Patriarch."

Hung Yen, the Fifth Patriarch, came out and saw the excited crowd. After he read Hui Neng's poem, he casually said, "This person hasn't seen the essential nature either." He proceeded to wipe off the poem with his shoe lest his jealous disciples should be tempted to do Hui Neng harm.

The next day, the patriarch came secretly to Hui Neng in the kitchen where he pounded the rice. The patriarch asked him, "Is the rice ready?" Hui Neng replied, "Ready long ago, only waiting for the sieve." The patriarch knocked on the mortar three times with his stick and left. Hui Neng understood the meaning of the message. At three o'clock in the morning, he went to the patriarch's room.

Using the robe as a screen so that no one could see them, the patriarch explained the Diamond Sutra to Hui Neng. When he came to the sentence "give rise to a mind which does not dwell anywhere," Hui Neng at once experienced great enlightenment and understood that all things in the universe were the Essence of Mind.

The patriarch passed the robe and begging bowl, which had originally belonged to Shakyamuni Buddha and symbolized the Dharma seal of enlightenment, to Hui Neng and said, "You are now the Sixth Patriarch."

To the knowledge of no one, the Dharma was transmitted to Hui Neng in the middle of the night.

The two verses composed by Shen Hsiu and Hui Neng are often quoted in the Zen tradition. They portray the characteristics of Zen practice, especially the meaning of enlightenment in the course of attaining buddhahood, and they illustrate the two paths of practice: before and after enlightenment.

Let us examine how we carry out our practice.

Our original mind is often compared to a mirror. Like the mirror our mind is covered by the dust of greed, anger, wandering thoughts, and delusions. The practitioner's task is to remove the dust so that the original brightness of our buddha nature will be revealed. This is spiritual practice. This is the way of most practitioners, and it is not restricted to Buddhists.

Yet when the enlightened Hui Neng read the first poem, he immediately realized that it was not the poem of an enlightened mind.

Hui Neng's approach to the practice was different. As Hui Neng's poem asks, if there is no mirror, how can the dust alight? If there is no air, the wind cannot blow. Likewise, if there is no mirror, dust (including unwholesome desires and wandering thoughts) cannot accumulate. Hui Neng's poem signifies the importance of enlightenment on the path to attaining buddhahood.

It is said that there are two paths for cultivating the mind, for spiritual practice. One is called "out-of-house practice," and it is the practice before enlightenment, before awakening to the real nature of our minds. The other is called "in-house practice," and it is the practice after enlightenment, after one realizes one's true nature.

In contemporary society many methods of spiritual cultivation focus on health and serenity, ranging from tai chi to yoga to qigong. These ways of practice help people to calm, focus, and pacify their minds. These disciplines enhance physical, mental, and emotional health; however, these practices do not lead us to a life with complete, unconditional, indestructible happiness and freedom. These ways of practice do not ultimately solve the grave matter of life and death, nor free us from samsara. This is because these practices are not fundamentally based on the realization of our true nature.

In-house practice is that practice that is based on the realization of no-self. After being awakened to the empty nature of reality, our way of practice becomes substantially different. Our practice becomes effortless and natural, leaving no karmic traces. In-house practice is founded on the realization that there is nothing to cultivate and there is no one practicing. This is the path of practice after being awakened to our true self.

The root of suffering is "I." Many situations or environmental causes lead us to suffer; however, the source of suffering remains the same: "I."

Enlightenment is the realization of no-self. It is the awakening to the emptiness of our ego. Enlightenment is the realization that we are just the five aggregates (see chapter 3) that arise and cease, depending on conditions, without any underlying substance. This realization is like severing the root of suffering, or like awakening from a dream where endless stories unfold, all created by the main character called "I." Just as in Hui Neng's poem, if there is no mirror, how could dust (such as wandering thoughts, desires, and anger) alight?

After being awakened, all our wandering thoughts and unwholesome desires lose their ground (our sense of self); therefore, thoughts and desires cannot take root.

Due to our past habits, thoughts and desires may arise, yet they are short-lived. In the mind of the enlightened one, they cannot take root and grow. Whenever thoughts arise, the enlightened one reflects upon the empty nature of all reality and then all wandering thoughts immediately vanish. When the lights go on, the darkness disappears. A Zen master compared this dispersal of thoughts to snowflakes falling on a fireplace.

After seeing into our original nature, when thoughts arise we can reflect upon our authentic self, dwelling in our empty self-nature. Thoughts (which are like thieves) cannot invade our mind, just as when the light is on in the house and the master is wide-awake, thieves cannot enter the home.

After enlightenment, the object of meditation changes. We are more easily absorbed in meditation. Before seeing our no-self, when thoughts arose we came back to the object of meditation, whether it was the breath or some bodily sensation. To settle the mind and stay focused, we needed to pay attention constantly to the object of meditation. The unenlightened person needs a leash to prevent the monkey-like mind from wandering off. But after seeing the self-nature, whenever thoughts arise we can just reflect upon and dwell in our true selves; thieves cannot invade our house. Reflection immediately loosens the grip of our thoughts, which arise from our sense of self. When we reflect upon the empty nature of our reality, all discursive thoughts become powerless and cannot continue. In Zen tradition, this reflection is called *hyeokwang-bancho*: directing the light inward, returning to the source.

That is why practice becomes natural and effortless after enlightenment. Since practice becomes far more efficient after enlightenment, Sotaesan, the founding master of Won Buddhism, said that it is like practitioners reaching buddhahood as if they were traveling by jet plane. Master Sotaesan compared the meaning of enlightenment in the course of attaining buddhahood to "knowing alphabets when studying languages." He compared the enlightened person to "a carpenter who has obtained a ruler and a straight-edge."[162]

Daesan, the Third Head Dharma Master of Won Buddhism, said that practice without enlightenment is like a tree planted in a pot, whereas practice after enlightenment is like a tree rooted in the earth. Since enlightenment, or attaining prajna, is so important in the course of attaining buddhahood, the Heart Sutra says, "The Bodhisattva *relies* on prajna paramita," and "All buddhas of the past, present, and future *rely* on prajna paramita and attain supreme enlightenment." "Rely" is the translation of the Sanskrit *asram,* which literally means "take refuge" or "dwell." The Heart Sutra says that not just the Bodhisattva of Great Compassion but also all buddhas of the past, present, and future have relied on prajna in order to attain buddhahood.

Attaining prajna does not lead directly to attaining buddhahood, however. As for the necessity of the follow-up practice after enlightenment, Master Sotaesan said:

> Being enlightened to one's nature is like a person who wishes to learn calligraphy, and eventually meets a good teacher, whose work can serve as a model for the practice of calligraphy. Another example would be a person who wishes to learn embroidery and acquires a good design. Therefore, a person who has seen his original nature and feels satisfied with his awakening, and thus neglects to continue practicing, is like a person who wishes to learn good calligraphy but stops and does nothing after acquiring a good sample of calligraphy. Similarly, it is like a person who wishes to learn embroidery but stops and does nothing after acquiring a good design. In truth, to be enlightened to our original nature is not difficult to do. What is immensely difficult is to become a buddha who has accumulated many blessings by practicing all types of good karma, and who obtains power and wisdom by using his original nature in a complete, bright, and upright manner.[163]

The enlightenment of a practitioner can differ from that of Shakyamuni Buddha in terms of its depth. There are very many levels of enlightenment. The deepest level of enlightenment is called *anuttaram samyak sambodhi* in Sanskrit, which literally means "unexcelled, ultimate, and complete enlightenment," or "supreme enlightenment." After attaining prajna, one should endeavor to attain this supreme enlightenment.

...The Bodhisattva relies on prajna paramita, therefore the mind has no hindrance...

All hindrances originate in the mind. The root of all hindrances is our sense or notion of self. Fears, disappointments, depression, frustration, jealousy, pride, low self-esteem, and other hindrances come from "I." After being awakened to the empty nature of self and all phenomena, the notion of self vanishes, and as a result, all hindrances vanish (see chapters 3 and 4).

Master Hui-chung said, "As long as there is the lightest Dharma, there is an obstruction. But the mind and the world are empty. No matter how we think or act, nothing at all happens. How could there be an obstruction?"[164]

Furthermore, he added, "Deluded people cling to the existence of the Five Skandhas and the Eighteen Elements and obstruct their own nature and don't see its light. This is what is meant by 'ignorance.' Once they discover the nature of their own mind, the roots and dust of sensation turn out to be empty at heart, and conceptual consciousness ceases to function. How could there be any obstruction?"[165]

Master Ching-mai said, "Dharmas are empty inside and out, the vision of one's wisdom is not blocked by the nature of existence."[166]

...without any hindrance, no fears exist...

Since the source of all our fears is "I," after enlightenment, our sense of self and all hindrances disappear. So do our fears.

People become fearful when they want something that seems hard to acquire, whether it is some material thing, social status, a better body, or the experience of enlightenment. Fears also tend to arise when we think we are lacking something. In English, "want" implies the lack of something. When we realize that we lack nothing and are complete and perfect, this "want" vanishes.

Fears disappear entirely when our sense of self and our idea of possession disappear. All hindrances disappear and indestructible happiness and freedom arise after we realize that we are already perfect. There is nothing to cultivate, there is nothing to improve; we are no different from the universe, and all things in the universe are ours. Enlightenment leads to that peace which cannot be broken.

...free from delusion, one dwells in nirvana...

A Dharma teacher who supervised a psychotherapy trainee wrote that he had a psychotic patient who said, "I am the sun and all of you are planets who orbit around me." That delusion is not so different from our way of thinking or living because we always think and act based on "I" or "me."

There was a king in China whose mentor was an ascetic. Before the king invaded a neighboring country, he strategized with his generals. In the early morning before going to the front, he asked his mentor, "Venerable Sir, is today auspicious?" The ascetic replied, "Your majesty, if today is an auspicious day for us, then it is inauspicious for them."

A man who had been divorced seven times said to his friend, "Don't you think it is odd that I have met the same kind of woman seven times?" Just as planets revolve around the sun, our lives are moving around the idea of self.

All sorts of delusions originate from the notion of self. "Delusion" is the translation of the Sanskrit term *vipa ryasa*, which literally means "inverse" or "upside down."

Just as a concave or convex mirror does not reflect an image accurately, ego-based thoughts are always *vipa ryasa*, delusion.

Since the realization of no-self dissolves our sense of self, all delusions, hindrances, or fears vanish on their own after enlightenment. That is why attaining prajna directly leads to nirvana.

...All buddhas of the past, present, and future rely on prajna paramita and attain supreme enlightenment...

One summer, while living in Korea, I went to the airport to fly to the United States. At the airport, I discovered that my passport had expired the previous year. I had already bought my ticket and had business to attend to in the States, yet there was no way that I would be able to fly there. Just as I could not fly to the States without a valid passport, likewise Master Sotaesan said that without enlightenment, there is no way to be free from samsara and to enter buddhahood.[167]

Without attaining prajna, our practice is inefficient and limited.

One day while I was working at the Seoul Meditation Center in Korea, I cleaned the floor in the meditation hall with a mop. Despite mopping the hall, it still smelled because the mop was not clean. Likewise, without realizing the nature of our original mind, our practice is not complete and wholesome. That is why, in the Rinzai tradition, it is said that the practice before enlightenment is called *o-ryun-soo*, which means tainted or misleading practice.

In Buddhist practice, one is told to empty or purify the mind. Yet without seeing into the empty nature of our mind, it is hard to let go of our thoughts and desires. However, when we realize our authentic self, our practice becomes effortless, natural, and efficient. Master Daesan said that when thoughts or desires arise, an enlightened person brushes them away, like brushing dust from a leather coat. Another Buddhist master used the analogy of water sliding off a leaf.

Just as one needs a net to catch fish, practitioners need the realization of no-self to reach buddhahood. Without attaining prajna, we can never sever the root of our suffering, which is "I."

Since enlightenment is fundamental to reaching buddhahood, just as the Heart Sutra says, the Bodhisattva of Great Compassion and all buddhas attained supreme enlightenment by relying on prajna paramita.

Practitioners, therefore, should endeavor to attain enlightenment and also continue the practice of cultivating their minds until they realize buddhahood. This is the universal path. Master Te-ch'ing says, "Not only do bodhisattvas rely on this prajna for their practice, there is no Buddha in the past, the present, or the future who does not rely on this prajna in order to realize unexcelled, perfect enlightenment."[168]

Prajna paramita, wisdom paramita, is the culmination of all paramitas and also informs the other paramitas. Without prajna paramita, the other paramitas cannot be complete, nor can they function well. For example, without the guidance of prajna, *dana* (generosity) paramita cannot be complete and authentic. The following story illustrates this principle:

> There was a wealthy man who, after saving his poor neighbors by releasing some money and grains in a famine year, kept wishing he would be eulogized for his virtue. The villagers conferred and erected a stele, but the man was still dissatisfied, so he spent more of his own money to erect a new stele and to construct a tremendous stele pavilion. The villagers thought his actions ludicrous, so there were many criticisms and disparaging remarks made. Kim Kwangson heard about this and presented it during a conversation session. The Founding Master [of Won Buddhism] listened and said, "This is a living scripture about warning people who compulsively seek honor. Although that person did this deed in order to enhance his reputation, didn't he actually lose even his previous reputation, not to speak of enhancing it? Thus, a foolish person in seeking honor only damages it instead; a wise person does not intentionally seek to be honored; instead, merely by performing proper actions, great honor naturally comes to him."[169]

Dana paramita after enlightenment becomes pure. It does not leave any trace of pride or conceit. The enlightened person's *dana* practice is performed without the concept of "I" or sense of self. In the awakened mind, there is no giver, no gift, and no recipient. These are called the three purities and are authentic *dana* practice.

Bodhidharma once told his disciples, "And since that which is real includes nothing worth begrudging, practitioners give their body, life, and property in charity, without regret, without the vanity of giver, gift, or recipient, and without bias or attachment."[170]

Similarly, after awakening one can practice *virya* (effort or diligence) paramita in a more consummate way. Some of the biggest egos can be found in monasteries or secluded places. Those practitioners may believe that they are holier than common people, and consequently they become judgmental and narrow-minded. I have seen many judgmental devotees in churches and temples.

Enlightened practitioners, when practicing, do not have any lingering thoughts or feelings such as "I am practicing some sacred work."

Just as with the previously discussed examples, prajna paramita is the blueprint of all paramitas. The author Red Pine says, "And the paramita is the helm, ingenious enough to give the boat direction... Thus bodhisattvas who practice the paramitas embark on the greatest of all voyages to the far shore of liberation."[171]

Master Fa-tsang said, "Prajna is the substance and means 'wisdom,' which is the spiritual awakening to the subtlest mysteries and the wondrous realization of the true source. Paramita is the function and means 'to reach the other shore,' which is to use this marvelous wisdom to transform samsara until one reaches completely beyond it to the realm of true emptiness."[172]

There is a small pond at the Jung Do Retreat Center in Korea that caused some difficulties when the Center first opened. For example, during droughts, people had to carry buckets of water to keep the pond full, and during rainy seasons, the water in the pond grew murky. One day a spring was discovered, and when it was linked to the pond, all the problems vanished completely.[173]

Prajna is like that spring water. Just as spring water replenished and purified the pond, so our prajna, our inexhaustible wisdom, will provide fresh water to our practice and purify our karma.

A huge forest fire is often caused from a small flame. Prajna, or the light of our inner wisdom, may not be as bright as the sun at the start of our practice, but it will grow and eventually dispel the darkness of our ignorance.

When Gun-Su, a Won Buddhist minister, first entered the order, Master Chongsan gave him his Dharma name, which means "diligent practice," and asked him to practice diligently not only before but also after enlightenment.

Master Daesan said that if a practitioner becomes self-satisfied with small goodness and small wisdom, then that transgression would be more serious than killing, thievery, or adultery.[174]

Practitioners should make a single-minded effort to attain prajna. After attaining prajna, practitioners should continue to endeavor to reach supreme enlightenment.

THE ULTIMATE SONG OF FREEDOM

One can enter the ocean of Dharma only through faith.

—Buddha

Therefore know that prajna paramita is the great mantra,
is the great enlightening mantra, is the unsurpassed and
unequalled mantra, which is able to eliminate all suffering. This is true, not false.

THE CONCLUSION of the Heart Sutra begins with these
words, and it ends with the Prajna Paramita mantra: *gate,
gate, paragate parasam gate, bodhi svaha.*
A mantra is a power-laden syllable or series of syllables that represents the ultimate reality and manifests certain cosmic forces and
aspects of the buddhas. A mantra is the manifestation of the universal
truth. In Chinese, the word *mantra* is translated *jin-eun,* which literally means "words of truth." Since the ultimate reality or universal
truth is utterly mysterious and profound, it can hardly be depicted by
any other means. Mantra is a way of expressing ultimate reality.
The author Red Pine describes mantra, saying, "In ancient India,
many schools of thought maintained, or at least paid homage to the

idea, that sound vibrations are the ultimate constituents of reality."[175] For instance, *aum* is said to be the primordial sound of the universe, the sound of the origin of all things, or ultimate reality. Mantra is simultaneously a representation of ultimate reality and the path leading to ultimate reality or the universal truth.

A boxer, while sparring with an opponent, becomes so exhausted that his coach is careful not to say much during the rest between the rounds. A coach usually says only a handful of words that he thinks are the most crucial, such as "Use your left hand," or "Watch out for his hook." Just as the coach uses simple words, the Buddha many times summarized his teachings in a mantra, a highly simplified form of truth so that the average practitioner could understand and use the Dharma. Many Mahayana Buddhist sutras conclude with mantras. The Heart Sutra explains and praises this mantra in the passage, "Prajna Paramita mantra is the great mantra, is the great enlightening mantra, is the unsurpassed and unequalled mantra..." Since Prajna Paramita mantra represents the ultimate reality, which is none other than the mind of all buddhas, or the original mind of all sentient beings, this passage means not only the Prajna Paramita mantra, but also the mind of all buddhas (our original mind) is great, unsurpassed, and unequalled. The Heart Sutra then ends with the Prajna Paramita mantra.

Master Hui-chung says, "A mantra is simply a person's own mind. Because these words point to the mind, it is called the mantra of Prajna Paramita."[176]

...the great mantra...

"The great mantra" is the translation of the Sanskrit *mahamantram*. The first characteristic of the Prajna Paramita mantra, and therefore of the ultimate reality, is *maha*, which in Sanskrit means "great." In Islam, they chant "Allah Akbar," or "God is great." According to the Bible, God's nature is great:

The Lord is great and certainly worthy of praise! No one can fathom his greatness! (Psalms 145:3)

In Won Buddhism, *il-won* is the name for the ultimate reality or universal truth (*il* means "one"; *won* means "circle"). The nature of *il-won* is *dae*, which literally means "great" or "large." The following story of Vimalakirti's room illustrates the great (*dae*) nature of our minds.

Vimalakirti was a highly realized lay practitioner in India. From time to time, the Buddha would send his best disciples to learn Dharma from Vimalakirti. His room was said to have strange characteristics. When ten people visited, it could accommodate them; when 100 people visited, it could accommodate all of them. His room was said to have held as many as 32,000 people at one time.

His room symbolizes the ultimate reality, i.e., our minds, which can become as large as the limitless universe or as minute as a particle of dust. In the *Hsui-hsiu-An Discourse on Tso-ch'an*, Zen Master Te-i stated that the mind "is as vast as to envelop what has no boundary and it is as minute as to enter what has no inside."[177] Our mind, when open and awakened, becomes unified with the universe or absolute truth, as great as the mind of all buddhas, and as empty and pure as space.

...the great enlightening mantra...

"Enlightening" is a translation of the Sanskrit *vidya*. *Vidya* originates from the root verb *vid*, which means "to know," "to understand," or "to perceive." *Vidya* means "understanding" or "perceiving" (and its opposite, *avidya*, or "ignorance," is discussed in detail in chapter 9). In English, *vidya* has also been translated as "illuminating," or "bright," or "clear." In the Chinese version of the Heart Sutra, *vidya* is translated as *myeong* (明), which means "bright" or "illuminating." Its Chinese character is made up of two parts; on the left is *il* (日), which means "the sun," and on the right is *wol* (月), which means "the moon."

Without light, we cannot see and distinguish things. In English, when we say that we see, it often means that we know. *Vidya* is *prajna* or the inner light of our original mind. *Vidya* is the lucid awareness of the universe. This awareness or brightness of the universe, or our original mind, is symbolized by the image of Avalokiteshvara Bodhisattva, who has countless eyes. In Hua-yen Buddhism, the ultimate reality is personified as Vairochana Buddha, the Buddha of Great Illumination.

This light or lucid awareness is our true self. Many meditators experience this light when they are deeply absorbed in meditation. If we practitioners are restored to our original mind, we will become as bright and illuminating as Vairochana Buddha. The chanting of the Prajna Paramita mantra will lead us to that brightness or light.

Since the Prajna Paramita mantra is the great enlightening and illuminating mantra, functioning to dispel the darkness or unwholesome energy, chanting of this mantra, or the full Heart Sutra, or the Diamond Sutra, has been used to invoke the power of the universe or the absolute truth.

...is the unsurpassed and unequalled mantra, which is able to eliminate all suffering...

This passage also praises the Prajna Paramita mantra. It means not only that the Prajna Paramita mantra is unsurpassed and unequalled but also that our original mind is like this. This passage implies that no words, no gods, and no truths can exceed the Prajna Paramita mantra, or the ultimate reality.

The practice of prajna paramita transforms us into great and enlightened beings. When we attain prajna and become united with the truth, we find ourselves completely free from all suffering and distress. As the Heart Sutra says, "The Bodhisattva of Great Compassion, when deeply practicing prajna paramita, realized that all five aggregates are empty and became free from all suffering and distress... The Bodhisattva relies on prajna paramita, therefore the mind has no hindrance... one dwells in nirvana. All buddhas of the past, present, and future rely on prajna paramita and attain supreme enlightenment."

Since enlightenment, or realizing no-self, is the only path to dispel the darkness of ego, or to sever the root of suffering ("I"), then the Prajna Paramita mantra, which is the pathway to enlightenment, "is able to eliminate all suffering." Prajna Paramita—which dissolves our ego, awakens us from our illusory dream, and frees us from the cycle of birth and death—is the only path we can follow to become permanently free from all suffering and distress

...this is true, not false...

This straightforward phrase means that the ultimate reality or the Prajna Paramita mantra is true, genuine, and real, not false or inauthentic.

This phrase also refers to the truth and genuineness of the words spoken by the Buddha, especially the teachings of the Heart Sutra. They are spoken from the perspective of faith. If we are enlightened and see into reality with our own eyes, then we have no need for these words in order to believe or not believe something. In other words, attaining supreme enlightenment is the best and greatest form of belief. However, unrealized practitioners need a faith, a guide, or Dharma. For this reason, the Buddha offers these sincere words, so that we may totally trust his teachings and walk confidently with a strong, unwavering faith toward nirvana.

The ultimate reality is mysterious, profound, and difficult to comprehend. The universal truth is often contrary to our conventional beliefs. Consider this from a scientific perspective. It was not that long ago that the big bang theory and the idea of an expanding universe were proven to be true. It may not appeal to our common sense, but according to modern physics, the reality is that the universe and all of its many galaxies and stars originated from an infinitely small hot entity, tinier than the tiniest dust particle. Another example is Einstein's theory that gravity curves the space-time continuum, which is hard to understand for even the best minds but was also proven to be true. According to his theory, if a man fired a gun and if the bullet traveled infinitely, then it would eventually strike the back of his head.

There are innumerable truths that are contradictory to our common sense. On this matter, Jesus said:

> If I have told you about earthly things and you don't believe, how will you believe if I tell you about heavenly things? (John 3:12)

Since the ultimate truth is hard for the unawakened mind to grasp, when Jesus taught a truth, he said many times to assure his followers: I truly, truly say this to you.

The Buddha also emphasized in the Diamond Sutra that what he spoke was not false, nor exaggeration, but the truth:

> Subhuti, the Tathagata is He who declares that which is true; He who declares that which is fundamental; He who declares that which is ultimate. He does not declare that which is deceitful, nor that which is monstrous...
>
> Subhuti, if I fully detailed the merit gained by good men and good women coming to receive, retain, study, and recite this Discourse in the last period, my hearers would be filled with doubt and might become disordered in mind, suspicious and unbelieving. You should know, Subhuti, that the significance of this Discourse is beyond conception; likewise the fruit of its rewards is beyond conception.[178]

When you board a plane to fly to another country, you need to trust the pilot; likewise when practitioners walk the path in order to reach buddhahood, they need to trust the words of the buddhas.

Practice can also be compared to driving a car to an unfamiliar destination. Before actually driving, we need an accurate map. The map, drawn in order to lead practitioners to reach nirvana, is the Dharma, or the words of the buddhas who have already walked on that path.

Many of our life decisions start from a certain belief. Our lives are unfolding directed by that belief. What we believe determines our destiny, and the destiny of society as well.[179] Just as the choice of seed is crucial to a farmer, so what practitioners believe is crucial on their path toward buddhahood. Without the foundation of strong faith, one cannot actualize one's practice.[180]

The Buddha said in the Avatamsaka Sutra that one can enter the ocean of Dharma only through faith.

Sotaesan, the founding master of Won Buddhism, said:

> The reason religious orders check a practitioner's belief and dedication is because belief is none other than the vessel that holds the dharma, the driving force that resolves all cases for questioning, and the foundation for observing all the precepts. Practice without belief is like fertilizing a dead tree: ultimately, you will never see any result. Therefore, you must first establish genuine belief, so that you may deliver yourself. In teaching others as well, arousing belief in those who lack it is the primary merit.[181]

Just as a baby completely trusts its mother when it rests at her bosom, practitioners need to trust completely the words of the buddhas and Dharma teachers.

When practitioners entirely trust the Dharma and their teachers, and their minds and hearts unite with their teachers, without having any doubts whatsoever, then this level of faith is called *teuk-shin* in Won Buddhism, which literally means "special faith."

Daesan, the Third Head Dharma Master of Won Buddhism, said that from this stage the tree of supreme enlightenment takes root in the mind of the practitioner. One's progress toward attaining great enlightenment becomes accelerated. Zen Buddhist traditions refer to this stage as *ilcho-jigip-yeorae*, which means "one jump and one reaches buddhahood." *Shin*, or faith, is sometimes called *shin-geun*, which means "the root of faith." These terms are used interchangeably because faith is the foundation of the practice of all practitioners, just as the root is the foundation of a tree.

Just as a root continuously grows, our faith or belief also grows and strengthens. The more we understand the Dharma, the more we practice, the more we associate with our teachers and dharma friends, the deeper and more firm our faith becomes. All practitioners need to grow and nurture their faith consistently by studying Buddhadharma and doing spiritual practice. Let us reflect upon how unwavering and special our faith is.

Master Chongsan said:

> The roots of faith vary in depth. If you are drawn to various theories and assertions without a fixed view of your own, and are shaken hither and thither and ruin your life by acting as you please, the root of your faith is an unstable one like fallen leaves. If you have a firm faith in the true dharma such that your faith is not shaken by minor adverse conditions but is shaken by major ones, though you do not become depraved thereby, the root of your faith is like that of a tree. If your faith is deep such that you are never shaken by any adverse circumstances or difficult situation, and such that you do not fall into the suffering of transgression, because your conscience leads you, the root of your faith is like that of a huge mountain.[182]

15

YOU ARE WHAT YOU SEEK

The seeker of truth should drop the bait of the world.

—Buddha

So proclaim the Prajna Paramita mantra, which says *gate gate paragate parasamgate bodhi svaha.*

THE ESSENCE of Buddhadharma is contained in the prajna paramita literature, and these scriptures are condensed into the Heart Sutra. The Heart Sutra concludes with the Prajna Paramita mantra discussed in the last chapter: *gate gate paragate parasamgate bodhi svaha*, or "Gone, gone, gone beyond, gone altogether beyond! Now awakened." Therefore this mantra is not only the finale of the Heart Sutra but also the conclusion of all Buddhadharma.

When my mother was a child, the Korean War broke out. The North Korean army swiftly occupied many areas of the country and was rapidly moving south. My grandfather decided to leave for Pusan, the southernmost port city. Leaving his home was extremely difficult, and he was greatly concerned because he had six small children of whom my mother was the eldest at ten years of age. Her father knew that the road was inundated with refugees, and what frightened him most was losing his children. My grandmother had to carry her three-year-old boy on her back while clutching her one-year-old baby to her breast. With her free hand, she gripped their bag, which they could not afford to lose. My grandfather asked my mother to do many things: hold the hands of her brothers (six- and eight-year-old boys), remember not to drink the dirty water, and constantly check whether the money—which he had given her just in case they became separated—was secure in her pocket. He asked my mother to repeat these instructions several times so that she would not forget.

The sight of the overwhelming number of refugees appalled him, and he immediately reduced the number of instructions my mother was to follow. He told my mother, "Just remember, do not let go of your little brothers' hands! Do not let go of your little brothers' hands!" That was all he asked of my mother on that trip, for fear of losing his family.

Just like my grandfather's singular entrusting words, so Prajna Paramita mantra is one last statement imparted by the Buddha, who said of it, "You may forget all that I taught, but you should not fail to remember this."

Whenever I recite the Heart Sutra, especially this mantra, I am reminded of what my grandfather asked of my mother, and of the great compassion of the Buddha and Avalokiteshvara Bodhisattva. This Prajna Paramita mantra is what the Buddha truly wants to say to us; this is what is really, really important for us.

The universal truth, or the wisdom that the Buddha and Avalokiteshvara Bodhisattva attained through their supreme enlightenment, has become a poem, a song, and a mantra: *gate gate paragate parasamgate bodhi svaha.*

The Prajna Paramita mantra is both the path leading to enlightenment as well as the truth itself, which all buddhas have realized. It is the customary practice not to translate the meaning of the mantra, just as *hallelujah* is not translated. However, for academic and explanatory purposes, the mantra can be translated as follows: *Gate* implies "gone," and *paragate* implies "gone beyond" (*para* means "across to the other side or shore"). The preposition *sam* means "with" or "together"; therefore, *parasamgate* implies "gone altogether beyond to the other shore." *Bodhi* means "awakening" or "enlightenment." *Svaha* is exclamatory, similar to *amen* or *hallelujah*. (Hindu priests say "*svaha!*" during the climax of Vedic rituals, especially when they made oblations of fire.) *Svaha* implies a wish that the previous words be fulfilled, like saying, "well said!" or "so be it!" It can also mean "now awakened!" or "oh, what an awakening!" So *gate gate paragate parasamgate bodhi svaha* means "Gone, gone, gone beyond, gone altogether beyond! Now awakened!"

Note the importance of the tense used here. The mantra does not state, "let us go, let us go, let us go altogether to the other side," but rather it says, "gone, gone, gone beyond, gone altogether beyond!" thus using the past perfect tense. This implies that we are already there. We do not have to struggle to reach the other shore. Since we are already whole, perfect, and complete, lacking nothing, our task is nothing more than to be fully awake.

The truth is that there is no one to go, and there is nowhere to go, and there is nothing to attain.

The Prajna Paramita mantra means that this very present moment is nirvana. We are already on the bus, so there is no need to wait at a bus stop for it. Let us just be awakened from this dream. Let us come back to the present moment, which is nirvana.

Enlightenment is the flower that blooms when we are awakened and come to this very instant (reality). Therefore the imparting words, *gate gate paragate parasamgate bodhi svaha*, mean "Let us be fully awake at this present moment. Let us be diligently mindful that nirvana is here and now."

Humans are continually moving somewhere—samsara literally means "continuous flow" or "moving around." We go to school, to our jobs, to the grocery store, and so on. Even while we are practicing sitting meditation, our minds are wandering in all directions. When it comes to our physical bodies, we are always moving toward old age and death.

Naong, who became a Korean Buddhist master later in his life, lost a close friend when he was a child. Devastated, he asked a village elder where his friend had gone. The elder replied, "I do not know." All the village people said the same thing, "I do not know." This situation caused Naong to search for something that is beyond life and death. His friend's death motivated Naong to walk on the spiritual path.

Where have we come from, and where are we going? Where is our mind going at this very moment? What is our life's destination?

Zen Master Whangbyuk was a counselor to a Chinese emperor. One day while visiting the lakeshore with many high-ranking officials, Whangbyuk and the emperor saw the many fancy boats of the dignitaries. The emperor exclaimed, "There are so many boats on the lake!" Whangbyuk, standing next to the emperor replied, "Your majesty, there are truly only two boats there. One boat pursuing fame, the other chasing after fortune."[183]

When the Buddha was born, his father gave him the name Siddhartha, which means "the one who achieves his aim," or "the one who fulfills his wish." When the Buddha saw the suffering and dissatisfaction of the human condition, what began to form in his mind was a wish to discover a truth or happiness that endures. That desire drove him to leave the palace in search of unconditional and everlasting happiness.

It is essential to distinguish between temporary happiness and eternal happiness, which is freedom. Sotaesan, the founding master of Won Buddhism, clearly differentiated worldly pleasure, which is temporary, and heavenly pleasure, which is everlasting:

> The worldly pleasures never last long; coming is the beginning of going, prosperity is the cause of wanting and birth is the cause of death. This is the universal way of the principle of nature. Wealth and fame are powerless before old age, illness and death. Wives, children, property or positions to which one becomes desperately attached are nothing but floating clouds in the face of one's death. Heavenly happiness is originally a matter of formless mind. Therefore even

if your body is transformed into another form the happiness will remain forever. This can be compared to the story which says that a talented person will still be talented even after moving to another house.[184]

A number of years ago when I taught the Buddhadharma and meditation at a college, a student said, "Reverend Yoo, I would rather have a happy life than work hard to attain enlightenment or buddhahood." To explain temporary happiness versus eternal, unconditional happiness, I asked him to read the above passage.

There was a man who died at an early age. He stood before God and asked, "Why did you not give me prior notice?" God replied, "Didn't you see men around you growing old, becoming sick, and dying?" When our hair begins to turn gray, and our eyesight and hearing are beginning to fail, and our close friends begin to leave this world, it is time for us to prepare for our death.

Some people say that they are too busy for spiritual practice and constantly postpone practicing Dharma. Yet when we grow old, we no longer have physical strength to practice meditation, and our mind is not lucid enough to study Dharma. When it comes to beginning our spiritual practice, the earlier, the better.

All foods are fresh and wholesome for only a certain length of time. Beyond that time, we cannot eat that food. Likewise only when we are born as humans and meet the Buddhadharma can we practice and have the opportunity to attain enlightenment.

Buddha says in verse 182 of the Dhammapada:

Rare is the attainment of a human birth.
Difficult is the life of mortals.
Rare is the opportunity to hear the dharma.
Rare is the appearance of the buddha.

Many masters have said that it is a rare opportunity to be born as a human. Yet I did not feel this deeply in my heart until I moved into the dormitory of the Won Institute of Graduate Studies, which is a very old building. When we first moved in, we were startled to discover many centipedes there, especially in the basement. Whenever I went down to the basement and turned on the light, I would see at least two dozen of them on the floor. I would catch them and release them outside. Even though we cleaned and fumigated the basement frequently over the next two years, I continued to see a lot of centipedes when the light was on. I realized then that the number of centipedes living in the building might well be dozens of times more than the number of human residents. Considering that there were also various insects, the total number of arthropods were perhaps hundreds or thousands of times more than the number of people living there.

Indeed, the chance to be born as humans is rare and precious. Master Sotaesan said, "Your meeting me is much like a blind person grabbing hold of a door handle. Since you have already held it, you are to keep hold of it firmly. If you are careless and let it go, it will not be easy to take hold of again."[185]

We should not lose this precious chance or postpone searching for the truth, so that we can discover our authentic self. We need to embark on our spiritual journey right now. Kabir, the Indian mystic poet and saint said, "If you cannot cross over alive, how can you cross when you're dead?"

We humans are all patients whose minds are not well. Our minds are tainted with greed, anger, jealousy, and ignorance, which has made us unable to use our minds at will. Like a patient wishing to leave a hospital, only when we can attain prajna and thereby obtain freedom of mind can we be free from the cycle of samsara.

Our life is like school and we are like students who must study well in order to graduate. Because we have been given the rare opportunity to be born as humans and meet the Dharma, we should diligently study and practice so that we can graduate from the cycle of birth and death.

There once was an Indian man who received his Ph.D. at a young age. When he returned to his hometown, a small and poor village by the sea, many people welcomed him. He started a class for the illiterate townsfolk in order to improve the level of their education.

One day, he asked one of his students, an old fisherman, "Have you ever heard of meteorology?" The old man replied, "No sir, I have never heard of that word before." The proud young doctor exclaimed, "You are a fisherman! Yet you are ignorant about meteorology. What a great pity! You have wasted many years of your life."

Several weeks later, the young man began to teach oceanography. At the beginning of the class, he asked his students, "Have you ever heard of oceanography?" Again the old fisherman replied, "No sir, I have never heard of this before." "What do you mean?" exclaimed the doctor. "You live by the ocean but do not know about oceanography. You have wasted half of your life."

In the middle of his lecture, a boy rushed into the room, shouting, "Tsunami is coming, tsunami is coming! It will be here within minutes!" Everyone panicked and rushed to leave the building. The fisherman said to the teacher, "Sir, are you able to swim?" "No," said the anxious doctor. "Sir, you have wasted your *whole* life," the old man responded as he left the building.

There are many urgent things that we need to take care of. What are the most important things in our lives? What is the most imperative? As long as all people wish to attain eternal and unconditional happiness and freedom, which is possible only when we attain prajna, nothing is more important than our practicing toward buddhahood.

As for the grave matter of life and death, Master Sotaesan often told his students the story of Mung Bau. In Korean, *mung* means "dumb" and *bau*, a very common name of male servants, means "rock." One day while Mung Bau was sweeping the yard of a rich man he was working for, he saw his friend walking out front. He asked his friend, who was also working as a servant in another nobleman's house, "Where are you going?" His friend replied, "I am going to the market." Mung Bau wanted to spend time with his friend, so they went to the market together.

The master of the house looked for Mung Bau all day long, but could not find him. At dusk, he saw Mung Bau returning and asked, "Where have you been?" Mung Bau replied, "I have been to the market." "What did you buy at the market?" asked the rich man. "I did not buy anything. I just went there because my friend was going there." The rich man sighed and said, "When you go to the market, you should tell me first when you are going, and what time you will be back, and what you are going to buy. I have never seen such an idiot as you! I will now give you this wooden club that you can attach to your belt. This is to remind you that you are an idiot. When you find someone who is more stupid than you, you can give this club to that person."

Mung Bau found the dangling club around his waist cumbersome. However, it was his master's order, so he always carried the club, constantly looking for someone to whom he could pass it on.

One day the old rich man fell very ill, and the doctor was summoned. The doctor examined the rich man and said there was no chance for him to recover, and that he was about to die. Every family member gathered together to be with him during his final minutes, and the servants were also called to his bedroom. Everyone cried when the master said his last words. The old man had many words of gratitude for Mung Bau, who was sad that this was the last time he would see his master. He cried and asked the old man, "Sir, where are you going?" The master replied, "I do not know." Mung Bau asked again, "When are you leaving?" The old man answered, "I do not know." Mung Bau had one more question: "Do you know when you will be back?" His master gathered his energy and said, "I have no idea." Mung Bau suddenly exclaimed, "Master, today I have finally found the one who is dumber than me! Now this club belongs to you!"

Just as soldiers become desperate when they lose their weapons, so too should all humans be desperate if we are not aware of where we have come from and where we are going. The poorest person is the one who does not understand this truth, who does not know who he or she is. Confucius said, "If I know the truth in the morning, it will be fine to leave this world at night."

In Korea, when a person has lived well and dies in old age, it is called *ho-sang*, which means "auspicious passing." However, it does not matter when people die if they do not realize their authentic selves.

Considering that our practice takes time and requires sweat and blood, we need to prioritize our activities and put the Dharma first. Buddhist masters have said, "Practice as if your head is on fire. Practice as if your hair is aflame."

In modern times, everyone is busy, whether at school or at work. Yet we need to reflect on why we are so busy. Are we busy dissipating or gathering our mind and energy?

One day a Zen master found one of his students doing many things but not focusing his energy on his practice. The master asked him to bring a bucket and move a large pile of stones, a large pile of gravel, and a large pile of sand. The master asked the student to pour the sand inside the bucket first, and then asked him to do the same thing with the gravel, and finally with the stones. After the student put in the sand and gravel, he found that there was no room left in the bucket for the stones.

Next, the master asked him to empty the bucket and put the large stones in first, then the gravel, and lastly the sand. Following this order, the student found that when the gravel was poured in, it settled easily between the stones. The sand, when added last, fit naturally between the gravel and the stones.

Through this demonstration the master taught his student how to prioritize activities, to do what is essential, i.e. his practice, first.

We should reflect on the biggest stones in our lives. What is the most important thing in your life? What is your top priority? There is a need to differentiate what is essential from what is nonessential.

Verses 11 and 12 of the Dhammapada say:

> Those who mistake the unessential to be
> The essential and the essential to be the unessential,
> Dwelling in wrong thoughts, never attain the essential.

Those who know the essential to be
The essential and the unessential to be the unessential,
Dwelling in right thoughts, attain the essential.

Chongsan, the Second Head Dharma Master of Won Buddhism, said:

A deer loved her magnificent antlers, and was ashamed of her ugly-looking legs. One day, being chased by a hunter, she was escaping danger through the bush; her magnificent horns impeded her escape but her unsightly legs ran well and saved her life. Although this is only a fable, if we reflect it on ourselves, we can say that it is a warning critique that truly depicts the world.[186]

There was a well-known Korean millionaire who, when he was in his late sixties, had surgery to remove a cancerous tumor. It was his third operation since developing cancer some years earlier. After the surgery, he asked the surgeon in charge how it went and what the prospects were for his recovery. The doctor candidly told him that since the cancer was so widespread, it would be hard for him to recover completely this time. Although this news had been expected, the millionaire was still very upset. To refresh himself, he went to the bathroom to brush his teeth and wash his face. As he raised his toothbrush, he had the profound realization that he could not take even this simple toothbrush with him when he left this world.

Master Sotaesan said:

No matter how much a person might have accumulated grains and money throughout his life, he cannot take anything with him when he dies. How can we call that which we cannot take along with us our eternal possessions? If we want to create eternal possessions, then while we are alive we must work hard for others' benefit in every possible way, but must do so without dwelling on any sign that benefit is conferred so that we may accumulate merit that is free from the outflows. Our true, eternal possession is the vow regarding the right dharma and the power of the mind that has cultivated it. By devoting ceaseless efforts to this vow and to mind practice, we will become a master of wisdom and merit in the infinite world.[187]

Master Chongsan said:

> An ephemeral creature can see only one day, and a mantis can see only one month, hence, an ephemeral creature does not know a month, and a mantis does not know a year. Deluded beings can see only one life without knowing eternal life, but Buddha-bodhisattvas can see the eternal life, and hence, they make the longest-term plan and exert themselves in the most fundamental matters.[188]

It is said that art is long but life is short. Practitioners should work for something everlasting. As long as we realize that our lives are endlessly unfolding, we cannot help but practice Dharma. Our understanding of eternal life is directly tied to our spiritual practice.

Gunpowder had been known in China for a long time and had been used in fireworks for the amusement of children. It was the Mongols, however, who used it to conquer the world. We are all given the same basic resources, but to what use will we put them during our lives?

Master Sotaesan said, "Among the many kinds of work, only moral work is boundless and everlasting."[189]

Saint Paul made tents for a living. The philosopher Spinoza polished eyeglasses to make ends meet. However, no one identifies Saint Paul or Spinoza as a tent-maker or an eyeglass polisher. Likewise, our authentic occupation is to discover our true self and seek eternal life (attain buddhahood). People are engaged in various activities, but our authentic occupation is always the same: attaining supreme enlightenment. Our secular job in the mundane world is just to make ends meet. We need to make clear what is primary and what is secondary.

Gate gate paragate parasamgate bodhi svaha means that we should change the direction of our lives. Our life goal should not be directed toward making more money, possessing more things, or gaining more recognition or fame. Our goal or final destination is reaching nirvana. We need to establish a new life goal. We need to live with a new value system.

Often I ask new practitioners what motivated their interest in Buddhism or meditation. Many of them answer that they would like to practice sitting meditation in order to reduce their stress, to have a peaceful, calm mind, and to stay focused in their daily lives. These are very good reasons. However, our ultimate goal of practice and life is to attain enlightenment and sever the root of suffering. Our ultimate goal is to awaken from our long, long dream.

Jesus said, "What good is it to gain the whole world if you lose your soul?" (Matthew 16:26; Mark 8:36). It is time that we embark on the pathless path with original mind.

Establishing a new life goal does not necessarily mean that practitioners should become monks or nuns in order to seriously practice, as the Buddha did when he left the palace, leaving behind his wife and son. Having a new life goal implies having a new value system and living our daily lives with mindfulness.

There were two loggers who worked in the same camp. Both were equally strong and worked the same amount of time. However, one logger discovered that his friend cut down more trees and made more money than he did. This made him wonder why his friend was able to work more efficiently. One day when they took a rest, he discovered that his friend always sharpened his ax during the rest period. We may spend the same amount of time at work as our colleagues. We may have the same amount of available free time. However, depending on how we live and how mindful we are, the quality of our lives as well as our final destination will be very different.

True practitioners live mindfully. When you have available time, what do you do? Do you watch TV, or read magazines, or do you read scripture, or do you practice meditation? How do you spend your time on weekends? Do you go to the movies, or meet friends, or do you meditate, or go to the Dharma service? When you have money and can afford a vacation, what do you do? Do you go to a meditation retreat, or do you go skiing or relax on a beach?

For true practitioners, the criteria used to choose an occupation are also different. They do not choose occupations based on how much money they will make. Rather, they consider whether the occupation in question is "right livelihood," whether the work atmosphere is supportive to encourage spiritual progress.

Paltawon was a female disciple of Master Sotaesan. She was one of the richest people in Korea and financially helped Sotaesan during the early stages of Won Buddhism. One hot summer day, they went hiking together. As a noble and well-cultured lady, Paltawon was heavily dressed and so she was extremely hot. When she saw a running brook, she became so delighted that she jumped wildly, without caution or hesitation, into the middle of the brook, and splashed her face with the cool water.

After watching this scene, Master Sotaesan said to her as she came out of the brook, "Paltawon, one should not use water in that fashion. Let me show you how to use water." Although Master Sotaesan was a large man, he cautiously approached the brook close to the bank, gathered water with his hands, and carefully washed his face. Upon returning, Master Sotaesan added, "Even though water is free and abundant, if one uses water unsparingly, one's karma may be to be reborn in a place where water is scarce and difficult to find."

At the end of each summer, Master Sotaesan would rewrap his mosquito net in the same newspaper he had used for five years. Even though Won Buddhists were poor at that time, newspapers and water were abundant and cheap. Nevertheless Master Sotaesan always asked his followers to practice frugality.

These stories illustrate the life of a true practitioner, who knows and pursues eternal life. A practitioner should live in a simple and moderate fashion. The life of a true practitioner, a searcher for enlightenment, has nothing to do with luxurious or extravagant living. Possessing fancy clothes, living in expensive houses, or driving fancy cars does not interest him or her. True practitioners understand that this kind of lifestyle taints their minds and dulls their spirituality, reinforcing their egos and strengthening their ignorance. The primary interest of practitioners lies in calming, purifying, and training their minds.

Contemporary practitioners should avoid mindlessly following the lifestyle of the majority, but rather, as the Buddha said, they should "swim against the stream." They should not be afraid of being different from others. Tigers and eagles are solitary animals. We should be like tigers and eagles, making friends with ourselves, our authentic selves, and not blindly following the herd. Practitioners need to spend more time in silence and meditation, turning the light inward and seeing prajna.

The poet Rilke wrote:

> I am too alone in the world
> And not alone enough
> To make every moment holy.

If we are constantly surrounded by nonpractitioners, it becomes very difficult to encounter our authentic self.

Jesus said, "You are in this world, but you are not of this world." If we live following the majority's value system, our final destination will be far from nirvana. It can be painful to live outside of the mainstream, yet it is far more painful to repeat the same habits and remain wandering in samsara. Jesus said, "For my yoke is easy to bear, and my load is not hard to carry" (Matthew 11: 30), and "I have told you these things so that in me you may have peace. In the world you have trouble and suffering, but take courage—I have conquered the world" (John 16:33). When we practice the Dharma, we are like a satellite launched into the sky. At first the satellite will have to struggle against gravity, but once it enters outer space, it orbits easily and automatically without effort. Initially our practice is a struggle. We must fight against our tenacious habits, yet as time passes, our practice becomes natural and effortless. This is especially true when we have the help of a *sangha* or spiritual community—when we have the support of dharma friends and teachers. That is why one of the three jewels, along with Buddha and Dharma, is Sangha. Since the pattern of obstacles in the course of our practice is similar, we can easily overcome temptations and hindrances with the help of experienced sangha members.

Parasamgate means "gone altogether (everyone) to the other shore." Let us go to the other shore, to nirvana, with our loved ones, as well as all the people around us, and eventually with all sentient beings.

To our friends, parents, and children, our words are far more powerful than the words of the Dalai Lama, Thich Nhat Hanh, or some other prominent master, because we are far more available and close to our loved ones than these masters are.

The best way to help others is to open their eyes and guide them on the spiritual path toward buddhahood. When circumstances allow, we should lead them to learn and practice Dharma and encourage them to attend Dharma services or retreats.

The elemental composition of coal and diamonds is the same even though they look entirely different. Diamonds are formed deep inside the earth by intense heat and pressure. Coal is gradually transformed into diamonds by this heat and pressure. Attaining buddhahood requires our intense effort, blood, sweat, and energy. The door is open, but it is up to us to enter the house. The path is known, but we have to actually walk on it.

According to the Diamond Sutra, the person who has come upon prajna paramita literature such as the Heart Sutra or the Diamond Sutra is extremely blessed, a person who has planted many meritorious seeds in his or her previous lives. The Buddha said in the Diamond Sutra that the teaching of emptiness, the core Dharma of the Heart Sutra, is for those initiated in the supreme way.

The Tathagata has declared this teaching for the benefit of initiates of the Great Way; He has declared it for the benefit of initiates of the Supreme Way. Whosoever can receive and retain this teaching, study it, recite it and spread it abroad will be clearly perceived and recognized by the Tathagata and will achieve a perfection of merit beyond measurement or calculation—a perfection of merit unlimited and inconceivable.[190]

Let us not lose this rare and precious opportunity. Keep with you this story from *The Sutra of Forty-Two Sections*, section 27:

The Buddha said, "Those who follow the Way are like a piece of wood which is drifting along a stream. If it stays clear of either shore, and it is not picked up by men, and if it faces no obstructions by ghosts or spirits, and if it is not hindered by whirlpools and does not rot, then I assure you that that piece of wood will finally reach the ocean. If students of the Way are not deluded by their feelings and desires, nor led astray by some evil influences, and if they are vigorous in their cultivation of the unconditioned, I guarantee that they will certainly attain the Way."

ACKNOWLEDGMENTS

M ANY PEOPLE have supported the evolution of this book. To them I offer my sincerest gratitude.

First, I am most grateful to my teachers who have guided me on my spiritual path: Venerable Chwasan, Venerable Kyungsan, Jungtawon, and Jasungheng, and Chotawon. My deepest gratitude of course goes to the Venerable Sotaesan, founding master of Won Buddhism, and finally to the compassionate Buddha himself.

Throughout the years of my practice, I have been lovingly supported by my parents, siblings, uncles, and aunts; I hold them all close to my heart.

I am thankful for the assistance of my many Dharma friends for proofreading the manuscript. I would especially like to thank Rev. Domyung Won, Dr. Carol Craven, Mr. Joel Ostroff, and Dr. David Low for their editing and valuable comments.

I extend my deep appreciation to my editors, Mr. Josh Bartok and Ms. Laura Cunningham, who brought clarity to this work.

I also offer deep appreciation to Rocky Bracero who created the illustration of the Wheel of Life on page 122.

Finally, I thank from the bottom of my heart Shintawon, Dotawon, and Wonsan, whose vision, dedication, and financial support was critical for the establishment of the Won Dharma Meditation Center, a spiritual community where people from diverse backgrounds can study and practice the Dharma together, so that they may enlighten their own minds and our world.

May the dharma live in many hearts.

1. Garfield, trans., *The Fundamental Wisdom of the Middle Path*, 69.

2. The Second Patriarch of Zen Buddhism. As a young man, Hui Ko was well versed in classical Chinese and Buddhist philosophy. Upon meeting Bodhidharma, the First Patriarch of Zen Buddhism, Hui Ko received the Dharma seal from Bodhidharma, and he later transmitted the Dharma lineage to his successor, Seng Tsan, the Third Patriarch.

3. I have based my translation on the original Sanskrit and Chinese versions of the Heart Sutra.

4. Red Pine, *The Heart Sutra*, 29.

5. "The Gospel of Thomas," v.3, in Willis Barnstone and Marvin Meyer, eds., *The Gnostic Bible*, 45.

6. Brach, *Radical Acceptance*, 307.

7. See the third section of chapter 11, "The Third Noble Truth."

8. Price and Mou-lam, trans., *The Diamond Sutra and The Sutra of Hui-Neng*, 45.

9. Ibid., 31.

10. One of the Buddha's ten names. "Tathagata" literally means both one who has thus gone (Tatha-gata) and one who has thus come (Tatha-agata). Hence, the Tathagata is beyond coming and going. This means the one who has transcended the endless cycle of birth and death.

11. Price and Wong Mou-lam, *The Diamond Sutra and the Sutra of Hui-Neng*, 22.

12. Buswell, Jr., trans., *Tracing Back the Radiance*, 115.

13. See Red Pine, *The Heart Sutra*, 38.

14. According to the Mahayana School, an authentic Buddhist sutra begins with the background of the scripture: the speaker of the sutra, the time when the sutra was delivered, the place where the sutra was delivered, and to whom the sutra was spoken. Many of the Tibetan versions of the Heart Sutra start with this standard introduction and also

conclude in a standardized way. Since longer versions did not appear until after the shorter versions had become established texts, most scholars believe that the standard introduction and conclusion were added later in order to establish the authority of the sutra. See Red Pine, *The Heart Sutra*, 39–42.

15. Lopez, *Elaborations on Emptiness*, vii.

16. A koan is a seemingly nonsensical, puzzling, often paradoxical statement, story, or question used in Zen Buddhism. The koan is for contemplation, and it defies rational understanding and works to exhaust analytic thinking. Koan practice is a means to stay centered and eventually to attain enlightenment.

17. Kyongbong, *Touch the Door Latch In the Middle of the Night*, 15–17.

18. Some versions of the Heart Sutra begin with the standard introduction, "Thus have I heard," but the authenticity of the phrase is doubted. Buddhist scholars believe that this introduction was added later to make the sutra look more authentic. See Red Pine, *The Heart Sutra*, 41–42.

19. Watson, trans., *The Lotus Sutra*, 299–305.

20. Nalanda is the name of an ancient monastic university in Bihar, India. It was established in about the fifth century B.C.E., and developed into the greatest ancient center of Buddhist learning. It is considered one of the first great universities in recorded history. Nalanda was often visited by the Buddha during his numerous sojourns, and he taught several important discourses there. According to Tibetan sources, Nagarjuna was ordained and taught there. At its peak, Nalanda University attracted scholars and students from many parts of the world including China, Korea, and Greece. When Hsuan-tsang was studying at Nalanda in the seventh century, there were 1,510 teachers and 8,500 students.

21. The first Chinese translation of the Heart Sutra was made by a central Asian monk, Chih-lou-chin-chan, some time between 200 and 250 C.E. He entitled his translation *Prajnaparamita Dharani*. Red Pine, *The Heart Sutra*, 16–27.

22. See Seung Sahn, *The Compass of Zen*, 224–27.

23. Price and Mou-lam, trans., *The Diamond Sutra and The Sutra of Hui-Neng*, 18–19.

24. *The Scriptures of Won-Buddhism*, 169.

25. The Third Patriarch of Zen Buddhism. Seng Tsan was the Dharma successor of Hui Ko, the Second Patriarch. Seng Tsan is best known as the author of the famous Zen text *Hsin-hsin Ming*.

26. Kornfield, ed., *Teachings of the Buddha*, 19.

27. Joeng, trans., *The Mirror of Zen*, 66.

28. Indra's net (also called Indra's jewels or Indra's pearls) is a metaphor to illustrate the idea of the interdependence or interconnectedness of all things in Mahayana Buddhism. This metaphor came from the Avatamsaka Sutra, one of the most important Mahayana Buddhist sutras, which describes a vast net that spans infinitely across space in all directions. Every intersection on this vast net hosts a shining jewel, which reflects every other jewel as well as the net as a whole. This metaphor illustrates the teaching of totality, which states that the nature of the entire universe is contained in each particle.

29. Red Pine, *The Heart Sutra*, 53.

30. Ibid., 67.

31. Hanh, *The Heart of the Buddha's Teaching*, 52.

32. Rahula, *What the Buddha Taught*, 22.

33. Bhikkhu Bodhi, trans., *The Connected Discourses of the Buddha*, 896.

34. For the philosophical explanation of the emptiness of the five aggregates, see Garfield, trans., *The Fundamental Wisdom of the Middle Path*, 12–13.

35. Rahula, *What the Buddha Taught*, 33.

36. Ibid., 70.

37. Ibid., 70.

38. Ibid., 25.

39. Red Pine, *The Heart Sutra*, 91.

40. Patrul Rinpoche, *The Words of My Perfect Teacher*, 56.

41. In fact, "apple" or "orange" are also just concepts because what really exists is some specific apple or orange. Yet, for the sake of simplicity, let us say that some specific fruit is what really exists.

42. In fact, sensations, perceptions, impulses, and consciousnesses are also concepts, not reality. For instance, consciousness is a concept for visual, auditory, olfactory, or mental consciousnesses. Yet, for the sake of simplicity, let us say that the particular elements of our mind (sensations, perceptions, impulses, and consciousnesses) are what really exist.

43. Warren, *Buddhism in Translations*, 133–34.

44. Rahula, *What the Buddha Taught*, 26.

45. Kornfield, ed., *Teachings of the Buddha*, 18.

46. Hanh, *Zen Keys*, 105–6.

47. Red Pine, *The Heart Sutra*, 87.

48. Geshe Tsultim Gyeltsen, *Mirror of Wisdom*, 100.

49. Goldstein, *Insight Meditation*, 109–13.

50. Red Pine, *The Heart Sutra*, 71.

51. The longer Tibetan version of the Heart Sutra contains the following:

> "Then, by the power of the Buddha, the venerable Shariputra said this to the bodhisattva, the *mahasattva*, the noble Avalokiteshvara, 'How should a son of good lineage who wishes to practice the profound perfection of wisdom train?' He said that and the bodhisattva, the *mahasattva*, the noble Avalokiteshvara said this to the venerable Shariputra, 'Shariputra, a son of good lineage or a daughter of good lineage who wished to practice the profound perfection of wisdom should perceive things in this way: form is emptiness; emptiness is form. Emptiness is not other than form; form is not other than emptiness. In the same way, feeling, discrimination, conditioning factors, and consciousnesses are empty...'"

> See Lopez, *Elaborations on Emptiness*, vii–viii.

52. Ricard and Thuan, *The Quantum and the Lotus*, 94.

53. Fraser, Lillestol, and Sellevag, *The Search for Infinity*, 9–13.

54. Schrödinger, *Science and Humanism*, 47.

55. Ricard and Thuan, *The Quantum and the Lotus*, 84.

56. Price and Mou-lam, trans., *The Diamond Sutra and The Sutra of Hui-Neng*, 31.

57. Ricard and Thuan, *The Quantum and the Lotus*, 130.

58. Red Pine, *The Heart Sutra*, 80.

59. Ibid., 82.

60. *The Scriptures of Won-Buddhism*, 327.

61. Newland, *Introduction to Emptiness*, 65.

62. Ibid., 61.

63. Ibid., 79.

64. Cho, *Seclusion*, 290.

65. Vairochana is the embodiment of Dharmakaya Buddha, which literally means "Truth Body" Buddha. In Sanskrit, Vairochana means "coming from the sun, illuminating." Vairochana, or the Buddha of Great Illumination, represents the ultimate reality or emptiness.

66. Price and Mou-lam, trans., *The Diamond Sutra and The Sutra of Hui-Neng*, 47.

67. Ibid., 21.

68. Chung, trans., *The Scriptures of Won Buddhism*, 184.

69. There are various English translations of the phrase *sarva dharma sunyata laksana*, for example, "all dharmas are the expression of emptiness." Another translation is "all dharmas are characterized by emptiness."

70. Just as there are so many meanings or interpretations of dharmas, the explanation of the phrase "All dharmas are empty" also has many interpretations. See Red Pine, *The Heart Sutra*, 89.

71. According to Descartes, substance is that which requires nothing else for its existence. Substance is something that can exist by and in itself, without depending on anything else. Therefore in Western philosophy, God is the only substance.

72. Ricard and Thuan, *The Quantum and the Lotus*, 158.

73. The distinction between "I" and "mine" can be subtle. For instance, is my hair "I" or "mine"? Or is the higher intellect that I speak from "me" or "mine"?

74. Dilgo Khyentse Rinpoche, *The Heart Treasure of the Enlightened Ones*, 8.

75. "No servant can serve two masters, for either he will hate the one and love the other, or he will be devoted to the one and despise the other. You cannot serve God and money." (Luke 16:13).

76. *The Scriptures of Won-Buddhism*, 360.

77. "Do not be obsessed by the pursuit of gold, silver, and precious gems." *The Scriptures of Won-Buddhism*, 73.

78. *The Scriptures of Won-Buddhism*, 328.

79. Garfield, trans., *The Fundamental Wisdom of the Middle Path*, 78.

80. Suzuki, trans., *The Lankavatara Sutra*, 4.

81. Luke 24:36, John 20:19, John 14:27.

82. Garfield, trans., *The Fundamental Wisdom of the Middle Path*, 73.

83. *The Scriptures of Won-Buddhism*, 240.

84. Red Pine, *The Heart Sutra*, 94–95.

85. *The Scriptures of Won-Buddhism*, 61.

86. Garfield, trans., *The Fundamental Wisdom of the Middle Path*, 78.

87. Kornfield, ed., *Teachings of the Buddha*, 143.

88. Kyongbong, *Touch the Door Latch in the Middle of the Night*, 26.

89. Rahula, *What the Buddha Taught*, 14.

90. Nearman, trans., *The Shobogenzo*, 56.

91. Sometimes "dharma" is used here instead of "the object of mind." Here "dharma" means all ideas, thoughts, religious teachings, creeds, principles.

92. Red Pine, *The Heart Sutra*, 108.

93. Hanh, *The Heart of the Buddha's Teaching*, 222.

94. Soeng, *Trust in Mind*, 14–16.

95. Red Pine, *The Heart Sutra*, 80.

96. Ricard and Thuan, *The Quantum and the Lotus*, 168.

97. Ibid., 121.

98. Wigner, *Symmetries and Reflections*, 172.

99. Lee, *The Heart Sutra*, 256.

100. Yasutani, *Flowers Fall*, 102.

101. Here "mind" does not mean the mind which is one of the six sense organs, but universal mind.

102. In Sanskrit, this is expressed as *manoja*; *mano* means "mind," and *ja* means "birth" or "arise."

103. Chungwha, *The Heart Sutra*, 156.

104. Kornfield, ed., *Teachings of the Buddha*, 144.

105. Goldstein, *Insight Meditation*, 116.

106. Hanh, *The Heart of the Buddha's Teaching*, 226.

107. *Pratitya* means "dependent"; *sam* means "co," "with," or "together"; and *utpada* means "arise" or "originate." *Pratityasamutpada* is variously translated into English as "dependent arising," "conditioned genesis," "dependent co-arising," "interdependent arising," or "contingency."

108. Bhikkhu Bodhi, trans., *The Connected Discourses of the Buddha*, 575.

109. When Shakyamuni Buddha was born, a hermit, who lived in the mountains not far away, noticed a radiance and came down to the palace. When he saw the child, he announced to the king, the father of Shakyamuni Buddha, "If your son succeeds to your throne, he will become a great ruler who will unite all kingdoms in India. If he leaves the palace to become a monk, he will become a Buddha, a greatly enlightened one, who will

save numerous sentient beings." After hearing the prophecy, the king asked his men to remove all unpleasant environmental things in order not to motivate Buddha to leave the palace to become a seeker of truth.

110. Chung, trans., *The Dharma Master Chongsan of Won Buddhism*, 119–20.

111. Piyadassi, *The Buddha's Ancient Path*, 75.

112. Hanh, *The Heart of the Buddha's Teaching*, 227.

113. Garfield, trans., *The Fundamental Wisdom of the Middle Path*, 78.

114. *The Scriptures of Won-Buddhism*, 325.

115. Ibid., 328–29.

116. Ibid., 340–41.

117. Garfield, trans., *The Fundamental Wisdom of the Middle Path*, 78.

118. See chapters 3 and 4 for details.

119. From the standpoint of this present life, old age and death can be considered the link following birth. From the perspective of the next life, however, old age and death can be considered the link before birth. "Birth" and "old age and death" are like the riddle of the chicken and the egg—we cannot tell which comes first. Therefore, in the absolute sense there is no old age and death.

120. Red Pine, *The Heart Sutra*, 114.

121. Price and Mou-lam, trans., *The Diamond Sutra and The Sutra of Hui-Neng*, 26–27.

122. The Sanskrit *mano* means "mind," and *maya* means "illusion."

123. Red Pine, *The Heart Sutra*, 126–27.

124. Price and Mou-lam, trans., *The Diamond Sutra and The Sutra of Hui-Neng*, 50.

125. Red Pine, *The Heart Sutra*, 118.

126. *Yad aniccam tam dukkham.* Rahula, *What the Buddha Taught*, 25.

127. *The Scriptures of Won-Buddhism*, 210–11.

128. Bhikkhu Bodhi, *The Noble Eightfold Path*, 25.

129. Catherine, *Focused and Fearless*, xiii.

130. Nepo, *The Book of Awakening*, 143.

131. *The Scriptures of Won-Buddhism*, 212.

132. Rahula, *What the Buddha Taught*, 36.

133. See chapter 9 to know that ultimately "becoming" (*bhava*) is the cause of rebirth.

134. Kornfield, ed., *Teachings of the Buddha*, 143.

135. Yamada, trans., *Gateless Gate*, 62.

136. Garfield, trans., *The Fundamental Wisdom of the Middle Path*, 69.

137. Chon, trans., *The Scripture of Won Buddhism*, 113–14.

138. See Bhikkhu Bodhi, *The Noble Eightfold Path*, 23–27, and Hanh, *The Heart of the Buddha's Teaching*, 51. Buddha also said, "You, bhikkhus, when you realize that the five aggreagates (*skandhas*) are empty, you will attain right view."

139. *The Scriptures of Won-Buddhism*, 242.

140. Bhikkhu Bodhi, *The Noble Eightfold Path*, 16.

141. For details of this, see Bhikkhu Bodhi, *The Noble Eightfold Path*, 29–42.

142. Chung, trans., *The Dharma Master Chongsan of Won Buddhism*, 204.

143. *The Scriptures of Won-Buddhism*, 363–64.

144. Ibid., 73–74.

145. Bhikkhu Bodhi, *The Noble Eightfold Path*, 17.

146. Joeng, trans., *The Mirror of Zen*, 55.

147. *The Scriptures of Won-Buddhism*, 235.

148. Ibid., 219.

149. Ibid., 127–28.

150. Rahula, *What the Buddha Taught*, 48.

151. *The Scriptures of Won-Buddhism*, 142.

152. Ibid., 176–77.

153. Cho, *Seclusion*, 204.

154. Garfield, trans., *The Fundamental Wisdom of the Middle Path*, 70.

155. According to the Samyukta Agama, the Buddha also taught his disciple stage by stage; from teaching five skandhas, then eighteen elements, then dependent origination and then finally the empty nature of all things. See Red Pine, *The Heart Sutra*, 114.

156. Garfield, trans., *The Fundamental Wisdom of the Middle Path*, 67.

157. Ibid., 67.

158. Kyongbong, *Touch the Door Latch In the Middle of the Night*, 18.

159. Red Pine, *The Heart Sutra*, 126.

160. Ibid., 126.

161. Price and Mou-lam, trans., *The Diamond Sutra and The Sutra of Hui-Neng*, 53.

162. Chon, trans., *The Scripture of Won Buddhism*, 257.

163. *The Additional Discourses of Venerable Sotaesan*, 61–62.

164. Red Pine, *The Heart Sutra*, 134.

165. Ibid., 112.

166. Ibid., 134.

167. *The Scriptures of Won-Buddhism*, 280.

168. Red Pine, *The Heart Sutra*, 143.

169. *The Scriptures of Won-Buddhism*, 229–30.

170. Red Pine, trans., *The Zen Teaching of Bodhidharma*, 7.

171. Red Pine, *The Heart Sutra*, 54.

172. Ibid.

173. Hahn, *The Happiness which Increases as We Practice*, 10.

174. Daesan, *The Essence of the Won Buddhist Canon*, 153.

175. Red Pine, *The Heart Sutra*, 156.

176. Ibid., 155.

177. Chung, *An Introduction to Won Buddhism*, 62.

178. Price and Mou-lam, trans., *The Diamond Sutra and The Sutra of Hui-Neng*, 33–36.

179. Chwasan, *The Principle of Belief and Its Power*, 13–14.

180. Ibid., 78. See also chapter 3 of *The Principle of Belief and Its Power* for a more detailed explanation of the importance of having a sound belief and selecting our beliefs wisely.

181. *The Scriptures of Won-Buddhism*, 347.

182. Chung, trans., *The Dharma Master Chongsan of Won Buddhism*, 151.

183. Jang, *Hill of Freedom*, 88.

184. Chon, trans., *The Scripture of Won Buddhism*, 269–270.

185. *The Additional Discourses of Venerable Sotaesan*, 28.

186. Chung, trans., *The Dharma Master Chongsan of Won Buddhism*, 181.

187. *The Scriptures of Won-Buddhism*, 328.

188. Chung, trans., *The Dharma Master Chongsan of Won Buddhism*, 107.

189. Chon, trans., *The Scripture of Won Buddhism*, 339.

190. Price and Mou-lam, trans., *The Diamond Sutra and The Sutra of Hui-Neng*, 35.

BIBLIOGRAPHY

WORKS IN ENGLISH

Barnstone, Willis, and Marvin Meyer, eds. *The Gnostic Bible*. Boston: New Seeds, 2006.

Batchelor, Stephen. *Buddhism without Beliefs*. New York: Riverhead Books, 1997.

Bhikkhu Bodhi. *The Noble Eightfold Path*. Onalaska: BPS Pariyatti Editions, 2000.

Brach, Tara. *Radical Acceptance*. New York: Random House, 2003.

Buswell, Robert Jr., trans. *Tracing Back the Radiance: Chinul's Korean Way of Zen*. Honolulu: University of Hawaii Press, 1991.

Catherine, Shaila. *Focused and Fearless: A Meditator's Guide to States of Deep Joy, Calm, and Clarity*. Boston: Wisdom Publications, 2008.

Chon, Pal Khn, trans. *The Scripture of Won Buddhism*. Iksan: Won Kwang Publishing Co., 1988.

Chung, Bongkil, trans. *The Scriptures of Won Buddhism*. Honolulu: University of Hawaii Press, 2003.

———. *The Dharma Master Chongsan of Won Buddhism*. Albany: State University of New York, 2012.

———. *An Introduction to Won Buddhism*. Iri: Won Buddhist Press, 1994.

Dilgo Khyentse Rinpoche. *The Heart Treasure of the Enlightened Ones*. Translated by the Padmakara Translation Group. Boston: Shambhala Publications, 1992.

Fraser, Gordon, Egil Lillestol, and Inge Sellevag. *The Search for Infinity*. New York: Fact On File, 1994.

Garfield, Jay L., trans. *The Fundamental Wisdom of the Middle Path: Nagarjuna's Mulamadhyamakakarika*. New York: Oxford University Press, 1995.

Geshe Tsultim Gyeltsen. *Mirror of Wisdom*. Long Beach, California: Thubten Dhargye Ling Publications, 2000.

Goldstein, Joseph. *Insight Meditation*. Boston: Shambhala Publications, 1994.

Hanh, Thich Nhat. *The Heart of the Buddha's Teaching*. New York: Broadway Books, 1998.

Hanh, Thich Nhat. *Zen Keys: A Guide to Zen Practice*. New York: Three Leaves Press, 1994.

Joeng, Boep, trans. *The Mirror of Zen*. Boston: Shambhala Publications, 2006.

Kornfield, Jack, ed. *Teachings of the Buddha*. Boston: Shambhala Publications, 1996.

Lopez, Donald. *Elaborations on Emptiness*. Princeton, New Jersey: Princeton University Press, 1996.

Nearman, Hubert, trans. *The Shobogenzo*. Mount Shasta, California: Shasta Abbey, 1992.

Nepo, Mark. *The Book of Awakening*. Boston: Conari Press, 2000.

Newland, Guy. *Introduction to Emptiness*. Ithaca, NY: Snow Lion Publications, 2008.

Patrul Rinpoche. *The Words of My Perfect Teacher: A Complete Translation of a Classic Introduction to Tibetan Buddhism*. Translated by the Padmakara Translation Group. Rev. ed. Boston: Shambhala Publications, 1998.

Piyadassi, Thera. *The Buddha's Ancient Path*. United Kingdom: Rider and Company, 1964.

Price, F., and Wong Mou-lam, trans. *The Diamond Sutra and The Sutra of Hui-Neng*. Boston: Shambhala Publications, 1990.

Rahula, Walpola. *What the Buddha Taught*. New York: Grove Press, 1974.

Ricard, Matthieu, and Trinh Xuan Thuan. *The Quantum and the Lotus: A Journey to the Frontiers Where Science and Buddhism Meet*. New York: Broadway Books, 2004.

Red Pine. *The Heart Sutra*. Shoemaker & Hoard, an Imprint of Avalon Publishing Group, 2004.

—————, trans., *The Zen Teaching of Bodhidharma*. San Francisco: North Point Press, 1987.

Sahn, Seung. *The Compass of Zen*. Boston: Shambhala Publications, 1997.

Schrödinger, Erwin. *Science and Humanism*. Cambridge, England: Cambridge University Press, 1951.

—————. *Mind and Matter*. Cambridge, England: Cambridge University Press, 1958.

The Scriptures of Won-Buddhism. Iksan: Won Kwang Publishing Co., 2006.

Soeng, Mu. *Trust in Mind: The Rebellion of Chinese Zen*. Boston: Wisdom Publications, 2004.

Suzuki, D. T., trans. *The Awakening of Faith*. New York: Dover Publications, 2003.

—————. *The Lankavatara Sutra*. Boulder, CO: Prajna Press, 1978.

Warren, Henry Clarke. *Buddhism in Translations*. Delhi: Moltilal Banarasidass Publishers, 1998.

Watson, Burton, trans. *The Lotus Sutra*. New York: Columbia University Press, 1993.

Wigner, Eugene. *Symmetries and Reflections*. Bloomington: Indiana University Press, 1967.

Yamada, Koun, trans. *The Gateless Gate: The Classic Book of Zen Koans*. Boston: Wisdom Publications, 2004.

Yasutani, Hakuun. *Flowers Fall: A Commentary on Zen Master Dogen's Genjokoan*. Translated by Paul Jaffe. Boston: Shambhala Publications, 2001.

WORKS IN KOREAN

All excerpts in this book were translated into English by the author.

The Additional Discourses of Venerable Sotaesan. Iksan: Won Kwang Publishing Co., 1985.

Cho, Hyun. *Seclusion: The Longest Spiritual Journey.* Seoul: Hankyoreh Publications, 2008.

Chungwha. *The Heart Sutra.* Seoul: Dharma Offering Publications, 2005.

Chwasan. *The Principle of Belief and Its Power.* Iksan: Won Kwang Publishing Co., 2009.

Daesan. *The Essence of the Won Buddhist Canon.* Iksan: Won Kwang Publishing Co., 1996.

Hahn, Dukchun. *The Happiness which Increases as We Practice.* Seoul: EZAnn Pulbications, 2009.

Jang, Eungchul. *Hill of Freedom: Commentary on The Heart Sutra.* Iksan: Dongnam Poong Publications, 2000.

Kyongbong. *Touch the Door Latch in the Middle of the Night.* Seoul: Millahl Pulications, 1989.

Lee, Chungdam. *The Heart Sutra.* Seoul: Bosung Publications, 1990.

D OSUNG YOO was ordained in the Won Buddhist Order in Korea in 1994. Since then, he has led retreats and taught meditation, as well as Buddhism and Won Buddhist Dharma in Seoul, Korea, and in the U.S. He was a minister at the Won Buddhist Temple of Philadelphia and has taught at the Won Institute of Graduate Studies near Philadelphia, as well as at other Won centers throughout North America. He is also a leading Korean-to-English translator of Dharma teachings and has helped to translate several Won Buddhist texts.

Currently, Rev. Yoo is the retreat director and a resident teacher at the Won Dharma Center in Claverack, NY, where he is building a spiritual community that supports people from all walks of life in finding inner light and peace, the cornerstones of a better and more enlightened world. More information on the center can be found at www.wondharmacenter.org.

About Wisdom Publications

W ISDOM PUBLICATIONS is dedicated to offering works
relating to and inspired by Buddhist traditions.
　　　To learn more about us or to explore our other books,
please visit our website at www.wisdompubs.org.

You can subscribe to our e-newsletter or request our print catalog
online, or by writing to:

Wisdom Publications
199 Elm Street
Somerville, Massachusetts 02144 USA

You can also contact us at 617-776-7416 or info@wisdompubs.org.

Wisdom is a nonprofit, charitable 501(c)(3) organization, and
donations in support of our mission are tax deductible.

Wisdom Publications is affiliated with the Foundation for the Preservation of the Mahayana Tradition (FPMT).